Regional Disparities in the Enlarged European Union

The last 20 years have seen an increase in European integration and the emergence of the technological revolution. Although tighter integration coupled with technological innovation should facilitate cross-regional convergence, some European regions have managed to jump ahead while others have been left behind. This book examines the regional characteristics that favour growth and analyses the relevance of innovation, socio-economic and structural factors in shaping regional economic disparities.

In this book, particular attention is devoted to the EU enlargement towards the east, to its consequences on Europe's traditional north–south divide and to the increasing regional disparities in new member states after the transition. It demonstrates the growing importance of innovation and human capital in explaining the increase in income and employment disparities in old EU members, particularly after the 2008 financial crisis. It also shows that, for newcomers, regional disparities are essentially linked to socio-economic factors as capital regions approach western standards, while others – mainly old industrial regions and peripheral ones - lag behind.

This book integrates theoretical discussion with empirical evidence and will appeal to regional scientists interested in regional inequalities and to policymakers concerned with devising effective strategies to tackle regional disparities in Europe.

Valentina Meliciani is Full Professor of Applied Economics at the University LUISS Guido Carli, Rome, Italy.

Routledge Advances in Regional Economics, Science and Policy

Regional Disparities in the Enlarged European Union

Geography, innovation and structural change

Valentina Meliciani

Routledge
Taylor & Francis Group

LONDON AND NEW YORK

First published 2016 by Routledge

2 Park Square, Milton Park, Abingdon, Oxfordshire OX14 4RN

52 Vanderbilt Avenue, New York, NY 10017

Routledge is an imprint of the Taylor & Francis Group, an informa business

First issued in paperback 2019

British Library Cataloguing in Publication Data
A catalogue record for this book is available from the British Library

Library of Congress Cataloging in Publication Data
Meliciani, Valentina, 1968-
Regional disparities in the enlarged European Union : geography, innovation and structural change / Valentina Meliciani.
Includes bibliographical references and index.
1. Regional disparities–European Union countries. 2. Regional economics–European Union countries. 3. European Union countries–Economic conditions–Regional disparities. I. Title.
HC240.M454 2015
337.1'42–dc23
2015018932

ISBN: 978-0-415-74171-2 (hbk)
ISBN: 978-0-367-86946-5 (pbk)

Typeset in Times New Roman
by Cenveo Publisher Services

Contents

Figures

Tables

Appendices

Acknowledgements

I would like to thank first of all Sheila Chapman, co-author of some papers strictly related to this book, who has greatly contributed to shape many of the views expressed in this work. In particular, Chapter 4 draws on the joint paper 'Behind the Pan-European Convergence Path: the Role of Innovation, Specialization and Socio-economic Factors' forthcoming in Growth and Change.

I am also greatly indebted to the University of Teramo, particularly to the Faculty of Political Science, for allowing me to devote time to the writing of this book during a sabbatical year and for the stimulating multidisciplinary environment from which I have learn a lot.

Some chapters of this book were written while I was visiting the Department of Geography and Environment of the London School of Economics and Political Science and I am really grateful to Simona Iammarino and Riccardo Crescenzi for this stimulating experience.

It was during my doctoral thesis that I started working on regional convergence and I learnt a lot from close cooperation with my supervisor and co-author Franco Peracchi, to whom I am greatly indebted.

Many co-authors and friends have also shaped my views on some of the topics of this book. Among them, I would like to thank especially Stefania Cosci, Rinaldo Evangelista and Maria Savona. The book has also benefited from conversations with my father Alessandro Meliciani.

Finally, I wish to thank Paolo, Elena, Stefano, Giovanni and Lucilla for the enjoyable environment they never failed to provide.

The book is dedicated to my mother Giovanna and to my first daughter Elena.

1 Introduction

Starting from the 1990s a series of events at global and European level have transformed the landscape in which firms, regions and countries operate, opening up new questions, stimulating new theoretical approaches and informing new policies.

First, the 1990s and 2000s have seen a sharp intensification in the process of European integration. This included the liberalization of capital movements, the creation of the European Monetary Union and the progressive enlargement of the European Union (EU) to eastern, formerly planned economies. These events created new opportunities for laggard regions but also raised new problems, especially for Southern European regions. Trade and capital liberalization, coupled with new technologies, allows multinational enterprises to relocate their activities in order to minimize production costs. This process may favour, on the one hand, regions with lower wages and less-regulated labour markets, and, on the other, regions with a strong innovation capability and efficient institutional systems, leaving behind intermediate regions. It can also lead to a race among laggard regions to become more attractive by lowering wages and dismantling regulations (and rights) perceived as detrimental by foreign investors.

Monetary unification and the adoption of a single currency is generally expected to lead to a fall in the importance of national factors in explaining regional disparities in income and employment. Adopting a common currency should make regions more independent from the countries they belong to since movements in exchange rates affecting simultaneously the international competitiveness of all regions of a country are no longer possible. Moreover, for each region, there is now only one common central monetary policy rather than different policies for regions belonging to different countries. However, countries still keep their power in most domains that are crucial for long-run growth and employment. These include the management of fiscal policies, the regulation of labour markets, operating the juridical system, the school system, the health system, etc. All these factors might be more important than monetary policy for driving convergence or divergence processes. Differences across countries in these factors, together with lower labour mobility, may lead to a much more dispersed location of economic activity in Europe than in the USA, despite further economic integration.

Finally, in 2008 the financial crisis, originated in the USA, strongly affected European countries and regions, leading to a simultaneous crisis of sovereign debt. This macro-economic shock cannot be disregarded when studying the evolution of regional disparities since not all regions were hit in the same way. In particular, regions located in Southern European countries suffered more because of the higher public debt (this is particularly the case for Greece and Italy) that led them to adopt restrictive fiscal policies in a period of recession. On the contrary, public debt in former socialist countries is much lower, allowing them more flexibility in fiscal policy. This applies also to countries recently joining the Eurozone. Finally, the integration of former socialist economies in the EU has led to a shift of EU structural funds previously mostly devoted to Southern European regions towards the East. Moreover, the lower costs of production have encouraged foreign direct investment (FDI) in eastern regions, changing regional specialization patterns in Europe. All these elements might lead to a different performance of newcomers with respect to old members and suggest the importance of controlling for country-effects when studying the evolution of regional disparities.

Another important event conditioning the evolution of regional disparities in the 1990s and 2000s is the technological revolution based on information and communication technologies (ICTs), which strongly reduces transportation costs and drastically changes the ways in which goods and services are produced and delivered across countries. In particular, it allows fragmentation of the production process domestically (outsourcing) and internationally (offshore outsourcing). In a recent and very popular book, Friedman (2005) argues that the new technologies have changed firms' and individuals' opportunities, favouring an a-spatial distribution of economic activity, thus creating a 'flat world'. From this perspective, thanks to advances in connectivity, in global supply chain software and in outsourcing, insourcing, offshoring and supply chaining, every territory, no matter how remote, has the potential to become a global player (see the discussion of Friedman by Rodríguez-Pose and Crescenzi, 2008). However, the concept of a flat world has been challenged by many authors (Rodríguez-Pose and Crescenzi, 2008; Prager and Thisse, 2012). Rodríguez-Pose and Crescenzi (2008) note that, even with the sharp reduction in transport and communication costs, there are several forces that favour the agglomeration of economic activity, thus contributing to create 'mountains in a flat world'. These include innovation, knowledge spillovers, backward and forward linkages, diversification benefits, social capital, etc. Moreover, while technological improvements in communication infrastructures have allowed 'codified information' to be transmitted over increasingly large distances, this is not the case for 'tacit' knowledge, which remains geographically bounded (Prager and Thisse, 2012; Ciarli et al., 2012) – contributing to the increasing concentration of innovation (Audretsch and Feldman, 2004; Cantwell and Iammarino, 2003). Similarly, the existence of backward and forward linkages favours the co-location of producers and users whenever they have to exchange tacit knowledge (Meliciani and Savona, 2014).

Therefore, although advances in technology and deregulation may allow for economic activity to take place virtually everywhere, favouring the emergence of new actors in the global world, at the regional level globalization appears to favour some regions, leaving others well behind.

This raises the question of which endogenous characteristics of territories favour the concentration of innovation and economic activity. One of the aims of this book is to answer this question, with particular attention to regional socio-economic characteristics, specialization patterns, geographical location and levels of knowledge and human capital.

Starting from the evidence that there are only weak signs of regional convergence in per capita GDP, labour productivity and employment rates in Europe, we will argue that the new growth and new geography models are insufficient to explain the complexity and diversity of regional growth dynamics. In particular, reading the process of convergence/divergence along the lines of the neoclassical (old and 'new') growth theory and/or of the new economic geography paradigms misses important features of growth and transformation processes that are relevant for regional disparities. These include the sectoral composition of the economy and processes of structural change, the way in which local territories are able to introduce and assimilate new technologies and socio-economic factors.

The main purpose of this book is to investigate, beyond the more traditional role of geographical factors, the relevance of knowledge, socio-economic and structural factors in the evolution of income and employment disparities in the enlarged Europe at the regional level over the last 20 years.

We argue that disparities are often tied to regions' particular structural or socio-economic characteristics and to their ability to produce and assimilate knowledge. Let us consider, first, the role of regional specialization: the underlying assumption is that growth is often accompanied by a process of structural change where some sectors offer better opportunities than others. For example, in the last 20 years knowledge intensive services have grown more than other services and more than the rest of the economy (Rubalcaba and Kox, 2007), while manufacturing (in particular medium-low-tech manufacturing or heavy industry) has faced important restructuring problems and has lagged behind. Since specialization patterns tend to be sticky, they might provide favourable (unfavourable) conditions for income and employment growth.

Second, also socio-economic factors may be important. Following the approach developed by Rodríguez-Pose (1998a; 1998b; 1999) that divides the EU-12 regions into four groups (capitals and urban areas; old industrialized and restructuring regions; intermediate regions; peripheral ones) it appears that groups of regions with similar initial structural features generally show a similar capacity to respond to the challenges posed by socio-economic restructuring and hence experience similar trends in per capita GDP, once national factors are wiped out. The process of globalization is fostering the concentration of capital and decision-making powers in a limited number of core urban spaces (Harvey, 1985; Cheshire and Hay, 1989; Frenken and Hoekman, 2006) where the concentration of skilled labour, of headquarter functions of multinational firms

(Duranton and Puga, 2000) and of a dynamic service sector can lead to self-enforcing mechanisms of economic growth. On the contrary, old industrialized regions have rigid social and economic conditions that may negatively affect their performance (Rodríguez-Pose, 1999). Finally, many peripheral regions due to their distance from the core of Europe may not be able to benefit from technological advances and the agglomeration of industrial and service activities.

Structural features and socio-economic ones can be interlinked. In particular, knowledge intensive business services tend to locate in urban areas, while peripheral areas often specialize in agriculture and old industrialized areas in manufacturing. We will ask whether changes in technology and, in particular, the rise and diffusion of ICTs, contribute to a process of convergence in specialization patterns and in income and employment levels at the regional scale or, rather, if agglomeration economies and local regional advantages still play a large role, leading to an increasingly uneven distribution of knowledge intensive activities and to growing income/employment divergence across territories sharing different structural and socio-economic characteristics.

Structural and socio-economic characteristics can also affect the mechanisms through which knowledge is transmitted across various agents (firms, research centres, universities, etc.), both within a country and across countries with important implications on regional convergence. The literature on knowledge diffusion shows that spillovers are very localized and occur only within short distances (Bottazzi and Peri, 2003; Peri, 2004; Crescenzi, 2005; Crescenzi and Rodríguez-Pose, 2011). Moreover, even when knowledge is identically available for all, regions may still show very different levels of ability in absorbing new technologies and transforming them into (endogenous) growth. Among the different local factors that affect a region's absorption capacity, the literature emphasizes the role of human capital. The population's level of education also matters for the creation of innovative networks among institutions aiming at creating, adopting and/or modifying new technologies (i.e., learning organizations; Lundvall, 1992). Following this approach, Crescenzi (2005) introduces human capital combined with innovation as an explanatory variable of regional growth in the EU. Crescenzi and Rodríguez-Pose (2011) find that this variable interacts with local innovative activities in a statistically significant way, allowing each element to be more (or less) effectively translated into economic growth.

These factors may be differently linked to geography, producing different effects on growth and convergence. For instance, if, on the one hand, knowledge flows easily across contiguous areas this creates geographic clusters of innovating (or of technologically backward) regions (Rodríguez-Pose and Crescenzi, 2008). If, on the other hand, ICTs allow knowledge to spread to distant places, new investments may locate in peripheral areas creating a more homogeneous economic space (Friedman, 2005). Specialization patterns may lead to the same results, either creating localized clusters or spreading across far-away regions. Socio-economic factors generally interrupt geographic homogeneity: urban areas surrounded by less developed neighbours often follow growth patterns that are more similar to those of other distant urban areas than to those of their neighbours. Also national borders could act in the same way, determining differ-ent outcomes in areas that are contiguous but belong to different nations.

In a seminal paper, Boschma (2005) underlines that, apart from geographic closeness, contiguity – or proximity in a general sense – may be important too. In this framework proximity becomes largely, even if not uniquely, a-spatial. This poses the question of what type of proximity is relevant for convergence. In other words, which one(s) among the various types of closeness is decisive for determining convergence patterns in the EU?

This book analyses the relative role of four types of 'proximity' – country-effects, similarities in socio-economic features, in specialization patterns and in innovation and human capital – in determining convergence in per capita GDP, labour productivity and employment rates in the enlarged EU; it aims to assess whether convergence occurs across: 1) regions of the same nation; 2) regions sharing similar socio-economic characters; 3) regions specialized in the same sector; or 4) regions with similar levels of innovation and human capital.

Particular attention in the book is devoted to the EU enlargement towards the east. This process raises new questions concerning the ties between integration and convergence, given the very special features of the countries involved in the last two enlargements. First, the overwhelming bulk of new members is composed of former centrally planned economies. These countries share a record of some 40 years of centralized communist regimes under which regional disparities were kept artificially low; at the same time, at the onset of integration income dispari-ties with older members were far bigger than in previous accessions; also, the eastern location of most new members adds a new geographical dimension to Europe's traditional north–south divide. In addition, sometimes a different loca-tion entails a different historical background and also different regional culture and traditions. For example, until World War I Poland was divided among centralized Prussia and Russia and the relatively decentralized Hapsburg Empire, which granted some degree of local self-government. The Banat region in Romania was under the highly centralized Hungarian crown up to 1918 and so on (see Yoder, 2003). The end of the strongly centralized socialist regimes opened the way to regional development paths that may differ also in relation to history, local traditions and culture.

Finally, the book theoretically discusses and empirically analyses the implica-tions of the financial crisis for the evolution of regional income and employment disparities in European countries/regions, distinguishing between countries inside and outside the European Monetary Union.

The book is organized as follows. Chapter 2 reviews the main theoretical and empirical analyses on regional income convergence. It starts from the neoclassical growth model and then moves to discuss the new growth and new economic geography models. The chapter also reviews the main methodologies used to assess the evolution of income disparities/income convergence. Starting from regression analyses (and β-convergence), it focuses on approaches explicitly taking into account the role of spatial factors and on non-parametric methodologies.

The last part of the chapter presents and discusses a series of stylized facts on the evolution of regional income disparities in Europe.

Overall, the chapter argues that the simultaneous reduction in some disparities and the emergence of new ones cannot be fully understood within the framework of the old and new growth theories. Other approaches emphasizing the role of structural change, regional systems of innovation and socio-economic factors offer new categories that might prove more powerful for accounting for such differentiated patterns of growth and convergence.

These categories are introduced in Chapter 3. After discussing the role of each factor, the chapter classifies European regions – first, according to their specialization, then with respect to their knowledge profiles and, finally, on the basis of their socio-economic characteristics.

The position of European regions in each classification and their transitions over time are investigated with the purpose of assessing, in the following chapters, the explanatory power of the groups for regional convergence/divergence in levels of per capita GDP, labour productivity and employment rates.

Chapter 4 analyses regional disparities in per capita GDP, also focusing on the Eurozone after the 2008 crisis, while Chapter 5 looks at disparities in labour productivity and employment rates.

In both chapters we use different methodologies to investigate the role of the different explanatory factors on regional disparities including the analysis of variance, conditioned distributions and spatial regression models.

The analyses reveal that the general trend of falling variability in per capita income across EU-27 regions actually conceals different and diverse phenomena: on the one hand, income disparities among old EU members grow, especially after the 2008 crisis while, on the other, newcomers reduce their distance from the EU average at the expense of increasing inequalities within countries.

Coming to the determinants of these phenomena, for the EU as a whole, country factors lose importance in explaining regional income disparities. However, this does not hold for older members alone, where country factors regain importance, especially after the crisis. This result runs counter to current wisdom concerning the most likely outcome of 50 years or so of economic integration and raises the question of what determines different reactions to exogenous shocks across countries, most of which share full monetary integration but only partial real integration.

For all regions (either in old or new EU member states) innovation and socio-economic groups gain importance over time. In particular, innovation groups explain differences in EU-relative per capita income better, while socio-economic groups do so with respect to income differences within countries.

But do the trends in per capita GDP reflect similar trends in productivity and employment or are there differences in the behaviour of these variables across regions and over time? There are several reasons for expecting that labour productivity and employment rates might follow different paths across regions and over time. First, we can expect that further economic integration and trade liberalization will raise competition, leading to convergence in labour productivity. In order to catch up with the leaders, regions with low productivity levels will be pushed to adopt new technologies and to raise investments (either domestically or by trying to attract FDI). However, if they lack absorption capacity and financial resources or the capability to attract FDI, they will be able to raise labour productivity only by cutting employment. If regions with low productivity levels also experience low employment rates (and are pushed to cut employment in order to raise labour productivity), convergence in labour productivity might go hand-in-hand with divergence in employment rates. Second, country factors are particularly important in affecting employment rates. The ratio of employment to population depends on both participation in the labour market and on unemployment rates. Southern countries lag behind Nordic ones in participation rates, especially when referring to females and old workers. Moreover, regulation of the labour market still occurs at the national level, leading to differences across countries in important features of the labour market affecting unemployment rates (difficulties in hiring and firing workers, power of the unions, labour taxation, minimum wages). Especially when confronted with downturns, country features can lead to different national responses with possible divergence in employment rates across countries. Although migration can work as a counterbalancing force, due to differences in languages and education, this may be easier within rather than across countries.

The results of the empirical investigations point at an overall process of convergence only in labour productivity consistent with increasing competition across EU regions. However, increasing regional disparities in the employment rate are found. Moreover, when old members are separated from newcomers, divergence occurs in both labour productivity and employment rates. At the same time, the overall convergence in newcomers hides growing disparities in both productivity and employment at the regional level.

Coming to the factors that are responsible for these disparities, the chapter shows that countries exhibit a great (and increasing) share of regional disparities in employment rates, especially in old members. This runs counter to the wisdom of the impact of further integration in the EU and the adoption of a single currency – that it should lead to a reduction in the explanatory power of national factors. However, as expected, countries lose importance in explaining disparities in regional labour productivity: convergence in labour productivity occurs within knowledge, socio-economic and specialization groups, but not within countries.

Finally, for newcomers, within-country disparities in both labour productivity and employment are increasingly explained by innovation and socio-economic groups, with innovation gaining importance especially for disparities in labour productivity, and socio-economic groups for disparities in both labour productivity and employment.

But what kind of transformation has affected regions in newcomers after the transition? In order to answer this question, Chapter 6 takes a longer-run perspective, examining the evolution of regional per capita GDP disparities from the beginning of the 1990s to 2011. Starting from the growing evidence that the shift from socialist regimes to market economies, European integration and trade liberalization have favoured the growth of former planned economies but, at the same time, have strongly increased within-country disparities, the chapter attempts to explain such disparities, making use of a modified categorization of the socio-economic groups introduced by Rodríguez-Pose (1998a). The classification in socio-economic groups may be particularly relevant in newcomers due to at least three reasons: 1) former socialist countries experienced planned industrialization mainly based on heavy industry. This poses strong problems of restructuring when moving from a planned to a market economy also as a result of the new geopolitical configuration, leading to a decline in the demand from the former Soviet Union; 2) capital regions, being the centres of political power and hosting the headquarters of banks, companies, universities and research centres, were far more rich than other areas already in the early 1990s and forged ahead after transition; 3) all Central and Eastern European Countries (CEECs) lie at the eastern borders of the EU; however, some regions are closer to the west and may benefit from this closeness in terms of higher demand, knowledge spillovers, etc. Moreover, sometimes a different location entails a different historical background and also different regional culture and traditions, so that the end of the strongly centralized socialist regimes opens the way to regional development paths that may differ also in relation to history, local traditions and culture.

Together with the traditional groups introduced by Rodríguez-Pose, the chapter suggests analysing a new category of regions: that of FDI-based restructuring regions. These are defined as those administrative units where specialization (country-relative) in industry or services grows over the 2000s and a relevant share of FDI (country-relative) is achieved. The analyses show that, over time, the explanatory power of socio-economic groups has increased, with urban areas and areas under restructuring forging ahead, while peripheral and old industrial regions lag behind.

The main results of the book are summarized in Chapter 7. The chapter also discusses the policy implications at both the national and regional level, with particular attention to innovation and industrial policy but without neglecting macro-economic policy and the impact of the financial crisis on regional (and national) inequalities.

References

Audretsch, D.B. and M. Feldman (2004), 'Knowledge spillovers and the geography of innovation'. In J.V. Henderson and J.F. Thisse (eds), *Handbook of Urban and Regional Economics, Vol. 4*. Amsterdam: Elsevier, pp. 2713–39.

Boschma, R.A. (2005) 'Proximity and innovation: a critical assessment', *Regional Studies*, vol. 39, pp. 61–74.

Bottazzi, L. and G. Peri (2003), 'Innovation and spillovers in regions: evidence from European patent data', *European Economic Review*, vol. 47, pp. 687–710.

Cantwell, J. and S. Iammarino (2003), *Multinational Corporations and European Regional Systems of Innovation*. London: Routledge.

Cheshire, P. and D. Hay (1989), *Urban Problems in Western Europe: An Economic Analysis*. London: Unwin Hyman.

Ciarli, T., V. Meliciani and M. Savona (2012), 'Knowledge dynamics, structural change and the geography of business services', *Journal of Economic Surveys*, vol. 26, pp. 445–67.

Crescenzi, R. (2005), 'Innovation and regional growth in the enlarged Europe: the role of local innovative capabilities, peripherality, and education', *Growth and Change*, vol. 36(4), pp. 471–507.

Crescenzi, R. and A. Rodríguez-Pose (2011), *Innovation and Regional Growth in the European Union*. Berlin, Heidelberg and New York: Springer.

Duranton, G. and D. Puga (2000), 'Diversity and specialisation in cities: why, where and when does it matter?', *Urban Studies*, vol. 37(3), March, pp. 533–55.

Frenken, K. and J. Hoekman (2006), 'Convergence in an enlarged Europe: the role of network cities', *Journal of Economic and Social Geography*, vol. 97, pp. 321–6.

Friedman, T. (2005), *The World is Flat: A Brief History of the Twenty-First Century*. New York: Farrar, Straus and Giroux.

Harvey, D. (1985), *The Urbanization of Capital*. Oxford: Basil Blackwell.

Lundvall, B.A. (1992), *National Systems of Innovation: Towards a Theory of Innovation and Interactive Learning*. London: Pinter.

Meliciani, V. and M. Savona (2014), 'The determinants of regional specialisation in business services: agglomeration economies, vertical linkages and innovation', *Journal of Economic Geography*, pp. 1–30, doi:10.1093/jeg/lbt038, IF=3.26, 5 years IF=5.02

Peri, G. (2004), 'Knowledge flows and productivity', *Rivista di Politica Economica*, March–April, pp. 21–59.

Prager, J.C. and J.F. Thisse (2012), *Economic Geography and the Unequal Development of Regions*. London and New York: Routledge.

Rodríguez-Pose, A. (1998a), *The Dynamics of Regional Growth in Europe: Social and Political Factors*. Oxford: Clarendon Press.

Rodríguez-Pose, A. (1998b), 'Social conditions and economic performance: the bond between social structure and regional growth in Western Europe', *International Journal of Urban and Regional Research*, vol. 22, pp. 443–59.

Rodríguez-Pose, A. (1999), 'Convergence or divergence? Types of regional responses to socio-economic change in Western Europe', *Tijdschrift voor Economische en Sociale Geografie*, vol. 90, pp. 365–78.

Rodríguez-Pose, A. and R. Crescenzi (2008), 'Mountains in a flat world: why proximity still matters for the location of economic activity', *Cambridge Journal of Regions, Economy and Society*, Cambridge Political Economy Society, vol. 1(3), pp. 371–88.

Rubalcaba, L. and H. Kox (eds) (2007), *Business Services in European Economic Growth*. New York: Palgrave Macmillan.

Yoder J.A. (2003), 'Decentralisation and regionalisation after communism: administrative and territorial reform in Poland and the Czech Republic', *Europe-Asia Studies*, vol. 552(2), pp. 263–86.

2 Regional income disparities
Theories and facts

Introduction

This chapter reviews the main theoretical and empirical studies on regional income convergence. It starts from the neoclassical growth model and then moves to discuss the new growth and new economic geography models. The most important prediction of the neoclassical growth model is that countries will convergence in growth rates and income levels. Such prediction, finding little empirical support, does not necessarily hold in new growth models and new economic geography models. In particular, new growth models introducing increasing returns allow for sustained income divergence, while new economic geography models offer some useful insights on the relationship between economic integration, agglomeration and income disparities.

The second part of the chapter is a review of the main methodologies used to assess the evolution of income disparities/income convergence. Starting from regression analyses (and β-convergence), it then focuses on approaches taking explicitly into account the role of spatial factors and, finally, focuses on the use of non-parametric methodologies.

The last part of the chapter presents and discusses a series of stylized facts on the evolution of regional income disparities in Europe.

Overall, the chapter argues that, although most studies support the existence of a catching-up process in Europe, convergence is not taking place uniformly across regions; rather, some areas leap ahead while others are left behind. The simultaneous reduction in some disparities and the emergence of new ones cannot be fully understood within the framework of the old and new growth theories. Other approaches emphasizing the role of structural change, regional systems of innovation and socio-economic factors offer new categories that might prove more powerful for accounting for such differentiated patterns of growth and convergence. From a methodological perspective, the adoption of those tools that allow study of the evolution of entire distributions rather than focusing on the behaviour of the 'average' region may be very useful for capturing the heterogeneity of regional growth processes.

Theories of growth, convergence and spatial agglomeration

This section reviews the main theories devoted to explaining the evolution of income disparities. It argues that the debate within the neoclassical tradition (old and new) has remained confined to examining the conditions for income convergence (growth theories) and the conditions favouring or hampering the spatial agglomeration of economic activity (new economic geography). However, this literature has largely neglected the role played by the structural and socio-economic characteristics of each territory and the ability to produce and absorb new knowledge, which appears to be an important factor for understanding the differentiated patterns of income growth and convergence across European regions.

Income convergence in the neoclassical growth model

Neoclassical growth models deal with a production function with constant returns to scale and decreasing marginal product for any single factor of production. Consequently, they assert that countries/regions with a higher capital–labour ratio must have a lower productivity of capital and lower growth rates compared with countries/regions with a lower capital–labour ratio. In this model, the increase in output is given by the increase in the labour force, the increase in the capital stock and the increase in the overall efficiency in the use of inputs. In the steady state, when output and capital grow at the same rate, the increase in per capita income is explained only by exogenous technical progress.

In the simpler neoclassical model, the production process can be illustrated by a Cobb–Douglas production function:

$$Y=AK^{\alpha}L^{1-\alpha} \tag{2.1}$$

where Y indicates real output; A the overall efficiency in the use of inputs; L the labour force; K capital; α the elasticity of output with respect to capital; $1-\alpha$ the elasticity of output to labour. This production function satisfies the following properties: 1) the marginal product of the factors of production is positive and declining:

$$F_K=\frac{\partial Y}{\partial K}>0; \quad F_L=\frac{\partial Y}{\partial L}>0; \quad F_{KK}=\frac{\partial^2 Y}{\partial K^2}<0; \quad F_{LL}=\frac{\partial^2 Y}{\partial L^2}<0$$

2) the function exhibits constant returns to scale:

$$F(\lambda K,\lambda L)=\lambda F(K,L);$$

3) the marginal product of the factors of production approaches infinity as the factors of production approach zero and approaches zero as they approach infinity (Inada conditions):

$$\frac{\lim(F_K)}{K\to 0}=\frac{\lim(F_L)}{L\to 0}=\infty; \quad \frac{\lim(F_K)}{K\to\infty}=\frac{\lim(F_L)}{L\to\infty}=0$$

There are two versions of the neoclassical model: one with exogenous savings rates (Solow, 1956; Swan, 1956) and one with consumer optimization (Ramsey,

1928; Cass, 1965; Koopmans, 1965). Here we will refer only to the first version as the conclusions do not differ substantially from those reached in the optimizing approach.

Assuming a constant savings rate and equality between investment and savings, we obtain the following expression for the rate of growth of capital:

$$\dot{k}=\frac{\dot{K}}{L}-nK=\frac{I}{L}-(d+n)k=\frac{sY}{L}-(d+n)k=sf(k)-(d+n)k \qquad (2.2)$$

where k is the capital–labour ratio, $\dot{k}$ denotes its time derivative, I is investment, s the savings rate, d the depreciation rate and n the rate of growth of the labour force. Figure 2.1 shows the dynamics implied by equation (2.2).

Whenever k is less than $k*$ savings per capita exceed the amount necessary for maintaining a constant stock of per capita capital so that k increases; the opposite happens when k is higher than $k*$ – therefore, the economy tends towards $k*$. In the long run, the capital–labour ratio is constant and capital grows at the same rate as the rate of growth of the labour force. Since k is constant in the steady state, y and c (consumption per capita) are also constant at the values $y*=f(k*)$ and $c*=(1-s)f(k*)$.

Considering two economies with the same production function, savings rate and rate of growth of population, the model predicts convergence in capital–labour ratios as the country with the lower capital–labour ratio has a higher capital productivity and a higher rate of growth. Moreover, in the long run all countries grow at the same rate given by the rate of exogenous technical change.

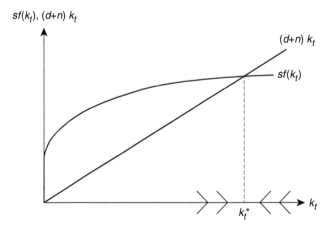

Figure 2.1 The dynamics of the neoclassical growth model.

Allowing for income divergence: the new growth models

Starting from equation (2.2) and introducing the Cobb–Douglas production function in per capita terms (denoting the coefficient on labour more generically with β rather than $1-\alpha$) we obtain:

$$\dot{k} = sK^{\alpha} L^{\alpha+\beta-1} - (d+n)k \tag{2.3}$$

Dividing both sides of (2.3) by k, indicating the rate of growth of the capital–labour ratio with γ and taking logarithms and derivatives, we obtain in the steady state, when all variables grow at a constant rate:

$$0 = (\alpha-1)\gamma + (\alpha+\beta-1)n \tag{2.4}$$

According to neoclassical growth theory, with constant returns to scale ($\alpha+\beta=1$) and decreasing marginal product for any factor of production ($\alpha<1$), the only possible steady state is $\gamma=0$: growth is explained by relying on exogenous technical progress.

Equation (2.4) is interesting because it shows different possibilities of having unbounded growth without relying on exogenous technical progress:

1) $\alpha+\beta=1$ and $\alpha=1$; this is the case of constant returns to scale and constant returns to reproducible factors;
2) $\beta>0$ and $\alpha=1$ so that $\alpha+\beta>1$; this is the case of increasing returns to scale and constant returns to the reproducible factors, in this case if $n>0$ equation (2.4) cannot be satisfied: the rate of growth is not constant but it increases over time.

The problem with a production function exhibiting increasing returns to scale is that it is inconsistent with the assumption of perfect competition: with increasing returns to scale the average cost is declining, and firms are tempted to increase production and acquire some market power. This problem has been solved following two different approaches:

2a) assuming that the factors that are paid their marginal revenues exhibit constant returns to scale and that the increasing returns are generated by the existence of externalities (Romer, 1986; Lucas, 1988);
2b) abandoning the hypothesis of perfect competition; in this case the existence of extra profits allows for the remuneration of inputs that are not directly productive such as R&D expenses (Romer, 1990; Grossman and Helpman, 1991).

We will not go into the details of these different models since it is outside the scope of this book. However, in both cases the presence of increasing returns to scale leads to self-sustaining growth and no convergence in (per capita) output levels.

In fact, assuming constant returns to the reproducible factors ($\alpha=1$), in a production function without non-reproducible factors ($\beta=0$) (so that we keep

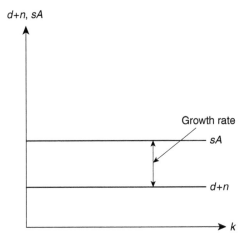

d+n, sA

Growth rate

sA

d+n

k

Figure 2.2 Persistent growth in the new growth models.

constant returns to scale), the per capita capital growth rate is given by the difference between the two lines *sA* and *d+n* (see Figure 2.2).

The same result applies with a production function exhibiting increasing returns to scale $\alpha+\beta>1$ and constant returns to the reproducible factor $\alpha=1$. Taking equation (2.3) with increasing returns to scale $\alpha+\beta>1$, adding the overall efficiency term *A*, and dividing by *k* we obtain:

$$\gamma = sAL^{\beta} - (d+n) \tag{2.5}$$

In this case the per capita capital growth rate is equal to the difference between the functions sAL^{β}, still independent of *k*, and *d+n*.

The new geography models and the agglomeration of economic activities

New economic geography's models seek to explain uneven spatial development on the basis of the interaction between economies of scale, monopolistic competition with product variety and iceberg transport costs. There are numerous contributions within this line of investigation (Krugman and Venables, 1990; Krugman, 1991a, 1991b; Krugman and Venables, 1995; Krugman and Venables, 1996; Puga, 1996; Venables, 1996; Puga, 1999; etc.) and a comprehensive review of this literature is outside the scope of this book (for reviews, see Ottaviano and Puga, 1998, and Ascani *et al.*, 2012). Here, we will focus on few examples of such models chosen since they can offer some useful insights on the impact of integration on agglomeration and income disparities in Europe. In particular, due to the relatively low level of labour mobility in Europe, we will start from models with labour immobility and conclude with Puga (1999), allowing for a different impact of integration on agglomeration and income disparities according to the mobility of labour.

Venables (1996) develops a new economic geography (NEG) model with inter-industry linkages. This model is particularly interesting since it allows location decisions of firms in one industry to depend on those in other (vertically integrated) industries. In the model, the manufacturing sector consists of two sub-sectors (upstream and downstream industries), both operating under increasing returns and imperfect competition, while the agriculture sector operates under constant returns to scale and perfect competition.[1] Demand and cost linkages between the two vertically linked industries favour agglomeration; however, due to labour immobility, final consumer demand and labour supply are tied to locations and this operates against agglomeration. The balance between centripetal and centrifugal forces depends on the relative strength of linkages and on transport costs. For high trade costs, the location decisions of firms are driven by market access considerations (final consumer demand is mostly served locally), so that manufacturing of final goods is equally distributed between the two locations. With increasing economic integration and trade costs approaching medium levels, the region with more producers of inputs offers cost advantages for downstream firms, which start to move towards this location. Although rising wages constitute a force towards dispersion for firms, the interaction of scale economies with vertical linkages and intermediate trade costs makes centripetal forces prevailing, and industry agglomerates. Finally, for low trade costs, the main driver of location decision becomes the wage rate and firms are again dispersed across regions. The overall result is a non-monotonic bell-shaped relationship between the decrease in transport costs and agglomeration. Applied to the European context, with limited labour mobility, we could predict agglomeration increasing during the first phases of economic integration, but dispersion forces acting again at higher levels of trade liberalization.

While the model of Venables (1996) explains agglomeration and predicts a non-monotonic relationship between integration and agglomeration, Krugman and Venables (1996) aim at explaining the relationship between economic integration and specialization. Starting from the observation that industry is much less concentrated in Europe than in the USA, they ask whether further integration will make Europe more similar to the USA. They consider two imperfectly competitive production sectors with firms producing both final and intermediate goods. Intra-industry input output linkages are higher than inter-industry, so that if one more firm locates in a region, the beneficial cost and demand linkages affect more intensely firms in the same sector, while the increased product and labour market competition harms firms in both sectors equally. With high trade barriers, each industry operates in both locations in order to supply final consumers. At intermediate values of transport costs we have more complex outcomes. If the economy starts with a fairly equal division of each industry between the two countries, it will converge to an outcome without agglomeration; but if the industries are initially very unequally distributed, specialization will occur. Finally, stronger economic integration leads to agglomeration of industries and each country specializes in one sector.[2]

Puga (1999) starts from the observation that not only is economic activity less geographically concentrated in the EU than in the USA, but also income disparities across EU members are much wider than across US states. In order to explain these patterns, Puga (ibid.) proposes a model allowing for both vertical linkages and labour mobility. The model shows that for high trade costs industry is spread across regions to meet final consumer demand. For intermediate trade costs, increasing returns interacting with migration and/or input output linkages between firms lead to agglomeration. Finally, in the case of low trade costs, the outcome depends on labour mobility. When workers migrate towards locations with more firms and higher real wages, this intensifies agglomeration and even for trade costs approaching to zero the process of concentration of production is not reversed. On the contrary, if workers do not move, firms become increasingly sensitive to cost differentials, leading industry to spread out again. The model, therefore, predicts that, because of a lack of interregional labour mobility, European integration may cause regional convergence both in terms of real wages and of production structures. However, the ability of the periphery to catch up in this context relies on integration going far enough and on a flexible response of wages to changes in industrial employment. In particular, in the presence of low mobility of the workforce and of centralized wage setting mechanisms (at the country level), trade liberalization may increase agglomeration, leading to a rise in income inequalities between regions within each country and to polarization in employment rates (Puga, 2002). With lack of sufficient wage flexibility, polarization in employment rates may occur also between countries as low productivity countries cut employment to gain competitiveness (Meliciani, 2006).

Overall NEG models offer very useful insights on the centripetal and centrifugal forces associated with the process of economic integration. However, locations are identical with the exception of allowing, in some cases, for an initial asymmetric distribution of industry across them. Therefore, these models may have difficulties in explaining why different typologies of regions experience very different outcomes as a consequence of economic integration, an issue we will come back in the next chapter.

Testing for convergence: main methodologies

This section reviews the main methodologies used to assess the evolution of income disparities (income convergence). Starting from regression analyses (and β-convergence), it then focuses on approaches taking explicitly into account the role of spatial factors and, finally, on the use of non-parametric methodologies.

Absolute and conditional convergence

The basic statistical model in the empirical literature on convergence is the deterministic linear trend model with AR(1) errors:[3]

$$Y_{it} = c_i + g_i t + U_{it} \tag{2.6a}$$

$$U_{it} = \lambda_i U_{i,t-1} + \varepsilon_{it} ; \tag{2.6b}$$

or equivalently:

$$Y_{it} = \mu_i + \lambda_i g_i + \theta_i g_i t + \lambda_i Y_{i,t-1} + \varepsilon_{it} \qquad (2.7)$$

with: $\mu_i = (1-\lambda_i)c_i + \lambda_i g_i$ and $\theta_i = (1-\lambda_i)g_i$

where Y_{it} is the log of per capita GDP of region i at time t, $\lambda \in (-1, 1)$ and ε_{it} is an innovation with constant variance σ_i^2. Notice that innovations may be contemporaneously correlated across regions. The parameters c_i and g_i respectively measure the mean initial level and the mean growth rate of per capita GDP in region i, whereas the autoregressive parameter λ_i measures the degree of persistence of the shocks to log per capita GDP in region i. The parameter $v_i = -\ln \lambda_i$, defined for $\lambda_i > 0$, measures the speed of convergence of per capita GDP in region i to its long-run growth path $c_i + g_i t$, and will be referred to as the 'rate of convergence'.

The model implies that, for any two regions i and j:

$$E = (Y_{i,t+k} - Y_{j,t+k}) = c_i - c_j + (g_i - g_j)(t+k) \qquad (2.8)$$

provided $-1 < \lambda_i, \lambda_j < 1$, where $E(Y_{i,t+k})$ denotes the unconditional mean of log per capita GDP at time $t+k$. This shows that convergence across regions depends on regional homogeneity in the parameters c_i and g_i. If $g_i = g_j = g$, then the difference (2.8) converges to the constant value $c_i - c_j$. We refer to this case as 'convergence in growth rates'. If, in addition, $c_i = c_j = c$, then the conditional expectation of log per capita GDP in the two regions converges to the same value $c + g(t+k)$ as $k \to \infty$. We refer to this case as 'convergence in levels'.

The growth equations that are often estimated in cross-section studies (the so-called 'Barro regressions') can be obtained from (2.6) by imposing equality across regions in all parameters $(c_i; g_i; \lambda_i)$, while the growth equations estimated in the context of fixed effects models can be obtained by imposing homogeneity in the parameters g_i and λ_i leaving the c_i unrestricted.

If $\lambda_i = 1$, the intercept c_i is not identifiable and model (2.6) reduces to $Y_{it} - Y_{i,t-1} = g_i + \varepsilon_{it}$, namely a random walk with drift g_i.

In this case it makes sense to talk about convergence only if the processes for log per capita GDP in the two regions are cointegrated.

Equation (2.6) may arise as the reduced form of several growth models including the Solow (1956) growth model (for a derivation, see Lee et al., 1997). In particular, in this model, convergence in growth rates is guaranteed by the fact that technology is an exogenous variable equally available to all countries and regions, so that $g_i = g_j$. Convergence in levels will occur whenever countries/regions have identical model parameters (savings rate, depreciation rate, growth rate of labour inputs, initial level of technology) resulting in $c_i = c_j$, otherwise regions/countries will experience conditional convergence – that is, each region/country will converge to its own steady state $c_i \neq c_j$. Differently, the existence of constant returns to the reproducible factors ($\alpha=1$) and constant or increasing returns to scale $\alpha+\beta=>1$ (characteristics of new growth models) is consistent with $\lambda_i=1$, implying the absence of convergence to a steady state level of per capita GDP. As stated before, in this case convergence across regions is a meaningful concept only if the per capita GDP series are cointegrated.

Testing for convergence with spatial correlation

Conventional growth regressions assume that regional observations are independent, but there is a growing consensus that regional income growth rates exhibit spatial dependence (Abreu *et al.*, 2004; LeSage and Fischer, 2008). The first studies investigating income convergence in the presence of spatial dependence (Armstrong, 1995, for European regions; Rey and Montouri, 1999, for US regions) have relied mainly on the spatial lag (or spatial autocorrelation) model (SAR) and/ or on the spatial error model (SEM). The first model assumes spatial autocorrelation in the dependent variable – that is, in the case of convergence studies it assumes that the level (or growth) of per capita GDP in region *i* is affected by the level (rate of growth) of spatially contiguous regions. This might occur because of knowledge spillovers, labour mobility, commodity flows, etc. The SEM model assumes spatial dependence in the disturbances – that is, unobservable factors affecting spatial contiguous regions have a feedback effect in the typical region.

More recently, LeSage and Fischer (2008) have suggested the adoption of a more general model allowing for spatial dependence: the Spatial Durbin model (SDM). This model allows for spatial dependence in both the dependent and explanatory variables and is appropriate, independently from economic considerations, when two circumstances are verified: 1) spatial dependence occurs in the disturbances of a regression model and 2) there is an omitted explanatory variable (variables) that exhibits non-zero covariance with a variable (variables) included in the model. LeSage and Fisher (ibid.) show that these circumstances are very likely to occur in the estimation of convergence equations. Another advantage of the SDM is that it nests most models used in the regional literature, including the SAR and SEM models.

The model can be represented as follows:

$$Y = \rho WY + X\beta_1 + WX\beta_2 + v \qquad (2.9)$$

where Y denotes a $Nx1$ vector consisting of the dependent variable, X is a NxK matrix of independent variables, W is an NxN non-negative spatial weights matrix with zeros on the diagonal. A vector or matrix premultiplied by W denotes its spatially lagged value, ρ, β_1 and β_2 are response parameters and v is a $Nx1$ vector of residuals with zero mean and variance σ^2.

In the case of a standard growth model, Y may denote the (log) level of per capita GDP and X may include the lagged level of per capita GDP and, in the case of conditional convergence, a set of explanatory variables which are assumed to affect countries/regions steady state per capita GDP (e.g., human capital, physical capital, etc.).

As stated above, the model encompasses several spatial models. In particular, imposing the restriction that $\beta_2=0$ leads to a spatial autoregressive (SAR) model that includes a spatial lag of the dependent variable from related regions, but excludes these regions' characteristics. Imposing the restriction that $\beta_2=-\rho\beta_1$ yields the SEM that allows only for spatial dependence in the disturbances. Imposing the restriction that $\rho=0$ leads to a spatially lagged X regression model (SLX) that assumes independence between the regional dependent variables, but includes characteristics from related regions in the form of explanatory variables. Finally, imposing the restriction that $\rho=0$ and $\beta_2=0$ leads to a non-spatial regression model.

In this model a change in a single explanatory variable in region i has a *direct impact* on region i as well as an *indirect impact* on other regions (see LeSage and Fischer, 2008, for a discussion). This result arises from the spatial connectivity relationships that are incorporated in spatial regression models and it raises the difficulty of interpreting the resulting estimates. There are two possible (equivalent) interpretations of indirect effects. One interpretation reflects how changing each explanatory variable of all neighbouring regions by some constant amount would affect the dependent variable of a typical region. LeSage and Pace (2009) label this as the average total impact on an observation. The second interpretation measures the cumulative impact of a change in each explanatory variable in region i over all neighbouring regions, which LeSage and Pace (2009) label the average total impact from an observation (see also LeSage and Fischer, 2008). LeSage and Pace (2009) provide computationally feasible means of calculating scalar summary measures of direct and indirect impacts that arise from changes in the explanatory variables.

Overall the inclusion of spatial effects into standard growth equations enriches the traditional neoclassical model by allowing the outcome of each region to depend on that of the surrounding regions. These models are very useful in the presence of spatial correlation and will be used in Chapter 4 to estimate growth regressions. However, apart from problems related to the choice of the appropriate spatial weight matrix, a major limitation of these models is that they allow for the formation of 'convergence clubs' only on the basis of geographical distance.[4] In the next section a more general methodology, potentially able to deal also with spatial factors and relying on non-parametric techniques, is illustrated. This methodology will complement the regression analyses throughout this book.

Non-parametric tests of convergence

Critiques of parametric tests of convergence (in particular β-convergence) go from statistical problems in estimating the rate of convergence to it being uninformative for a distribution's dynamics (Quah, 1996a). In particular, Quah (ibid.) shows that the uniformity in the estimation of the convergence rate around the value of 2 per cent might depend on a unit root in the series of per capita GDP (see also Meliciani and Peracchi, 2006). More relevant is also the fact that a negative β-coefficient is consistent with a stable or even increasing variance in the per capita GDP distribution. In fact, suppose Y's are independent and identically distributed cross-sections of per capita GDP with:

$$Y_{it} = bY_{it-1} + u_{it}, \quad |b| < 1, \quad Y_{i0} \text{ independent of } u_{it}$$

where u is iid also in time, and has a positive finite variance σ_u^2. This implies:

$$\sigma_t^2 = b^2 \sigma_{t-1}^2 + \sigma_u^2 \Rightarrow \lim_{t \to \infty} \sigma_t^2 = \left(1 - b^2\right)^{-1} \sigma_u^2$$

Therefore, β-convergence implies also σ-convergence (a decrease in σ^2 over time) only if $\sigma_0^2 \ll \left(1 - b^2\right)^{-1} \sigma_u^2$

In order to tackle with this problem several studies have complemented information on β-convergence with that on σ-convergence. However, also σ-convergence has important limitations when one is interested to distribution dynamics. For example, Quah (1996a) shows two situations that are radically different in terms of distribution dynamics but both involve a stable variance. In the first case (ibid., p. 1364, Fig. 1), economies show criss-crossing and leap-frogging while, in the second case (ibid., p. 1366, Fig. 3), there is persistent inequality: rich economies always remain rich; poor ones, poor. In both cases σ^2 remains unchanged, showing that information on just one characteristic of the cross-section distribution does not allow very different distributions dynamics to be distinguished. The natural way to study convergence empirics is to provide an empirical model for how distributions evolve (Quah, 1996a).[5]

Let F_t denote the distribution of incomes across countries at time t. Associated with such a distribution is a measure λ_t. The simplest model for the evolution of $\{F_t: \text{integer } t\}$, or equivalently $\{\lambda_t: \text{integer } t\}$, is an autoregression in measures:

$$\forall \text{ measurables sets } A : \lambda_{t+1}(A) = \int M(y, A) d\lambda_t(y) \tag{2.10}$$

where M is a *stochastic kernel*, mapping the Cartesian product of income values and measurable sets to the interval $[0,1]$. The kernel M maps one measure λ_t, into another λ_{t+1}, and tracks where in F_{t+1} points in F_t end up. Thus, M encodes information on intra-distribution dynamics; it therefore contains strictly more information than just aggregate statistics such as means or standard deviations.

Equation (2.10) is analogous to a standard time-series first-order vector autoregression, except its values are distributions (rather than scalars or vectors of numbers), and it contains no explicit disturbance or innovation. By analogy with autoregression, there is no reason why the law of motion in λ_t need be first order, or why the relation need be time-invariant. Nevertheless, (2.10) is a useful first step for analysing dynamics in $\{\lambda_t\}$. Rewrite (2.10) as the convolution $\lambda_{t+1} = M\lambda_t$ iterating yields (a predictor for) future cross-section distributions: $\lambda_{t+s} = M^s\lambda_t$. Taking this to the limit as $s \to \infty$, one can characterize the likely long-run or ergodic distribution of cross-country incomes. The speed of convergence of the evolving distributions and their cross-sectional mobility properties can be studied from certain spectral characteristics of the kernel M.

In order to estimate M, one possibility is to discretize the measures λ_t so that M becomes just a transition probability matrix; and λ's become non-negative vectors on the unit simplex. A second possibility is to estimate non-parametrically the infinite-dimensional kernel M.

To give an intuition of the use of kernel estimates for understanding distribution dynamics Figure 2.3 reports density estimates and contour plots[6] under extreme hypotheses on the behaviour of the economies over time: a) convergence, b) criss-crossing, c) polarization and d) stability.

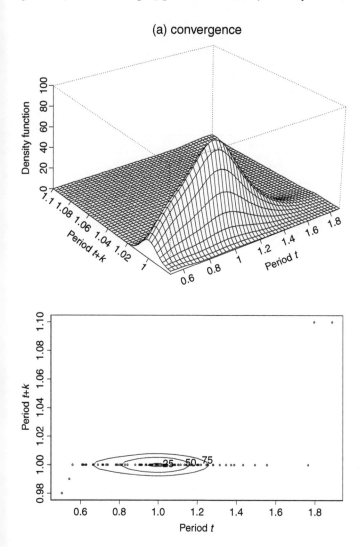

Figure 2.3 Convergence, criss-crossing, polarization and stability.

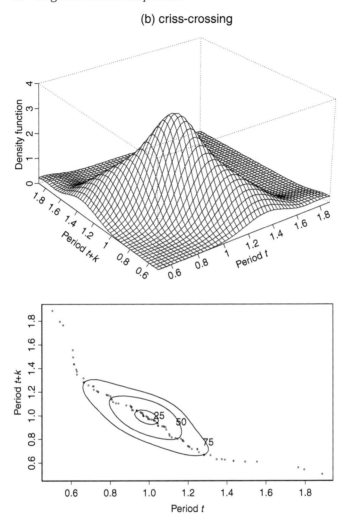

Figure 2.3 (Continued)

In the case of convergence, the distribution at time $t+k$ collapses to a point; in the case of criss-crossing, the density is concentrated around the secondary diagonal; in the case of polarization, the density at time $t+k$ has two modes; and in the case of stability the density is concentrated around the main diagonal.

If we consider the per capita GDP distribution, the first case would occur when all the economies, starting from different levels of per capita GDP, converge to the same level (absolute convergence). The second case means that poor economies are becoming rich while, at the same time, rich economies are becoming poor; this case is denoted as 'criss-crossing' and it is the less likely to be observed in reality. The third case occurs when two groups of economies converge to a

(c) polarization

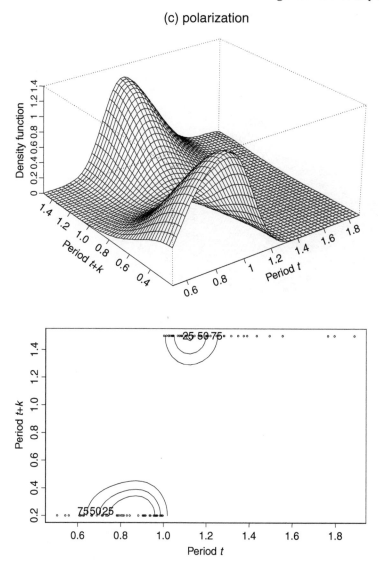

Figure 2.3 (Continued)

different level of per capita GDP (e.g., convergence clubs). The fourth case means that each economy maintains its relative position in the per capita GDP distribution (it can be consistent with conditional convergence if the economies have converged to different levels of per capita GDP). These are extreme cases but give an idea of the information that can be inferred from the study of the shape of a bivariate kernel density estimate. This information is much richer than that contained in σ and β measures of convergence.

(d) stability

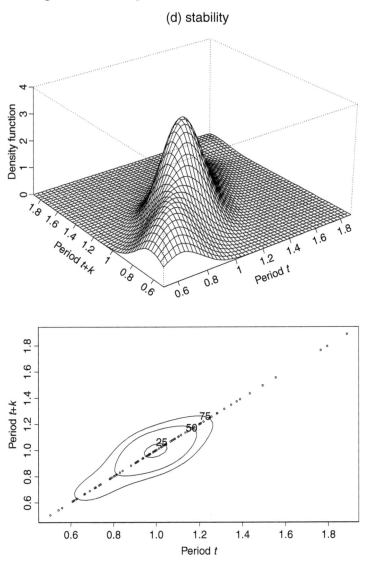

Figure 2.3 (Continued)

Testing for convergence across European regions: main results

So far several empirical papers have investigated convergence in the EU-25 (or 27) following different methodologies. Barro and Sala-i-Martin (1991), Sala-i-Martin (1996), Armstrong (1995) and Neven and Gouyette (1995) test for convergence in the context of cross-sectional 'Barro regressions'; Islam (1995), Canova and Marcet (1995) and de la Fuente (1996) use fixed effects models; Fischer and Stirböck (2005), Debarsy and Ertur (2006), Frenken and Hoekman (2006) and Paas *et al.* (2007) test for convergence across the enlarged EU in the context of regression analysis; Ertur and Koch (2006) use exploratory spatial data analysis; Ezcurra and Rapun (2007) adopt a non-parametric approach; Chapman *et al.* (2012) and Chapman and Meliciani (2012) use both non-parametric and spatial regression analyses.

Overall, we summarize the main results of these empirical analyses as a series of stylized facts.

Stylized fact 1: *Convergence, when occurs, is slow and it is limited to a group of European regions*

The results on convergence vary considerably depending on the regions included, the sample period and the estimation method. Using cross-sectional 'Barro regressions', Barro and Sala-i-Martin (1991) found that regions within the EU experienced convergent growth in per capita GDP over the period 1950–85 at an annual rate of about 2 per cent. Their analysis, however, is confined to the richest European countries. Fingleton (1999) finds that, from a neoclassical perspective, there is only weak evidence that EU regions are converging, requiring more than two centuries for approximate convergence to be achieved. Similarly, Armstrong (1995), enlarging the sample of Barro and Sala-i-Martin to Greece, Ireland, Luxembourg and Portugal, finds convergence rates of only some 1 per cent per year between 1970 and 1990.

Overall, there is agreement that rates of convergence, in particular within-country convergence, fell from their peak in the 1960s. Moreover, during the 1980s divergence between north and south Europe has emerged (Neven and Gouyette, 1995).

Studies using the fixed effects approach (Islam, 1995; Canova and Marcet, 1995; de la Fuente, 1996) obtain much higher convergence rates than those found in cross-country regressions. The convergence process has a different interpretation, however, for it is convergence to country- or region-specific steady-states.

Stylized fact 2: *Countries strongly condition the evolution of regional disparities but regional disparities within countries are persistent*

Rodríguez-Pose (1998a, 1999) underlines the importance of country effects in determining regional GDP dynamics in old EU members (an area grows because the country it belongs to grows).[7] In particular, he finds a strong national influence on regional growth rates in Europe between 1977 and 1993. Moreover, he finds no evidence of convergence between regions within countries: in many states the fastest-growing regions are precisely those that had the highest levels of GDP in 1977. The capital areas in many countries grew at a faster pace than other regions, although starting from above average levels of per capita GDP.

Similarly, Ezcurra *et al.* (2005) reveal the fundamental role of the country effect in accounting for regional disparities in income per worker in Europe between 1977 and 1999; Ezcurra *et al.* (2007) highlight the important role played in explaining the distribution dynamics of European regions (including newcomers) by the national component. Ezcurra *et al.* (ibid.) also find between-country convergence and within-country divergence. In the enlarged Europe 84 per cent of global inequality in the early 1990s was explained by inequality in average per capita income across countries. By 2001, however, this percentage had dropped to 29 per cent. Similar results are found by Chapman and Meliciani (2012), showing that between 1998 and 2005 income converges overall but disparities within countries rise; this is largely due to strong divergence emerging between the regions of newcomer countries.

Meliciani (2006) argues that, in investigating converge across regions, the national element should not be neglected. In fact, European regions are part of European countries and institutional differences operating at the national level can induce different dynamics in income and employment across countries. The paper finds evidence of a strong country effect in the dynamics of the employment rate across European regions over the period 1988–96. At the same time, it finds evidence of increases in within-country regional disparities.

Spiezia and Weiler (2007) distinguish between regional and national factors in explaining regional growth across OECD regions over the period 1998–2003. They find that changes in the GDP share of the country in total OECD explain more than half of the changes in the GDP share of the region in total OECD.

Stylized fact 3: *Geographical distance matters for regional convergence*

A large and increasing number of empirical analyses, focusing either on the more restricted pre-enlargement sample (Armstrong, 1995; López-Bazo *et al.*, 1999, 2004; Le Gallo and Ertur, 2003) or extending the analysis to the enlarged Europe (Ertur and Koch, 2006; Chapman *et al.*, 2012) have looked at spatial correlation in European regions' income levels or rates of growth. A general result is that the level and growth rates of per capita GDP are spatially correlated (for a review see Abreu *et al.*, 2004, and Rey and Janikas, 2005). In what follows the focus is on some of the main findings of the literature.

López-Bazo *et al.* (1999) find that over the 1980s European regions did not converge in GDP per capita. They also find persistence in the spatial clusters of low values in the traditional periphery, supporting the view that, despite the progressive dematerialization, the location and physical geography still matter in the EU. This might be due to the fact that technology diffusion is mostly restricted to within-country borders and may be significantly bounded by distance (López-Bazo *et al.*, 2004). The presence of local spatial spillovers from domestic neighbours is also found in Basile (2008), using a semiparametric SDM to analyse the growth behaviour of 155 European regions in the period 1988–2000. The study also finds evidence of global spillovers across countries.

Le Gallo and Ertur (2003), using a sample of European regions over the 1980–95 period, find strong evidence of global and local spatial autocorrelation in per capita GDP throughout the period, pointing to persistence of spatial disparities between European regions. Similarly, Eczurra and Rapun (2007) find a significant role for neighbouring regions in explaining the dispersion in GDP per worker, while LeSage and Fischer (2008) show that long-run steady-state

regional income depends on own-region as well as neighbouring region characteristics, the spatial connectivity structure of the regions and the strength of
spatial dependence.

Other studies complement the evidence on spatial correlation with the existence
of convergence clubs based on geographical clusters (Le Gallo and Dall'erba,
2006; Fischer and Stirböch, 2004;[8] Ramajo *et al.*, 2008). For example, Ramajo
et al. (2008) find strong support for the existence of two different spatial regimes
over 1981–96 concerning cohesion and non-cohesion regions, with convergence
being stronger for regions of the cohesion group than for non-cohesion ones.

When extending the analysis to newcomers, interesting results on changes in
regional geographical patterns emerge. In particular, Ertur and Koch (2006) using
an extended EU-27 sample of 258 European regions, including regions from
acceding and candidate European countries, over the period 1995–2000 find
evidence of a new north–west/east polarization pattern which replaces the previous
north–south one for the EU-15. This result is confirmed by regression analysis in
Chapman *et al.* (2012).

Stylized fact 4: *National factors and geography alone do not explain regional
disparities (and their evolution) in Europe*

Several studies, mainly overcoming the limitations of estimating simple convergence regressions and allowing for club convergence, find that new disparities are
emerging across European regions. Some of these disparities have a geographical
dimension but others are linked to factors not accounted for in either the simplest
neoclassical growth models or in the more articulated analyses embedded within
the NEG tradition. These include regional patterns of specialization, socio-
economic factors and the regional ability to introduce and adopt the new technologies. Such factors will be extensively analysed in Chapter 3 and will be the
main focus of this book. Here the main results are summarized.

Some authors find that the sectoral composition of production is often important in determining regional differences in growth processes. This holds for both
old member regions (Paci and Pigliaru 1997, 1999; Paci *et al.*, 2001; Mora *et al.*,
2005) and for the eight Central and East European countries (CEECs) that joined
the EU in 2004 (Ezcurra *et al.*, 2007).[9] However, other studies question this
conclusion (Esteban, 2000; Ezcurra *et al.*, 2005). Moreover, the different studies
use different methodologies and focus on different sectors.

European Commission (1999)[10] argues that regions specializing in dynamic,
high-growth sectors tend to perform better in terms of per capita income.
Similarly, Mora *et al.* (2005), studying convergence between 1985 and 2000, find
that European regions specialized in low-tech intensive industries before the
integration process do not show conditional convergence. They also find that
regions with lower specialization in low-tech industries but further from the core
showed a significantly higher convergence rate.

Paci and Pigliaru (1999), rather than focusing on specific sectors, use the
decomposition methodology proposed in Bernard and Jones (1996), and find that

76 per cent of the (weak) aggregate labour productivity convergence across 109 European regions in the period 1980–90 is due to sectoral dynamics. However, this study is silent on the role played by the different sectors. This is investigated in Paci *et al.* (2001), looking at convergence in per capita GDP, labour productivity and employment across European regions and distinguishing regions according to their specialization. They find that regions that start from a low agricultural share are the richest and grow relatively slowly. Regions that start from very high agricultural shares are characterized by a fast decline of that share and by higher than average growth rates but a limited decline in their employment rates. Regions specialized in service activities show a particularly slow rate of productivity growth and a rising employment rate.

Differently from the previous studies, Ezcurra *et al.* (2005) question the role of specialization in explaining regional inequalities in labour productivity over the period 1977–99. In fact, using a combination of shift-share analysis with various results reported in the literature on personal income distribution, they finds that industry mix contributed relatively little to regional dispersion in labour productivity. Similar results are found by Esteban (2000) using a more limited number of sectors and regions.

Also, when analysing the enlarged Europe, the results on the role of specialization are mixed. Ezcurra *et al.* (2007) examine the evolution of territorial imbalances in per capita income between 1990 and 2001 and find an important role played in explaining the distribution dynamics by regional productive structures. However, Ezcurra and Rapun (2007), focusing on spatial disparities in labour productivity over the period 1991–2003, find that industry mix is only partially able to explain the characteristics of the distribution under consideration.

Another source of income disparities across European regions are socio-economic factors (Rodríguez-Pose, 1998a, 1998b, 1999; Crescenzi and Rodríguez-Pose, 2011). Following the approach developed by Rodríguez-Pose (1998a, 1998b, 1999) that divides the EU-12 regions into four groups (capitals and urban areas; old industrialized and restructuring regions; intermediate regions; peripheral ones), Chapman and Meliciani (2012) show that regions with similar initial structural features experience similar trends in per capita GDP, once national factors are wiped out.

Moreover, several studies (Frenken and Hoekman, 2006; Chapman *et al.*, 2012; Chapman and Meliciani, 2012) find that urban areas converge more quickly than other areas and are responsible for growing inter-country disparities in Eastern Europe. In these countries regional disparities rose significantly starting from the 1990s (Artelaris *et al.*, 2010), mainly because of the strong dynamism of the major urban centres, fostered by the presence of skilled labour force, relatively developed infrastructure, advanced services and a marked increase in foreign investment (Ezcurra *et al.*, 2007).

Another strand of the literature stresses the importance of innovation in affecting regional income disparities. Differently from the contributions within the new growth theory, this line of research does not assimilate innovation to R&D (as in the linear innovation model) and recognizes the importance of local factors in affecting the relationship between innovation and economic performance (Rodríguez-Pose, 1999; Crescenzi, 2005).

Rodríguez-Pose (1999) distinguishes between 'innovation-prone' and 'innovation-averse' societies in order to explain regional differences in economic performance. He finds that, in Europe, regions with higher resources devoted to R&D tend to grow at a greater pace than the remaining spaces. Nevertheless, the passage from R&D to innovation and growth is not achieved in a similar way across Europe. In fact, even when knowledge is identically available for all, regions may still show very different levels of ability in absorbing new technologies and transforming them into (endogenous) growth. Local social conditions play an important role in the formation of these innovation-prone and innovation-averse societies, including the working of labour markets, human capital, migration and the age structure of the population (see also Crescenzi, 2005, and Crescenzi and Rodríguez-Pose, 2011).

All these factors contribute to define the so-called 'systems of innovation' – that is, 'the network of institutions in the public and private sector whose activities and interactions initiate, import, modify and diffuse new technologies' (Freeman, 1987: 1) – or, at the regional level, the 'regional innovation systems' (Cooke *et al.*, 1997; Cooke, 2001; Doloreux, 2002). Similar concepts are also at the core of the so-called 'smart specialization strategy' suggested by the 'knowledge for growth' expert group advising the European Commission (Foray, 2009; Foray *et al.*, 2009) and stressing the importance of the matching between investments in knowledge and human capital and the 'vocations' and competencies of territories. Overall, these studies contribute to overcome the simplistic dichotomy between an advanced research area (the core) and a technologically backward space (the periphery), in some cases also providing richer taxonomies of European regions (Regional Innovation Scoreboard various years; Camagni and Capello, 2013).

Conclusions

This chapter has shown that in Europe there is only weak evidence of regional income convergence and that while some disparities, especially between countries, are decreasing, others, particularly within countries, are increasing. These facts are at odds with the neoclassical growth model predicting convergence in income levels and growth rates. The new growth and new geography models are better able to account for income divergence. However, reading the process of convergence/divergence along the lines of the neoclassical (old and 'new') growth theory and/or of the new economic geography paradigms misses important features of growth and transformation processes that are relevant for studying the evolution of regional disparities. These include the sectoral composition of the economy and processes of structural change, the way in which local territories are able to introduce and assimilate new technologies and socio-economic factors. These factors are the focus of this book and their relevance for regional income and employment disparities is discussed at length in the next chapter.

The complexity of growth processes requires the use of more flexible methodologies than simple absolute or conditional growth regressions allowing for different behaviours of different groups of regions. For this reason, the empirical analyses conducted in Chapters 4–6 will complement the use of spatial regression analysis with non-parametric methodologies focusing on the behaviour of entire distributions and the estimation of bivariate kernel densities.

Notes

1 See also Krugman and Venables (1995), collapsing the upstream and downstream industries to a single imperfectly competitive sector in which the output of each firm is sold both as a final good to consumers and as an intermediate input to all other firms.
2 For an extension of this model to a continuum of imperfectly competitive sectors, see Venables (1996).
3 This paragraph draws on Meliciani and Peracchi (2006).
4 Recently, some authors (Boschma, 2005; Maggioni and Uberti, 2011) have argued that the importance of geographical proximity cannot be assessed in isolation, but should always be examined in relation to other dimensions of proximity that may provide alternative solutions to the problem of coordination (Boschma, 2005). However, the role of other types of distance in affecting regional convergence has been greatly overlooked.
5 In explaining stochastic kernels, we follow the definitions and notation provided in Quah (1996a).
6 In contour plots the height (the value of the density) is scaled so that each contour contains a specified quantile of the the the density, see Bowman and Azzalini (1997).
7 Spiezia and Weiler (2007) reach the same conclusion for OECD countries between 1998 and 2003.
8 They find that different regional economies obey different linear regressions when grouped by means of spatial tools (Getis and Ord's [1992] local clustering technique).
9 Other important elements in convergence processes are spatial and agglomeration factors, the share of GDP devoted to investments and country factors (see *infra*).
10 *Sixth Periodic Report on the Social and Economic Situation of the Regions in the European Union.* EC, Brussels.

References

Abreu, M., H.L.F. de Groot and R.J.G.M. Florax (2004), 'Space and Growth: a Survey of Empirical Evidence and Methods', Tinbergen Institute Working Paper No. TI 04-129/3.

Armstrong, H.W. (1995), 'Convergence among regions of the European Union 1950–1990', *Papers in Regional Science*, vol. 74, pp. 143–52.

Artelaris, P., D. Kallioras and G. Petrakos (2010), 'Regional inequalities and convergence clubs in the European Union new member-states', *Eastern Journal of European Studies*, vol. 1, pp. 113–33.

Ascani, A., R. Crescenzi and S. Iammarino (2012), 'New economic geography and economic integration: a review', WP1/02 Search Working Paper.

Barro R.J. and X. Sala-i-Martin (1991) 'Convergence across states and regions', *Brookings Papers on Economic Activity*, pp. 137–58.

Basile, R. (2008), 'Regional economic growth in Europe: a semiparametric spatial dependence approach', *Papers in Regional Science*, vol. 87(4), November, Wiley Blackwell, pp. 527–44.

Bernard, A. and C. Jones (1996), 'Productivity and convergence across US states and industries', *Empirical Economics*, vol. 21, pp. 113–35.

Boschma, R.A. (2005) 'Proximity and innovation: a critical assessment', *Regional Studies*, vol. 39, pp. 61–74.

Bowman, A.W. and A. Azzalini (1997), *Applied Smoothing Techniques for Data Analysis*. London: Oxford University Press.

Camagni, R. and R. Capello (2013), 'Regional innovation patterns and the EU regional policy reform: towards smart innovation policies', *Growth and Change*, vol. 44, pp. 355–89.

Canova, F. and A. Marcet (1995), 'The poor stay poor: non-convergence across countries and regions', CEPR Discussion Paper No. 1265.

Cass, D. (1965), 'Optimum growth in an aggregative model of capital accumulation', *Review of Economic Studies*, vol. 32, pp. 233–40.

Chapman, S. and V. Meliciani (2012), 'Income disparties in the enlarged EU: socio-economic, specialization and geographical clusters', *Tijdschrift Voor Economische En Sociale Geografie*, vol. 103(3), pp. 293–311.

Chapman, S., S. Cosci and L. Mirra (2012), 'Income dynamics in an enlarged Europe: the role of capital regions', *The Annals of Regional Science*, vol. 48, pp. 663–93.

Cooke, P. (2001), 'Regional innovation systems, clusters, and the knowledge economy', *Industrial and Corporate Change*, vol. 10 (4), pp. 945–74.

Cooke, P., M.G. Uranga and G. Etxebarria (1997), 'Regional innovation systems: institutional and organisational dimensions', *Research Policy*, vol. 26, pp. 475–91.

Crescenzi, R. (2005), 'Innovation and regional growth in the enlarged Europe: the role of local innovative capabilities, peripherality, and education', *Growth and Change*, vol. 36(4), pp. 471–507.

Crescenzi, R. and A. Rodríguez-Pose (2011), *Innovation and Regional Growth in the European Union*. Berlin, Heidelberg and New York: Springer.

de la Fuente, A. (1996), 'On the sources of convergence: a close look at the Spanish regions', CEPR Discussion Paper No. 1543.

Debarsy, N. and C. Ertur (2006), 'The European enlargement process and regional convergence revisited: spatial effects still matter', ERSA Conference Papers.

Doloreux, D. (2002), 'What we should know about regional systems of innovation?', *Technology in Society: An International Journal*, vol. 24, pp. 243–63.

Ertur, C. and W. Koch (2006), 'Regional disparities in the European Union and the enlargement process: an exploratory spatial data analysis, 1995–2000', *The Annals of Regional Science*, vol. 40, pp. 721–65.

Esteban, J. (2000), 'Regional convergence in Europe and the industry mix: a shift share analysis', *Regional Science and Urban Economics*, vol. 30, pp. 353–64.

European Commission (1999), 'Sixth periodic report on the social and economic situation and development of regions in the European Union', Brussels.

Ezcurra, R. and M. Rapun (2007), 'Regional dynamics and convergence profiles in the enlarged European Union: a non-parametric approach', *Tijdschrift voor Economische en Sociale Geografie*, vol. 5, pp. 564–84.

Ezcurra, R., P. Pascual and M. Rapun (2007), 'The dynamics of regional disparities in Central and Eastern Europe during transition', *European Planning Studies*, vol. 15, pp. 1397–421.

Ezcurra, R., C. Gil, P. Pascual and M. Rapun (2005), 'Regional inequality in the European Union: does industry mix matter?', *Regional Studies*, vol. 39(6), pp. 679–97.

Fingleton, B. (1999), 'Estimates of time to economic convergence: an analysis of regions of the European Union', *International Regional Science Review*, vol. 22(1), April, pp. 5–34.

Fischer, M.M. and C. Stirböck (2005), 'Pan-European regional income growth and club-convergence: insights from a spatial econometric perspective', *The Annals of Regional Science*, vol. 40, pp. 693–721.

Foray, D. (2009), 'Understanding smart specialisation'. In D. Pontikakis, D. Kyriakou and R. van Bavel (eds), *The Question of R&D Specialisation*, JRC, European Commission, Directoral General for Research, Brussels, pp. 19–28.

Foray, D., P. David and B.H. Hall (2009), 'Smart specialisation – the concept', *Knowledge Economists Policy Brief*, no. 9, June. European Commission, Directoral General for Research, Brussels.

Freeman, C. (1987), *Technology Policy and Economic Performance: Lessons from Japan.* London: Pinter.

Frenken, K. and J. Hoekman (2006), 'Convergence in an enlarged Europe: the role of network cities', *Journal of Economic and Social Geography*, vol. 97, pp. 321–6.

Getis, A. and J.K. Ord (1992), 'The analysis of spatial association by use of distance statistics', *Geographical Analysis*, vol. 24(3), pp. 189–206.

Grossman, G. and E. Helpman (1991), *Innovation and Growth in the World Economy.* Cambridge, MA: MIT Press.

Islam, N. (1995), 'Growth empirics: a panel data approach', *The Quarterly Journal of Economics*, vol. 110(4), November, pp. 1127–70.

Koopmans, T.C. (1965), 'On the concept of optimal economic growth', *The Econometric Approach to Development Planning.* Amsterdam: North Holland.

Krugman, P. (1991a), 'Increasing returns and economic geography', *Journal of Political Economy*, vol. 99, pp. 483–99.

Krugman, P. and A. Venables (1990), 'Integration and the competitiveness of peripheral industry'. In C. Bliss and J. Braga De Macedo (eds), *Unity with Diversity in the European Economy: The Community's Southern Frontier.* Cambridge: Cambridge University Press.

Krugman, P. and A. Venables (1995), 'Globalization and the inequality of nations', *The Quarterly Journal of Economics*, vol. 110, pp. 857–80.

Krugman, P. and A. Venables (1996), 'Integration, specialization, and adjustment', *European Economic Review*, vol. 40, pp. 959–67.

Le Gallo, J. and C. Ertur (2003), 'Exploratory spatial data analysis of the distribution of regional per capita GDP in Europe, 1980–1995', *Journal of Economics*, vol. 82, pp.175–201.

Le Gallo, J. and Sandy Dall'erba (2006), 'Evaluating the temporal and spatial heterogeneity of the European convergence process, 1980–1999,' *Journal of Regional Science*, vol. 46(2), Wiley Blackwell, pp. 269–88.

Lee, K., M.H. Pesaran and R. Smith (1997), 'Growth and convergence in a multi-country empirical stochastic Solow model', *Journal of Applied Economics*, vol. 12, pp. 357–92.

LeSage, J.P. and M.M. Fischer (2008), 'Spatial growth regressions: model specification, estimation and interpretation', *Spatial Economic Analysis*, vol. 3, pp. 275–304.

LeSage J.P. and R.K. Pace (2009), *Introduction to Spatial Econometrics.* Boca Raton: Taylor & Francis CRC Press.

López-Bazo, E., E. Vayá and M. Artís (2004), 'Regional externalities and growth: evidence from European regions', *Journal of Regional Science*, vol. 44, pp. 43–73.

López-Bazo, E., E. Vayá, A. Mora and J. Surinach (1999), 'Regional economic dynamics and convergence in the European Union', *Annals of Regional Science*, vol. 33, pp. 343–70.

Lucas, R.E. (1988), 'On the mechanism of economic development', *Journal of Monetary Economics*, vol. 22, pp. 3–42.

Maggioni, M. and T.E. Uberti (2011), 'Networks and geography in the economics of knowledge flows', *Quality and Quantity*, vol. 45, pp. 1031–51.

Meliciani, V. (2006), 'Income and employment disparities across European regions: the role of national and spatial factors', *Regional Studies*, vol. 40, pp. 75–91.

Meliciani, V. and F. Peracchi (2006), 'Convergence in per-capita GDP across European regions: a reappraisal', *Empirical Economics*, vol. 31(3), pp. 549–68.

Mora, A., E. Vayá and J. Surinach (2005), 'Specialisation and growth: the detection of European regional convergence clubs', *Economic Letters*, vol. 86, pp. 181–5.

Neven, D and C. Gouyette (1995), 'Regional convergence in the European Community', *Journal of Common Market Studies*, vol. 33, pp. 47–65.

Ottaviano, G. and D. Puga (1998), 'Agglomeration in the global economy: a survey of the "new economic geography"', *The World Economy*, vol. 21, pp. 707–31.

Paas, T., A. Kuusk, F. Schlitte and A. Vork (2007), 'econometric analysis of income convergence in selected EU countries and their NUTS 3 level regions', Working Paper Series 60, University of Tartu, Faculty of Economics and Business Administration.

Paci, R. and F. Pigliaru (1997), 'Structural change and convergence: an Italian regional perspective', *Structural Change and Economic Dynamics*, vol. 8(3), August, Elsevier, pp. 297–318.

Paci, R. and F. Pigliaru (1999), 'European regional growth: do sectors matter?'. In J. Adams and F. Pigliaru (eds), *Economic Growth and Change: National and Regional Patterns of Convergence and Divergence*. Chelthenham: Elgar, pp. 213–35.

Paci, R., F. Pigliaru and M. Pugno (2001), 'Disparities in economic growth and unemployment across the European regions: a sectoral perspective', Working Paper CRENoS 200103, Centre for North South Economic Research, University of Cagliari and Sassari, Sardinia.

Puga, D. (1996), 'Urbanisation patterns: European vs less developed countries', CEP Discussion Paper, no. 305, London School of Economics.

Puga, D. (1999), 'The rise and fall of regional inequalities', *European Economic Review*, vol. 43, pp. 303–34.

Quah, D.T. (1996a), 'Empirics for economic growth and convergence', CEPR Discussion Papers 1140.

Ramajo, J., M.A. Marquez, G.J.D. Hewings and M.M. Salinas (2008), 'Spatial heterogeneity and regional spillovers in the European Union: do cohesion policies encourage convergence across regions?', *European Economic Review*, vol. 52, pp. 551–67.

Ramsey, F. (1928), 'A Mathematical Theory of Saving', *Economic Journal*, vol. 38, pp. 543–59.

Rey, S.J. and M.V. Janikas (2005), 'Regional convergence, inequality, and space', *Journal of Economic Geography*, vol. 5(2), April, Oxford University Press, pp. 155–76.

Rey, S. and B. Montouri (1999), 'US regional income convergence: a spatial econometric perspective', *Regional Studies*, vol. 33(2), Taylor & Francis Journals, pp. 143–56.

Rodríguez-Pose, A. (1998a), *The Dynamics of Regional Growth in Europe: Social and Political Factors*. Oxford: Clarendon Press.

Rodríguez-Pose, A. (1998b), 'Social conditions and economic performance: the bond between social structure and regional growth in Western Europe', *International Journal of Urban and Regional Research*, vol. 22, pp. 443–59.

Rodríguez-Pose, A. (1999), 'Convergence or divergence? Types of regional responses to socio-economic change in Western Europe', *Tijdschrift voor Economische en Sociale Geografie*, vol. 90, pp. 365–78.

Romer, P.M. (1986), 'Increasing returns and long-run growth', *Journal of Political Economy*, vol. 94, pp. 1002–37.

Romer, P.M. (1990), 'Endogenous technological change', *Journal of Political Economy*, vol. 98, S71–S102.

Sala-i-Martin, X. (1996), 'Regional cohesion: evidence and theories of regional growth and convergence', *European Economic Review*, vol. 40, pp. 1325–52.

Solow, R. (1956), 'A contribution to the theory of economic growth', *Quarterly Journal of Economics*, vol. 70, pp. 65–94.

Spiezia, V. and S. Weiler (2007), 'Understanding regional growth', *The Review of Regional Studies*, vol. 37(3), pp. 344–66.

Swan, T.W. (1956), 'Economic growth and capital accumulation', *Economic Record*, vol. 32, pp. 334–61.

Venables, A. (1996), 'Equilibrium locations of vertically linked industries', *International Economic Review*, vol. 37, pp. 341–59.

3 Classifying European regions on the basis of specialization, knowledge and socio-economic groups

Introduction

This chapter discusses the role of regional specialization, the capability of producing and absorbing new knowledge and socio-economic characteristics for regional growth within different streams of literature. In particular, we argue that old and new theories of growth have neglected the role of socio-economic factors for local development. When coming to discuss technology and specialization, the new growth theory has recognized the important role of human capital for long-run growth and the fact that different activities can offer different learning opportunities. However, the representation of technology has been very simplistic, assuming a linear relationship between research and development (R&D) and innovation and neglecting the interaction between the local characteristics of each territory and its capability to introduce new knowledge and to absorb external knowledge. Similarly, the ways in which territories are able to undertake processes of structural change and the causes and consequences of shifts from agriculture to manufacturing and or from manufacturing to services and/or the capability to upgrade existing specialization patterns into related fields with higher growth opportunities have been out of the scope of neoclassical (old and new) growth theories.

After discussing those theoretical approaches accounting for the role of socio-economic factors, specialization and innovation for processes of economic growth and for the evolution of regional income and employment disparities, the chapter classifies European regions, first according to their specialization, then with respect to their knowledge profiles and, finally, on the basis of their socio-economic characteristics.

In particular, specialization clusters are identified with reference to Eurostat data on sectoral employment, thus distinguishing between regions specialized in: 1) agriculture; 2) low- and medium-low-technology manufacturing; 3) high- and medium-high-technology manufacturing; 4) knowledge intensive services; and 5) less knowledge intensive services. Knowledge groups are constructed on the basis of regions' capacity to innovate (proxied by patents) and to absorb new knowledge (proxied by education).

Socio-economic clusters are based on Rodríguez-Pose (1998a), who classifies EU-12 regions into four groups: 1) capital and urban areas, 2) regions affected by industrial decline, 3) intermediate regions and 4) peripheral regions, and on Chapman and Meliciani (2012), extending this classification to the countries that joined the EU later (EU-27).

The position of European regions in each classification and their transitions over time are then investigated with the purpose of assessing, in the following chapters, the explanatory power of these groups for regional convergence/divergence in income levels, labour productivity and the employment rate.

Regional specialization groups

The first classification of European regions proposed in this book is on the basis of their specialization profile. In this section, we first discuss why specialization might matter for regional growth and then introduce our classification, showing the position of European regions in 2004 and in 2011.

Does specialization matter?

Differences in technological opportunities and income elasticities of demand across sectors

Although the neoclassical growth model assigns no role for specialization in affecting economic growth, other approaches, also within the neoclassical tradition, highlight several mechanisms through which regions/countries with a different sectoral mix may enjoy different rates of growth. In the neoclassical tradition, some of the contributions within the new growth theory recognize that long-run growth is driven by innovation and different activities offer different opportunities for knowledge creation. A well-known example of this line of reasoning is the contribution by Grossman and Helpman (1991). They consider an economy with two sectors, one producing high-tech products and the other producing traditional goods, and assume that the resource composition of these two types of production and of their R&D activity is different – and, more precisely, that R&D requires the more intensive use of human capital and traditional manufacturing the less intensive. The effects of specialization will depend on the scope of spillovers. When knowledge capital is a national public good, the countries rich in human capital that specialize in R&D and high-tech sectors experience a faster rate of growth of output because of the higher opportunities for technological progress.

The same line of reasoning can be applied to regions: assuming that there are no transport costs across regions, regions will specialize according to their comparative advantage and the relationship between specialization and growth will depend on the extent of knowledge spillovers. Whenever spillovers are localized, regional growth can be affected by specialization with a positive impact for regions specialized in high-tech sectors.

Long before the development of the new growth theory, other non-mainstream approaches had identified several mechanisms linking structural change to economic growth. The two-sector model developed by Kaldor (1966) in the 1960s shows how trade might lead to 'wrong' specialization patterns hampering countries' growth. Assuming two sectors, agriculture with diminishing returns and manufacturing with increasing returns, the opening up of trade does not equally benefit countries that have a comparative advantage in agriculture and those which have a comparative advantage in manufacturing. Countries that specialize in manufacturing after the opening up of trade can enjoy the greatest gains as they are able to exploit economies of scale. On the contrary, countries that specialize in agriculture can also be damaged by the opening up of trade as their workforce previously employed in the manufacturing sectors might lose their jobs without the possibility of being re-employed in agriculture owing to the limits in the amount of land suitable for production.

The Kaldorian view that technical change can differ in the different sectors of the economy and that it is, therefore, important to explore the consequences of removing the assumption of one-sector models is further developed by Pasinetti (1981). Pasinetti develops a multi-sectoral approach to economic growth by taking into consideration the sector-specific elements of technical progress and demand. With respect to demand he notes that the proportion of income spent on any type of good changes as per capita income increases: in particular, the proportion of income spent on satisfying primary goods declines as income increases; moreover, for each good there is a saturation level so that, once it has been reached, further increases in income no longer lead to increases in expenditure. In this model, different sectors offer different opportunities for technical change and for the expansion of demand so that it is no longer a matter of indifference which activities countries are undertaking for their unemployment and growth rates.

Do economic sectors matter?

So far we have highlighted how various streams of literature have identified differences in technological opportunities and/or in income elasticities of demand as a rationale for specialization to affect economic growth. But are these differences somehow related to economic sectors? The idea that sectors matter dates back to the Physiocratic school of economics that was the first to see labour as the sole source of value. For the Physiocrats, only agricultural labour created this value in the products of society while industrial and non-agricultural labour was unproductive (Gray, 1948). The same distinction, but this time in favour of manufacturing, is found in Smith (1776). Two centuries later, the distinction between productive and unproductive labour was still relevant to the economic discipline and informed the debate on the superiority of manufacturing over services (Baumol and Bowen 1966; Baumol, 1967; Fuchs, 1977, 1968; Baumol et al., 1989). Nowadays the concern that the increase in the weight of services in the economy might be a threat to increasing productivity and growth has been replaced by the emphasis on the growth-enhancing characteristics of (some) services – in particular, knowledge intensive services (KIS). Some of the recent literature appears to suggest that it is no longer manufacturing that offers the better opportunities for growth, but is, in fact, (knowledge intensive) services: 'the knowledge intensive business service industry is replacing the manufacturing industry as the engine of the accumulation of competencies and knowledge in a knowledge-based economy' (Antonelli, 1998, p. 192).

In what follows we will briefly review the debate on manufacturing versus services showing how it has shifted from the initial emphasis on the capability of different activities to create a surplus to their different contribution to innovation and technical change. Finally, before discussing the new debate on smart specialization, we will emphasize the increasing interdependence between manufacturing and service activities suggesting that virtuous models of growth rely on a strict linkage between industry and KIS.

The superiority of manufacturing over services

After the Physiocratic school, the distinction between productive and unproductive labour based on their capability to contribute to capital accumulation and to the wealth of nations is found in the classical tradition. Adam Smith distinguishes between labour producing value that can be fixed in goods and accumulated (productive labour) and labour whose services perish in the instant of their performance (unproductive labour).

> There is one sort of labour which adds to the value of the subject upon which it is bestowed; there is another which has no such effect. The former, as it produces a value, may be called productive; the latter, unproductive labour. Thus the labour of a manufacturer adds, generally, to the value of the materials which he works upon, that of his own maintenance, and of his master's profit. The labour of a menial servant, on the contrary, adds to the value of nothing. (Smith, 1776, Book II, Ch. III)

Although Adam Smith does not explicitly identify unproductive labour with services, he makes several examples of unproductive labour that would be classified as services:

> In the same class [of unproductive labour] must be ranked, some both of the gravest and most important, and some of the most frivolous professions: churchmen, lawyers, physicians, men of letters of all kinds; players, buffoons, musicians, opera-singers, opera-dancers, etc. (Smith, 1776, Book II, Ch. III)

The Smithian concern about the different contribution of productive and unproductive labour to capital accumulation and growth resembles the later debate on the nature of services growth and its consequences on the productivity slowdown in the 1960s sparked by Baumol (Baumol and Bowen, 1966; Baumol, 1967; Baumol *et al.*, 1985, 1989; Baumol, 2001).

Baumol (1967), in his first influential paper, distinguishes between two types of activities 'technologically progressive activities in which innovations, capital accumulation, and economies of large scale all make for a cumulative rise in output per man hour and activities which, by their very nature, permit only sporadic increases in productivity'. What characterizes these activities is the role of labour:

> In some cases labor is primarily an instrument – an incidental requisite for the attainment of the final product, while in other fields of endeavor, for all practical purposes the labor is itself the end product. Manufacturing encompasses the most obvious examples of the former type of activity ... On the other hand there are a number of services in which the labor is an end in itself, in which quality is judged directly in terms of amount of labor. (Ibid., pp. 1–2)

In later contributions (Baumol *et al.*, 1985), Baumol recognizes that the equation of the service sector with the stagnant sector of his model requires modification, although there surely is a sub-class of the services which is a good approximation to the model's stagnant activities.

> Outputs, firms and industries do NOT follow into neat categories in terms of stagnancy and progressivity. They are all shades of gray rather than black and white, and even the most stagnant sectors of the economy have benefited from some technological change. Moreover, their relative shade of gray varies from one period of time to another. Second, an activity which is, say, relatively stagnant need not stay so forever. It may be replaced by a close substitute which is considerably more progressive, or it may benefit from an outburst of technological innovation for which it would not previously have been thought eligible. (Baumol *et al.*, 1984, p. 3)

A similar line of reasoning is found in Kaldor (1978, 1980), who argues that manufacturing has special properties as an engine of growth. According to Kaldor's laws, faster growth in manufacturing is (causally) associated with faster aggregate growth; productivity growth in manufacturing is endogenous to the growth of manufacturing output; and aggregate productivity growth is positively related with the growth of manufacturing output and employment. The reasons behind the importance of manufacturing include dynamic economies of scale; strong backward and forward linkages between manufacturing and other sectors of the domestic economy; strong properties of learning-by-doing; innovation and technological progress; and the importance of manufacturing for the balance of payments (Tregenna, 2011).

More recently – that is, since the growing emphasis of the literature on the importance of services in the knowledge-based economy (see next) – Rodrik (2004) again stresses the importance of industrialization for development identifying a series of stylized facts: 1) rapidly growing countries are those with large manufacturing sectors; 2) growth accelerations are associated with structural changes in the direction of manufacturing; 3) countries that promote exports of more 'sophisticated' goods grow faster; 4) some specialization patterns are more conducive than others in promoting industrial upgrading (manufactured goods present a better platform for jumping onto new economic activities).

One common theme of the advocates of the supremacy of manufacturing for increases in labour productivity and per capita GDP is the better opportunity that these activities offer for innovation and technical change. The materiality of manufacturing is also related to its exportability, which is crucial since an expansion of non-tradables is self-limiting as the domestic terms of trade eventually turns against non-tradables, choking off further investment and growth. However, both the limited scope for innovation in services and their non-tradability have been questioned by the new literature on KIS.

The new emphasis on growth-enhancing knowledge intensive services

Over time, the controversy around services has shifted to debating the role of innovation and knowledge creation within the service sector and, recently, there has been a change of perspective brought about by contributions within the knowledge-based economy emphasizing how services (and, in particular, KIS) may represent the new engine of growth (Antonelli, 1998; Rubalcaba and Kox, 2007).[1]

ICTs have played an important role for the emergence of a 'market for knowledge', increasing the stockability, transportability and tradability of information, releasing it from some time-spatial indivisibilities and constraints characterizing the production, storage and transmission of information and codified knowledge. From this perspective, the diffusion of ICTs and the growth of KIS take place as parallel interdependent processes reshaping the structure of knowledge flows and the technological interdependences in the economy as a whole (Castellacci, 2008). Moreover, developments in telecommunications and information technology have reduced the physical proximity requirement in the delivery of services, enhancing their tradability. In fact, since the early 1980s, international trade in services has expanded rapidly and faster than trade in merchandise, so that, in 1990, global services trade reached 20 per cent of global trade (Hoekman and Primo Braga, 1997). It, therefore, appears that one of the limits of services' specialization – that is, the constraints to their expansion due to their non-tradability – does not hold any longer, at least for the branch of producer services.

Not only can (producer) services no longer be identified with non-tradables, but also they no longer are seen as technologically laggard and as passive adopters of technology from elsewhere, but as creators of innovation and vehicles for the diffusion of technology across sectors (Antonelli, 1998; Evangelista, 2000; den Hertog, 2000; Tomlinson, 2001; Miles *et al.*, 2001; Tether, 2005; Cainelli *et al.*, 2006; Rubalcaba and Kox, 2007; Gallouj and Savona, 2009; Abreu *et al.*, 2010; Evangelista *et al.*, 2013). According to Rubalcaba and Kox, knowledge intensive business services (KIBS)[2] have a positive impact on the economy through three main channels, namely being major generators of innovations on their own, by diffusing knowledge throughout the economic system and by reducing human capital indivisibilities at the firm level (Rubalcaba and Kox, 2007). On the one hand, they 'provide products to client firms that are different (higher quality, more specialized) from the in-house services that the client firms produced in-house beforehand, or that are even completely new' (Kox and Rubalcaba, 2007b, p. 8). Therefore, they are likely to stimulate the innovation capacity of client firms, supporting the introduction of new process technologies as well as enhancing their capability to design, develop, introduce and effectively locate into the market new or improved products.

The new emphasis on KIS has led some authors to interpret the emergence and rapid growth of these activities as the sign of a more general paradigmatic change of the key actors responsible for the generation and diffusion of knowledge in modern economic systems (Antonelli, 1998).[3]

However, the idea that KIS might replace manufacturing as the engine of growth runs against the evidence of an increasing interdependence between KIS and manufacturing, suggesting that successful models of innovation and growth might be based on stronger links between KIS and manufacturing user sectors.

The interdependence between services and manufacturing

Several authors have argued that the rise of services, particularly of business services, over the last 30 years is mostly due to changes in the production processes in many sectors and to the ensuing increase in the demand for services as intermediate goods (Francois, 1990; Rowthorn and Ramaswamy, 1999; Guerrieri and Meliciani, 2005; Savona and Lorentz, 2005; Francois and Woerz, 2008). The growing complexity in the organization of manufacturing production and distribution resulting from new technologies and the significant increase in coordination problems has raised the service content of many manufactured goods, which goes well beyond the simple 'outsourcing' or 'contracting out' of services (Ten Raa and Wolff, 2001; Miozzo and Soete, 2001).

Recent studies investigate the pattern of inter-sectoral linkages between business services and manufacturing. Guerrieri and Meliciani (2005), using input–output data, show regularities across countries in the intensity of use of financial, communication and business (FCB) services. In particular, they find that knowledge intensive manufacturing industries make considerable use of FCB services, while labour and scale-intensive industries are, on average, low or medium users of these services. Similar results are found by Francois and Woerz (2007), who show how business services are in high demand especially by knowledge intensive industries. Empirical evidence showing the key role of intermediate demand – rather than final consumption or trade – in explaining business services growth is also provided by Savona and Lorentz (2005) (see also Kox and Rubalcaba, 2007a, 2007b, and Montresor and Vittucci Marzetti, 2011).

The interdependence between business services and manufacturing also depends on the type of interactions taking place between KIS and client industries. Using Miles's words, KIS are 'locating, developing, combining and applying various types of generic knowledge about technologies and application to the local and specific problems, issues and context of their clients' (Miles, 2005, p. 45). Furthermore, far from being constituted by pure market transactions of generic or abstract knowledge, in many cases these linkages can be best represented as a 'cooperative mode of innovation' in which both KIBS and client industries play an active role (Miles, 2005; Tether and Tajar, 2008; Muller and Doloreux, 2009). The role of tacit knowledge in the interaction between KIS and their clients increases the importance of spatial proximity (den Hertog, 2000; Muller and Zenker, 2001; Raspe and van Oort, 2007; Antonietti and Cainelli, 2008; Shearmur and Doloreux, 2008; Ciarli *et al.*, 2012) and suggests that the location of these services might not be independent from the location of user sectors.

In fact, Guerrieri and Meliciani (2005) show that international competitiveness in producer services depends on countries' capability to develop a comparative and absolute advantage in manufacturing user sectors. Similarly, at the regional level, Meliciani and Savona (2014) show that the spatial structure of intermediate sectoral linkages with high users' manufacturing sectors is an important determinant of specialization in business services. Moreover, Castellani *et al.* (2014), also at the regional level, find that the potential local demand from manufacturing user sectors strongly affects the location of foreign direct investments in business services. These findings suggest that there might be no trade-off between industrialization and tertiarization, but rather that the key factor in country/regional competitiveness in the knowledge-based economy might be linked to the capability of creating strong links between KIS and production activities.

The concept of smart specialization

So far we have adopted a broad sectoral perspective with the aim of reviewing the debate on which sectors offer the better opportunities for growth and development. However, the recent literature has identified new concepts that relate countries/regional growth opportunities to their existing comparative advantages. These approaches also favour place-based over place-neutral development strategies (Barca *et al.*, 2012) and are particularly relevant in a regional context.

One such concept is that of smart specialization, especially when applied to a spatial context (McCann and Ortega-Agilés, 2013). Originally, the concept lacked a spatial perspective and was designed as a tool for Europe to respond to the transatlantic productivity gap (Ortega-Argilés, 2012). It was recognized that Europe lagged behind the USA, especially in the ability to exploit ICTs in using sectors. This was due to the fact that, despite the single market, the linkages between sectors, institutions and places were limited also because of market segmentation, thus limiting knowledge flows, technology spillovers and innovation networks. In this framework, the European Research Area (ERA) was established, aiming at promoting knowledge spillovers within the EU through the creation of networks of researchers, innovators and firms. Within this initiative the 'Knowledge for Growth' (K4G) expert group advising the DG Research developed a policy-prioritization logic termed 'smart specialization' (Foray *et al.*, 2009, 2011; David *et al.*, 2009).

The smart specialization argument employs the concept of a domain, and argues that entrepreneurs will search out the innovation opportunities within their domain. The key ideas are those of embeddedness, relatedness and connectedness. Embeddedness refers to the fact that the potential development of an innovation system strongly depends on the inherited structures and existing dynamics; relatedness refers to the importance of the size of the domain intended as the range of the relevant sectors or activities in which new technological adaptations can most likely be applied and which can best benefit from knowledge spillovers. Finally, connectedness is important since domains that are highly connected with other domains will offer greater possibilities for knowledge flows and learning than less connected domains.

When translated to a spatial context (McCann and Ortega-Argilés, 2013) and taking the region as the unit of observation, the smart specialization concept implies increasing its embeddedness, related variety and connectivity (Frenken *et al.*, 2007; Frenken and Boschma, 2007; Boschma and Frenken, 2011; Boschma and Iammarino, 2009). Starting from the observation that regions have different comparative advantages, policies should be devoted to deepening the linkages within the region in the relevant fields of specialization, helping to foster a related diversification process and developing interregional networks on a region's most connected activities while at the same time maximizing local knowledge diffusion and learning networks.

Overall, the smart specialization strategy does not aim at 'picking winners', but rather at favouring a searching and learning process involving local actors and allowing regions to exploit potential unexploited opportunities. Moreover, the debate on which sectors offer better opportunities for growth and development (manufacturing vs services; high-tech industries; etc.) is overcome by the recognition that each region should build on its comparative advantage. However, there appears to be consensus on the fact that more (relatedly) diversified regions have better opportunities with respect to strongly specialized regions (Frenken *et al.*, 2007; Boschma and Iammarino, 2009; Boschma *et al.*, 2012).

Classifying regions on the basis of their specialization

The literature reviewed so far suggests that different patterns of specialization might offer different opportunities for regional growth. However, it is not necessarily true that specific activities/sectors (manufacturing, services, etc.) offer better opportunities than others. This is so for several reasons. First, the same sector/activity may present heterogeneous levels of productivity in different regions according to the regional capability to develop and adopt new technologies (an issue we will come back to later in this chapter). Second, the overall performance of the region can depend on how different activities are interrelated. Finally, each region may have different comparative advantages, so that deepening the linkages within the region in the relevant fields of specialization, helping to foster a related diversification process and developing interregional networks on a region's most connected activities might prove better strategies for development with respect to driving resources into new 'strategic' activities.

Therefore, whether different sectoral specializations help explain differentiated regional patterns of growth and convergence becomes an empirical issue. In order to test for this hypothesis, in what follows regions are classified according to their specialization profile. The explanatory power of this classification is then assessed in Chapters 4 and 5.

With reference to Eurostat data on sectoral employment the following groups are defined: regions specialized in 1) agriculture; 2) low- and medium-low-technology manufacturing; 3) high- and medium-high-technology manufacturing; 4) knowledge intensive services; and 5) less knowledge intensive services. Each region is assigned to a group on the basis of the sector in which it has the highest 'location quotient' or 'revealed comparative advantage' index in 2004.

The regional breakdown rests on the so-called nomenclature of statistical territorial units (NUTS). However, the NUTS classification does not always identify homogeneous regions across countries, even for a given level of breakdown.[4] Accordingly, following and extending Rodríguez-Pose (1998a), the most appropriate regional breakdown is selected on the basis of comparable levels of self-government for all countries (old and new) that have achieved at least moderate degrees of decentralization. For the others, the breakdown is identified with reference to comparable geographic extension and population. Thus the NUTS2 level is chosen for: Bulgaria, the Czech Republic, Ireland, Spain, France, Italy, Hungary, Austria, Poland, Portugal, Romania, Slovakia, Finland and Sweden;[5] the NUTS1 level for: Belgium, Germany, Greece, the Netherlands and the UK; the NUTS0 (i.e., country) level for: Denmark, Cyprus, Estonia, Latvia, Lithuania, Luxembourg, Malta and Slovenia. Croatia, which gained EU membership in mid-2013, is not included in the sample. In all, this leads us to consider 184 regions. The list of regions and their classification in specialization, knowledge and socio-economic groups is reported in Appendix 3.1.

In this and the following two chapters, the analysis starts from 2004, since this is the first year for which we have complete data for all the variables used to form our groups. A longer time span is covered in Chapter 6, focusing only on socio-economic groups for explaining within-country regional disparities in newcomers.

The revealed comparative advantage is computed as the share of employment (*EMP*) in sector *s* over total employment in the region *i* divided by the share of sector *s* in total EU employment:

$$RCA_s = \frac{EMP_{i,s} / \Sigma_s E_{i,s}}{\Sigma_i E_{i,s} / \Sigma_{i,s} E_{i,s}}$$

Figure 3.1 and 3.2 report the regions classified on the basis of their specialization in 2004 and in 2012 (the last year of observation) in a map, while Table 3.1 reports the transition between different specialization profiles over the same period.

As expected, the figures show regions specializing in agriculture clustering in the periphery of Europe; knowledge intensive service regions in the north of the EU, the UK and in some capital regions. Less knowledge intensive services appear less clustered, being located both in some capital regions (of Italy and Spain), in many islands and also in East Germany. Manufacturing predominates in the core of Europe, the more high-tech lines of production in West Germany and in Northern Italy and lower-technology ones in East Germany and in Central Italy – as well as in former Czechoslovakia and in some regions in Hungary (where high-tech areas are present too).

From Table 3.1 we can see, as expected, a high degree of persistence in specialization types between 2004 and 2012, particularly in knowledge intensive services (91 per cent of the regions maintain their specialization type) and in agriculture (where the share of regions remaining in the same class is 88 per cent). The higher degree of mobility is found in low- and medium-low-tech manufacturing, where 61 per cent of the regions maintain their specialization type. Looking at more frequent transitions, we find that regions specialized in

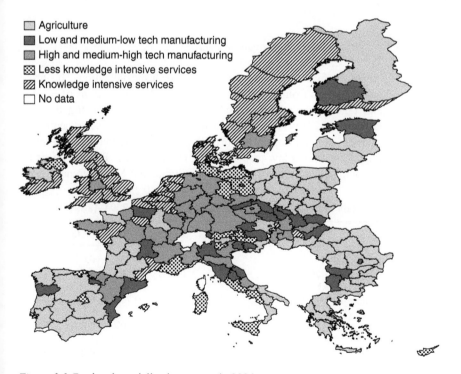

□ Agriculture
■ Low and medium-low tech manufacturing
▨ High and medium-high tech manufacturing
▦ Less knowledge intensive services
▨ Knowledge intensive services
□ No data

Figure 3.1 Regional specialization groups in 2004.

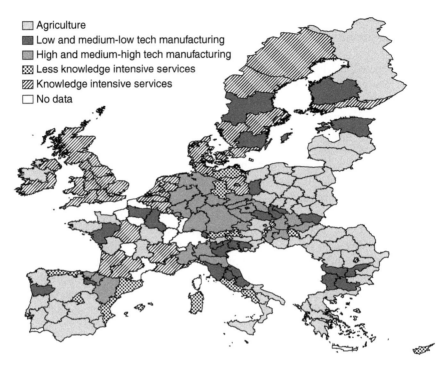

Figure 3.2 Regional specialization groups in 2012.

agriculture mainly move to low- and medium-low-tech specialization. This group mainly includes regions from newcomers (the two Bulgarian regions of Severen tsentralen and Yuzhen tsentralen and the Polish region of Lubuskie, together with Champagne-Ardenne). This is consistent with relocation processes whereby old members have delocalized important portions of the production chain in manufacturing, especially among low-tech products, to newcomers. Rather surprising, instead, is the shift of two French regions (Aquitaine and Midi-Pyrénées) from

Table 3.1 Transition in specialization types of European regions, 2004–12

2004/12	AGR	LMAN	HMAN	LKIS	KIS
Agriculture (AGR), N=56	0.88	0.07	0.00	0.02	0.04
Low- and medium-low-tech manufacturing (LMAN), N=28	0.11	0.61	0.18	0.11	0.00
High- and medium-high-tech manufacturing (HMAN), N=28	0.07	0.11	0.71	0.00	0.11
Less knowledge intensive services (LKIS), N=23	0.09	0.04	0.00	0.65	0.22
Knowledge intensive services (KIS), N=32	0.00	0.06	0.00	0.03	0.91

agriculture to KIS. Finally, Principado de Asturias (Spain) moves to less knowledge intensive services.

Regions specialized in low- and medium-low-tech manufacturing mainly move to high- and medium-high-tech manufacturing (Oberösterreich, AT; Severozápad, CZ; Severovýchod, CZ; Lombardia, IT; and Stredné Slovensko, SK). Moreover three regions move to agriculture (Steiermark, AT; Auvergne, FR; and Észak-Alföld, HU) and three regions to less knowledge intensive services (Cataluña, SP; Comunidad Valenciana, SP; and Bucuresti – Ilfov, RO).

In the case of less knowledge intensive services, the higher mobility is towards KIS; this is the case for Brandenburg (GE), Schleswig-Holstein (GE), Provence-Alpes–Côte d'Azur (FR), Malta and Northern Ireland (UK). Two regions move to agriculture (Kärnten, AT and Sicilia, IT) and one region to low- and medium-low-tech manufacturing (Provincia Autonoma Trento, IT).

Finally, very few regions specialized in KIS change their specialization profile between 2004 and 2012. This does happen for Pays de la Loire (FR) and Norra Mellansverige (SW), shifting to low- and medium-low-tech manufacturing, and of Közép-Magyarország (HU), shifting to less knowledge intensive services.

Changes in specialization types for each region are the consequence of what occurs in other regions (comparative advantage is a relative measure). Looking at which sectors increase their share in total EU employment (Table 3.2) there is a clear pattern of increases in KIS at the expense of all other sectors. In fact, the share of employment in KIS over employment in the five large sectors considered increases from 32 to 39 per cent in only eight years, while the share of all other sectors declines.

But are specialization patterns linked to economic development? Table 3.3 reports the level of per capita GDP, productivity and employment rate (the ratio of employment to total population) by specialization group in 2004 and in 2011 (the last year for which we have complete observations for all variables).

From Table 3.3 we can see that regions specialized in agriculture are those with the lowest levels of per capita GDP, labour productivity and employment. Regions specialized in low- and medium-low-technology manufacturing also present below average levels of per capita GDP and labour productivity, although their rate of employment is close to the EU average. Regions specialized in high- and medium-high-technology manufacturing have above average levels of all

Table 3.2 Sectoral shares in 2004 and in 2012

	2004	2012	Change
Agriculture	0.067	0.052	–0.015
Low- and medium-low-tech manufacturing	0.122	0.100	–0.022
High- and medium-high-tech manufacturing	0.068	0.057	–0.011
Less knowledge intensive services	0.335	0.306	–0.029
Knowledge intensive services	0.322	0.393	0.070
Other	0.086	0.093	0.007

Table 3.3 Per capita GDP, labour productivity and employment rate by specialization group

Specialization groups	Relative per capita GDP		Relative productivity		Relative employment rate	
	2004	2011	2004	2011	2004	2011
Agriculture	0.670	0.719	0.734	0.784	0.925	0.931
Low- and medium-low-tech manufacturing	0.917	0.913	0.900	0.916	1.017	0.995
High- and medium-high-tech manufact.	1.075	1.067	1.061	1.009	1.020	1.058
Less knowledge intensive services	1.088	1.159	1.109	1.199	0.987	0.984
Knowledge intensive services	1.372	1.254	1.264	1.169	1.099	1.078

variables while regions specialized in less knowledge intensive services, surprisingly, experience above average levels of per capita GDP and labour productivity but below average levels of employment. Finally, regions specialized in KIS are the richest, with the highest levels of labour productivity and employment.

Over time there is a tendency for differences to decrease among groups with regions specialized in agriculture improving their relative position and regions specialized in KIS reducing their advantages. This trend can depend on the behaviour of newcomer regions, with 'old' specialization types reducing their gap with regions from old Europe.

Finally, we may ask how similar/different regions with the same specialization profile are in terms of per capita GDP. Table 3.4 reports the minimum, maximum and some quantiles of the regional per capita distribution according to the specialization profile in 2004.

From Table 3.4 we can observe that the income gap between the poorest and the richest region is higher in agriculture (the richest region Bolzano in Italy had a per capita income more than six times larger than the poorest region Nord Est in Romania in 2004, declining to five times in 2011). Very high disparities are also found in low-tech manufacturing, where the richest region (Lombardia in Italy in 2004 and Vorarlberg in Austria in 2011) had a per capita income five times larger in 2004 and 4.8 times larger in 2011 of the poorest region (Severozapaden in Bulgaria). In high-tech manufacturing income gaps are also very large (in the order of 3.5 times) and do not decline over time (the poorest region is Észak-Magyarország in Hungary and the richest one is Hessen in Germany). The income gap between the poorest (Campania in Italy) and the richest (Salzburg in Austria) region in less knowledge intensive services is smaller (in the order of two times), but rising over time. Finally, the per capita GDP of the richest region specialized in KIBS (Luxembourg) is almost three times larger than that of the poorest region in 2004 (Languedoc-Roussillon) and more than 3.5 times larger than that of the poorest region in 2011 (Wales).

Table 3.4 Per capita GDP disparities across specialization groups

Sector	min.	max.	p25	med.	p75	max./min.	p75/p25
Agriculture 2004	4.94	31.78	8.43	11.99	18.19	6.43	2.16
Agriculture 2011	7.19	36.92	11.75	16.12	19.70	5.13	1.68
Low- and medium-low-tech manufacturing 2004	5.77	29.88	13.20	19.45	24.00	5.18	1.82
Low- and medium-low-tech manufacturing 2011	7.23	34.41	16.58	21.52	27.86	4.76	1.68
High- and medium-high-tech manufacturing 2004	8.91	31.35	18.29	22.08	25.60	3.52	1.40
High- and medium-high-tech manufacturing 2011	10.02	36.20	21.23	24.68	29.88	3.61	1.41
Less knowledge intensive services 2004	14.61	31.23	17.24	22.00	24.45	2.14	1.42
Less knowledge intensive services 2011	15.71	37.44	21.52	25.33	27.60	2.38	1.28
Knowledge intensive services 2004	18.70	54.48	22.77	25.18	28.88	2.91	1.27
Knowledge intensive services 2011	18.60	66.75	23.93	28.27	34.50	3.59	1.44

If disparities are measured looking at the ratio between the first and the last quartile, they are larger but declining in agriculture and low-tech manufacturing, more or less stable in high-tech manufacturing, declining in less knowledge intensive services and rising in knowledge intensive services. It is also interesting to observe that the lowest median income level is found in agriculture, followed by low- and medium-low-tech manufacturing, while the highest levels are found in knowledge intensive services and the intermediate levels in high-tech manufacturing and less knowledge intensive services. A similar pattern is found also for the 25th and the 75th quartiles. On the contrary, the maximum income level is very similar in all sectors (in the order of 30.000 euros in 2004 and 35.000 euros in 2011, slightly lower in low-tech manufacturing) but knowledge intensive services, where it is much higher (54.000 euros in 2004 and 67.000 in 2011).

Overall, these descriptive statistics show a great amount of variability in the dynamics of convergence/divergence within sectors. They also show that, while there appears to be a pattern between the specialization profile of regions and their income levels, income gaps for the same specialization profile can be very large. Moreover, the regions with similar specialization patterns may experience very different growth trajectories.

Regional knowledge groups

A second way of grouping regions proposed in this book is on the basis of their capability to create and absorb new knowledge. In order to classify regions into 'knowledge groups' we use data on innovation (patents per population) and human capital (share of the population with tertiary degree). In what follows, we first discuss the role of innovation and human capital for growth focusing on the regional dimension and then present the methodology used to classify regions into knowledge groups and comment on the position and dynamics of EU-27 regions between 2004 and 2010.

Innovation, human capital and regional growth

Innovation is the main source of economic growth in the long run. However, different theoretical approaches have given a different emphasis to technological change leading to different forecasts about its role for economic convergence/ divergence with very different policy implications.

While the neoclassical growth theory (Solow, 1957) treats innovation as an exogenous process freely available to all countries and forecasts convergence between countries/regions, the new growth theory (Grossman and Helpman, 1991; Aghion and Howitt, 1992) recognizes that knowledge is not a pure public good but is produced by human capital through investment in R&D, remunerated by the temporary extra rent provided by the economic exploitation of innovation. In 'new' growth models knowledge accumulation generates increasing returns to scale and an economy's steady-state rate of growth then depends *inter alia* on technology parameters, implying that economies with similar savings and investment rates may not converge (Romer, 1986; Lucas, 1988). Equally important, knowledge may spill over from one firm to another. Given that spillovers are more likely to occur locally, the possibility of unequal growth rates among regions is opened. This idea forms the basis of new economic geography models incorporating geographical space into endogenous growth theory. Any factor leading to a fall in trade costs – for instance, tighter economic integration – may lead firms to relocate, determining agglomeration and unequal development. 'Core–periphery' patterns may occur where cumulative causation 'can endogenously differentiate into rich "core" regions and poor "peripheral" regions' (Ottaviano and Puga, 1998). The neoclassical prediction that, given common features, laggard countries/regions grow more than rich ones no longer applies.

However, both the new growth and the new trade theory provide a very stylized picture of the process of technological change which is detached from the environment in which firms operate and from the set of possible relations between firms, local actors and institutions. Differently from the old and new neoclassical models, the technology-gap approach to economic growth highlights the country-specific character of technical change and the difficulties of transferring technological capabilities across countries (Fagerberg, 1987; Dosi *et al.*, 1988; Dosi *et al.*, 1990; Verspagen, 1993). These difficulties depend on the tacit and cumulative character of knowledge that is seen to be embedded within firms and organizations (Nelson and Winter, 1982; Lundvall, 1992; Nelson, 1993). This leads to the definition of 'systems of innovation' as 'the network of institutions in the public and private sector whose activities and interactions initiate, import, modify and diffuse new technologies' (Freeman, 1987, p. 1).

Translated at the regional level, the 'regional systems of innovation' framework arises from recognizing that the process of innovation is embedded in the (various) territorialized processes responsible for the economic performance of each economic space. Innovation thus needs to be linked to the cluster structure of the economy, and the regional innovation system should be understood in terms of the relationships and flows between the various actors and parts of the innovation system itself (Cooke, 1997; Crescenzi, 2005).

Among the different local factors affecting the capability to absorb and translate available knowledge into (endogenous) economic growth, the innovation systems approach emphasizes the role of human capital. Moreover, the level of education of the population also matters for the creation of innovative forms of organization (i.e., learning organizations, Lundvall, 1992). Following this approach, human capital is introduced as an explanatory variable together with innovation for explaining regional growth in the EU by Crescenzi (2005) and Crescenzi and Rodríguez-Pose (2011), finding that it interacts (in a statistically significant way) with local innovative activities, thus allowing them to be more (or less) effectively translated into economic growth.

Overall, having already captured some elements of the regional environment by the classifications based on regional specialization and socio-economic characteristics (see next section), this book, in order to interpret processes of uneven growth across regions, introduces a classification accounting simultaneously for regional innovation capabilities and absorption capacity.

Identifying regional knowledge groups

In the literature there have been several ways of classifying regions/countries according to their knowledge intensity.[6] The European Commission classifies countries and regions according to their innovation performance and publishes early the results in the European Innovation Scoreboard and in the European Regional Innovation Scoreboard. This classification takes into account three main types of indicators (enablers, firm activities and outputs) and eight innovation dimensions (three for enablers: human resources, open excellent research systems and finance and support; three for firm activities: firms' investments, linkages and entrepreneurship and intellectual assets and two for outputs: innovators and economic effects), for a total of 25 sub-indicators. Archibugi and Coco (2004) propose the so-called 'ARCo Indicator of Technological Capabilities' based on three main dimensions: the creation of technology, technological infrastructures and the development of human skills. In total, they consider eight basic indicators: two for the first category (patents and scientific articles), three for the second (internet penetration, telephone penetration and electricity consumption) and three for the third (tertiary science and engineering enrolment, mean years of schooling and literacy rate). Each basic indicator is standardized according to the following formula so that it ranges between zero and one:

$$\frac{Observed\ value - Minimum\ observed\ value}{Maximum\ observed\ value - Minimum\ observed\ value}$$

The synthetic indicator is derived from a simple average of standardized sub-indexes. Similarly, Crescenzi and Rodríguez-Pose (2011) define an innovation index based on R&D expenditures as a percentage of GDP, R&D personnel as a percentage of total labour force and the number of high-tech patents per million in the labour force.

Here, the interest is to find a very simple and synthetic way of classifying regions which takes into account two important dimensions of the capability of European regions to create and use new knowledge: their innovativeness and their absorption capacity. In order to proxy regional innovation capacity, we use the number of per capita patents that we prefer to R&D since it is an output of the innovation process. In order to proxy the regional absorption capacity, we use the percentage of the population with tertiary education. On the basis of these two indicators we construct five regional knowledge groups: 1) high innovation, high human capital (HINHHC); 2) high innovation and medium or low human capital (HINMLHC); 3) high human capital and medium or low innovation (MLINHHC); medium innovation and medium or low human capital or medium human capital and low innovation (MINMHC); and 5) low innovation and low human capital (LINLHC). The focus on five groups rather than nine groups, resulting from all possible combinations, is chosen in order to provide an adequately differentiated scheme of regional innovation types; moreover, it leads to consideration of a number of groups that is comparable with those obtained from specialization or socio-economic characteristics. The high, medium and low levels of the two indicators are identified on the basis of the tertiles of the regional distribution.

Figures 3.3 and 3.4 report the regions classified according to our knowledge groups in 2005 and in 2010, while Table 3.5 reports the transition of the regions between groups over the same period.

As expected the figures show the regions in the top category (high/high) concentrating in the south of England, in the core of Europe and in Scandinavia (including also some peripheral, agriculture-specialized areas). The regions in the bottom category (low/low) are instead mostly in the eastern and southern borders of the EU. High innovating regions with medium-low human capital concentrate in the core of Europe and include many German, French, Northern Italian and Austrian regions. CEECs, excluding capital regions, mostly fall in the low innovation classes, regardless of the education level.

Over time, Table 3.5 shows a high degree of persistence in regional knowledge groups, especially for those regions that are in the first tertile either in the patent indicator or in the education indicator, while the higher degree of mobility is found for intermediate regions. In particular, among regions improving their position in regional knowledge groups, we find eight regions moving from low levels of both patents and education to medium levels of such indicators and these include only regions from newcomers (mainly Polish regions: Lubuskie, Warminsko-Mazurskie, Wielkopolskie, Slaskie, Podkarpackie together with Jihovýchod, CZ, Moravskoslezsko, CZ and Yuzhen tsentralen, BG). Moreover, we find six regions moving from medium/low levels of either patents or education to high levels of education (North East, UK; Yorkshire and the Humber, UK;

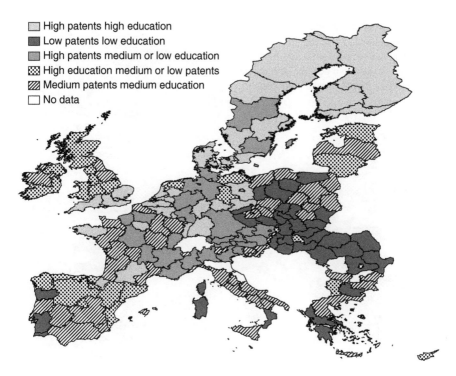

Figure 3.3 Regional knowledge groups in 2004.

Border, Midland and Western, UK; Mazowieckie, PL; Aquitaine, FR; Zahodna Slovenija, SI) and three regions moving to high levels of patents (Liguria, IT; Burgenland, AT and Pays de la Loire, FR). Finally, we find only two regions moving either from high levels of patents and medium levels of education to high levels of both indicators (Rhône-Alpes, FR) or from medium levels of patents and high levels of education to high levels of both indicators (País Vasco, SP).

Among losers with respect to the education indicator, we find four regions initially belonging to the first group (Bretagne, Hessen, Zuid-Nederland and Thüringen) and three regions previously belonging to the third group (Sachsen-Anhalt, GE; Comunidad Valenciana, SP; and Mecklenburg-Vorpommern, GE). Among losers with respect to the patent indicator, we find again four regions initially belonging to the first group (Övre Norrland, SW; Mellersta Norrland, SW; East of England, UK; and South West, UK) and three French regions previously belonging to the second group (Bretange, FR; Hessen, GE; Zuid Nederland, NL and Thuringen, GE). Finally, among losers in both education and patents moving from intermediate positions to low positions in both indicators we find seven regions, all belonging to Southern Europe (Nisia Aigaiou, Kriti, GR; Sicilia, IT; Basilicata, IT; Campania, IT; Molise, IT; Centro, PT; and Malta). Overall, while the pattern of movement among intermediate classes is variegated, there

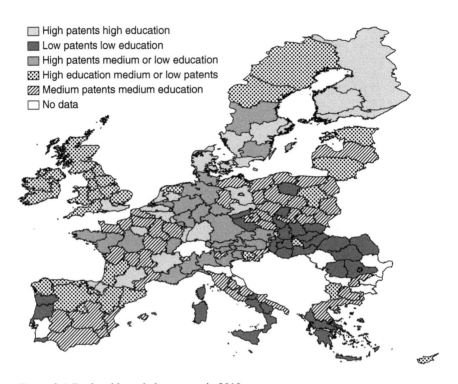

Figure 3.4 Regional knowledge groups in 2010.

appears to be a clear process of displacement of regions belonging to Southern Europe by regions of Eastern European countries and, in particular, from Poland.

We then ask how knowledge groups are linked to levels of per capita GDP, labour productivity and employment rate in 2004 and in 2011. This is shown in Table 3.6.

Table 3.6 shows that per capita GDP, productivity and employment are above the EU average for regions with high levels of at least one of the two knowledge indicators (patents or education). Differences appear to be larger in the case of GDP and productivity where patents seem to matter more than education. Over time, there are signs of convergence only between regions with low levels of the two indicators and regions with medium-low levels, while regions with high levels of both indicators increase their positive distance in both GDP and labour productivity.

Finally, Table 3.7 reports per capita GDP disparities within knowledge groups based on minimum, maximum values and quantiles of the distribution.

From Table 3.7 we can observe very large differences between the minimum and the maximum value within each group. Only for the group of regions with high patents and medium or high levels of education the ratio between the per capita GDP of the richest region (Wien in Austria) and that of the poorest region

Table 3.5 Transition of European regions between knowledge groups, 2005–10

2005\10	HINHHC	HINMLHC	HHCMLIN	MINMHC	LINLHC
High patents high education (HINHHC), N=32	0.75	0.125	0.125	0.00	0.00
High patents medium or low education (HINMLHC), N=33	0.03	0.86	0.00	0.10	0.00
High education medium or low patents (HHCMLIN), N=30	0.03	0.00	0.86	0.10	0.00
Both medium or one medium and one low patents medium or low education (MINMHC), N=54	0.00	0.06	0.12	0.68	0.14
Low patents low education (LINLHC), N=35	0.00	0.00	0.00	0.25	0.75

(Picardie in France) is less than two. In 2004, for the regions with low patents and low education the richest region (Algarve, Portugal) had a per capita GDP more than three times larger than the poorest one (Nord Est, Romania); the income gap reduced somewhat in 2011 (when the poorest region was still Nord Est and the richest region was Corse). Even higher differences are found in the group of regions with medium levels of both patents and education or medium levels of one indicator and low levels of the other. Here, the richest region in 2004 (Aland in Finland) had a per capita GDP almost six times larger than the poorest region (Severozapaden in Bulgaria); this gap was reduced to the order of almost five in 2011. Among regions with high levels of education and high or medium levels of patents, the richest region in 2004 (London) had a per capita GDP almost four

Table 3.6 Per capita GDP, labour productivity and employment rate by knowledge group

Knowledge groups	Relative per capita GDP		Relative productivity		Relative employment rate	
	2004	2011	2004	2011	2004	2011
High patents high education	1.364	1.394	1.292	1.323	1.077	1.073
High patents medium or low education	1.265	1.260	1.238	1.175	1.032	1.081
High education medium or low patents	1.121	1.122	1.064	1.086	1.055	1.037
Both medium or one medium and one low	0.872	0.811	0.923	0.870	0.949	0.946
Low patents low education	0.563	0.641	0.625	0.738	0.932	0.904

Table 3.7 per capita GDP disparities within knowledge groups

Knowledge group	min.	max.	p25	med.	p75	max./min.	p75/p25
Low patents low education 2004	4.94	18.52	8.43	10.05	14.11	3.75	1.67
Low patents low education 2011	7.19	22.77	11.12	14.82	17.65	3.17	1.59
Both medium or one medium and one low 2004	5.77	33.85	14.15	18.23	21.49	5.87	1.52
Both medium or one medium and one low 2011	7.23	34.79	15.96	19.69	23.16	4.81	1.45
High education medium or low patents 2004	11.03	43.61	18.81	21.79	25.51	3.95	1.36
High education medium or low patents 2011	16.94	46.66	21.25	23.69	30.66	2.75	1.44
High patents medium or low education 2004	18.96	36.69	22.30	24.04	28.22	1.94	1.27
High patents medium or low education 2011	20.83	41.33	26.52	27.94	33.15	1.98	1.25
High patents high education 2004	16.58	54.48	22.34	25.12	28.87	3.29	1.29
High patents high education 2011	21.21	66.75	23.89	28.66	33.68	3.15	1.41

times larger than the poorest region in the group (Yugozapaden in Bulgaria); the gap was substantially reduced in 2011 when the ratio went down to 2.7 (in 2011 the richest region was Bratislavský kraj in Slovakia and the poorest Lithuania). Finally, among regions with high patents and high education, the richest region (Luxembourg) had a per capita income 3.3 times larger than the poorest one (Thüringen in Germany) and the gap reduced to 3.1 in 2011.

When looking at disparities using the ratio of the first to the last quartile, the highest gaps are found among regions with low levels of education and patents, followed by regions with medium levels of both indicators or of medium levels of one indicator and low levels of the other. For both groups disparities decrease between 2004 and 2011. However, they increase for regions with high education and medium or low patents and between regions with high patents and high education.

Regional socio-economic groups

Another aspect that has been largely neglected in both traditional and new neoclassical models of geography and growth are location-based socio-economic characteristics. In what follows, we first discuss their relevance in the regional context and then propose a classification of European regions on the basis of these characteristics. The classification, together with that based on specialization and knowledge groups, is used in Chapters 4 and 5 for interpreting the evolution of regional income, productivity and employment disparities.

The relevance of regional socio-economic groups

The relevance of socio-economic groups in the process of regional development was clearly highlighted by Rodríguez-Pose (1998a) in the book *The Dynamics of Regional Growth in Europe: Social and Political Factors*. The author observed that the persistence of regional disparities in Europe (Dunford, 1993, 1996; Rodríguez-Pose, 1994; Martin, 1997) despite the increasing mobility of economic and technological factors could be, to a certain extent, connected to local social structures. In fact, existing social conditions may play a relevant role in affecting the capability of a territory to assimilate technological change and to respond to economic, organizational and structural transformation.

Among different ways to summarize regional socio-economic characteristics, the literature on post-Fordism and socio-economic restructuring has frequently identified four types of regions according to their economic performance and dynamism: capital and urban, industrial declining, intermediate and peripheral regions (Rodríguez-Pose, 1998a, 1998b). Capital and urban regions and some intermediate areas are often identified as the spaces more clearly benefiting from the processes of socio-economic restructuring and structural change. At the other extreme, old industrial regions are frequently perceived as the great losers of the new spatial configuration due to their inability to adapt to current changes and to undertake a process of restructuring. Finally, the position of peripheral regions is less clear since some authors stress the new possibilities which have opened up for these areas due to the ICT revolution, while others highlight the fact that the greater globalization of the world economy is leaving peripheral regions in Europe aside from major economic circuits.

A similar classification has been used by Todtling and Trippl (2005) in order to highlight how different types of regions may face different innovation and economic difficulties and may require different innovation policies. In particular, among peripheral regions the main problem can be 'organizational thinness' (the lack of support organizations), while old industrial areas may suffer especially from 'lock-in' in declining sectors and technologies and metropolitan regions from 'fragmentation' (the lack of networks and interactive learning).

In the remainder of this section we first focus on how new technologies have affected the relative strengths and weaknesses of urban and peripheral regions, and then analyse the specific features of old industrial areas.

New technologies and the location of activity in urban
and peripheral regions

The process of globalization is fostering the concentration of capital and decision-making powers in a limited number of core urban spaces (Harvey, 1985; Cheshire and Hay, 1989; Frenken and Hoekman, 2006). In these areas the concentration of capital and information, together with the endowment of a flexible and skilled workforce (Bacolod *et al.*, 2009), of headquarter functions of multinational firms and a dynamic service sector (Jacobs, 1969; Duranton and Puga, 2000) constitute the basis for the genesis of virtuous economic cycles.

The concentration of production and skilled labour in cities is linked to the importance of agglomeration economies for knowledge spillovers and increases in labour productivity (Combes *et al.*, 2011). Traditionally, different sources of agglomeration economies have been identified. Together with *localization externalities* stemming from sectoral density, which favours internal and external economies of scale (see, for instance, Combes, 2000; van Oort, 2007), the literature has highlighted the importance of *urbanization externalities*, which are independent from the sectoral structure and are due to urban and population density which facilitate knowledge spillovers (Glaeser *et al.*, 1992, 1995; Henderson *et al.*, 1995). Moreover, also the existence of *Jacobs's externalities* deriving from the variety of activities favours location within urban contexts (Jacobs, 1969; Duranton and Puga, 2000). This type of externality tends to be higher in regions with a relatively higher *related* rather than *unrelated* variety of urban activities (Frenken *et al.*, 2007; McCann and van Oort, 2009).

But has the importance of cities been reduced by the sharp decrease in transport costs due to the ICT revolution? And will this process favour the rise of intermediate and peripheral regions?

In a recent and very popular book, Friedman (2005) argues that the new technologies have changed firms' and individuals' opportunities, favouring an a-spatial distribution of economic activity, allowing for processes of production outsourcing and offshoring and increasing the possibility of networking, thus creating a 'flat world'. Taken to its limits, the flat world argument implies that 'location no longer matters' (O'Brien, 1992, p. 73) since advances in technology and telecommunications are eroding the traditional benefits of economies of scale, allowing for a much greater mobility of information and knowledge. From this perspective, thanks to advances in connectivity, in global supply chain software and in outsourcing, insourcing, offshoring and supply chaining, every territory, no matter how remote, has the potential to become a global player (see the discussion of Friedman by Rodríguez-Pose and Crescenzi, 2008). In this scenario, peripheral regions might benefit from the lower costs of their land, capital and labour and grow by attracting an increasing share of world economic activity.

However, the concept of a flat world has been challenged by many authors (Rodríguez-Pose and Crescenzi, 2008; Prager and Thisse, 2012). Rodríguez-Pose and Crescenzi (2008) note that, even with the sharp reduction in transport and communication costs, there are several forces that favour the agglomeration of economic activity, thus contributing to create 'mountains in a flat world'. These include innovation, knowledge spillovers, backward and forward linkages, diversification benefits, the role of social capital, etc. In the case of innovation, R&D investment has strong threshold effects (Dosi, 1988; Scherer, 1983) and its return heavily relies on the quality of the workforce conducting research and of the local human capital (Audretsch and Feldman, 1996; De Bondt, 1996; Engelbrecht, 1997), with the consequence that investments in R&D in peripheral areas may not yield the expected returns. Moreover, technological improvements in communication infrastructures have allowed 'codified information' to be transmitted over increasingly large distances, while this is not the case for 'tacit' knowledge which remains geographically bounded (Prager and Thisse, 2012; Ciarli *et al.*, 2012), contributing to the increasing concentration of innovation (Audretsch and Feldman, 2004; Cantwell and Iammarino, 2003). Similarly, the existence of backward and forward linkages favours the co-location of producers and users whenever they have to exchange tacit knowledge (Meliciani and Savona, 2014).

Overall, also in the presence of falling transportation and communication costs, there appear to be many factors favouring the concentration of economic activity in urban areas where economic and social actors can benefit from proximity to other economic and social actors with whom they can relate from a cognitive, organizational, social and institutional perspective (Boschma, 2005). Concentration of economic activity in urban areas creates a good environment for exchanges of ideas, Jacobs's type externalities, innovation and, ultimately, economic activity and growth (Rodríguez-Pose and Crescenzi, 2008).

Therefore, although advances in technology and deregulation may allow for economic activity to take place virtually everywhere, favouring the emergence of new actors in the global world, at the regional level globalization appears to have favoured large metropolitan areas which are the nodes within the global network of financial and business firms.

Regions affected by industrial decline and restructuring

Rodríguez-Pose (1998a, 1998b, 1999) places old industrial areas among the spaces that have been less able to adapt to the new socio-economic circumstances, due to a set of extremely rigid social and economic conditions (Quevit *et al.*, 1991; Tomaney 1994; Hudson, 1994a, 1994b). The early industrialization of these areas and the adoption of rigid economic and social models typical of the era of mass production have made these areas less able to adapt to the more flexible methods of the post-Fordism era and to compete in a larger and more open international market (Storper and Scott, 1989; Scott and Storper, 1992). When production became less homogeneous and standardized and more diverse and differentiated and the importance of economies of scale was replaced by that of economies of scope, these areas found themselves unprepared for the new production modes and for the related changes in organization and capabilities.

Originally, old industrial areas were identified as those having at least one third of their total employment in the secondary sector, with one third of total industrial employment in traditional industrial subsectors, such as coal, iron, steel and electricity (Quevit *et al.*, 1991). This group of regions was found to experience below average growth rates over the 1980s, while most of them had already started their decline in the 1950s and 1960s (Rodríguez-Pose, 1999). Moreover, when classifying regions on the basis of a battery of socio-economic indicators (labour force variables, employment variables, demographic structure, population change, educational enrolment and urban structure) old industrial areas were found to cluster in a group characterized by ageing population, below average educational enrolment levels, low rates of growth of working population, high unemployment in general and, in particular, high youth unemployment (Rodríguez-Pose, 1999).

A key feature of these regions is that they suffer from various forms of 'lock-in' (Todtling and Trippl, 2005), which seriously curtail their development potential and innovation capabilities. Analysing the innovation problems of the Ruhr area, Grabher (1993) identified functional lock-ins (too rigid inter-firm networks), cognitive lock-ins (homogenization of world views) and political lock-ins (strong, symbiotic relationships between public and private key actors hampering industrial restructuring). These are exacerbated by too strong ties both in the economic and political spheres (Todtling and Trippl, 2005).

The concept of old industrial areas is more generally linked to the problem of restructuring – that is, some territories may be locked into productions for which demand is declining and the scope for innovation is limited. Whenever this occurs, regions may lag behind and experience drops in both production and employment. We will come back to this point when discussing the criteria adopted to classify regions into old industrial areas.

Identifying regional socio-economic groups

On the basis of the reviewed literature, we expect that distinguishing between urban areas, peripheral regions and regions in industrial decline may be relevant for understanding processes of uneven growth across regions. We, therefore, adopt a classification of European regions based on socio-economic groups. These are identified with reference to Rodríguez-Pose (1998a), who classifies EU-12 regions into four groups: capital and urban areas, regions affected by industrial decline; intermediate regions; and peripheral regions. This grouping has been extended to the countries that joined the EU later – that is, to Austria, Sweden, Finland and to CEECs – by Chapman and Meliciani (2012), also checking whether the classification identified for old members by Rodríguez-Pose was still accurate more than ten years later.

Here, we refer to the Chapman and Meliciani (2012) classification for all groupings but the 'regions affected by industrial decline and restructuring', where we refer mainly to the criteria used by the European Union to identify former Objective 2 regions.

In particular, 'urban areas and capitals' include all areas previously identified by Rodríguez-Pose (2008) plus Bremen (that qualifies no longer as an industrial region) and all newcomer capitals (not having identified any significant urban area in the new members). Selecting the 'regions affected by industrial decline and restructuring' is more difficult. In the EU-12 Rodríguez-Pose identified a group of 21 among Europe's oldest industrial regions which had been facing considerable shrinkage of the relative weight of industry since the early 1970s; all presented below- average growth rates while the initial level of GDP sometimes was above, and more often below, the average. The selection is by no means non-controversial, as Rodríguez-Pose acknowledges (see 1998a, p. 96, n. 5). A more recent study (Cumbers and Birch, 2006), for instance, defines old industrial regions as based on old mining areas. For some countries this criterion is more restrictive while for others (the UK) it is more extensive. Even this study, however, warns that the designation is not unproblematic (ibid.).

The concern for problems linked to the capability of regions to undertake restructuring processes led the European Commission to devote part of the budget of Structural Funds to the conversion of the declining industrial regions (Objective 2). This Objective was reformed under Agenda 2000 into 'supporting the economic and social conversion of areas experiencing structural difficulties', to include not only industrial areas, but also rural and urban areas. The first classification of regions 'affected by industrial decline' (and thus eligible for assistance from the Structural Funds under Objective 2 before 2000) was based on the following criteria: 1) the share of regional industrial employment in total employment is above the national average. This characterizes the region as industrial; 2) regional unemployment is above the national average. This identifies the region as a problem area; 3) over time the region records a drop in industrial employment, implying that the origin of high unemployment is industrial decline.

Chapman and Meliciani (2012) observe that old industrial areas were particularly widespread in CEECs where, as a legacy of some 40 years of central planning, large-scale, materials- and labour-intensive plants predominated and were largely concentrated in traditional sectors (coal, iron and steel, chemicals, shipbuilding and textiles). New members defined the areas of industrial decline in their territory; however, the classification was generally carried out with respect to territorial units below the NUTS2 level – counties or groups of municipalities and, therefore, does not always help in defining regions of industrial decline at the NUTS2 level. Moreover, reference to the EU criteria is not always helpful when dealing with CEECs, given that in these countries restructuring followed very diverse paths. Thus, for instance, Slaskie, the largest industrial district producing iron and steel in Poland, continued to record unemployment rates that were well below the national average, albeit growing fast, until after the turn of the century. The same occurred in other heavily industrialized Polish regions, such as Lodskie, Malopolskie and Wielkopolskie, as well as in some of the heaviest industrialized regions of Romania. However, EU criteria give satisfactory results for the other new members (including Austria, Finland and Sweden). Thus, in identifying NUTS2 regions of industrial decline Chapman and Meliciani (ibid.) refer to the areas indicated by national authorities, checked on the basis of EU criteria. This led the authors to identify 40 regions of industrial decline, 26 belonging to new members (of these, 21 belong to CEECs) and 14 to older ones (i.e., seven less with respect to Rodríguez-Pose, 1998a).[7]

Here we decided simply to apply the EU criteria to define old industrial areas since these are easy to apply, can be replicated in other contexts and give precise information on the three main characteristics of industrial decline: a relatively high share of industry in total employment, a declining industry and a relatively large unemployment rate.

As far as the remaining regions are concerned, following Rodríguez-Pose (1998a), they are divided into 'peripheral regions' and 'intermediate regions' (the terms refer to their geographical position). The former includes relatively far-off, isolated areas, often displaying above the national average specialization in agriculture, while the latter are a residual group. Due to their geographical position and to their socio-economic features most new member regions fall into the peripheral group, while only few classify as intermediate.

Figure 3.5 shows a map with the classification of the regions in socio-economic groups.

Comparison of Figure 3.5 with maps based on specialization and knowledge groups shows some overlap among groupings. On the one hand, for instance, capitals mostly specialize in services (both knowledge intensive and less knowledge intensive ones) and never present low levels of innovation and human capital. However, a few capitals in newcomers specialize in low-tech manufacturing. On the other hand, while it is generally true that peripheral regions specialize in agriculture, nevertheless a few far-off regions in Sweden and the UK specialize in knowledge intensive services and present high levels of education coupled with high, or medium, innovation.

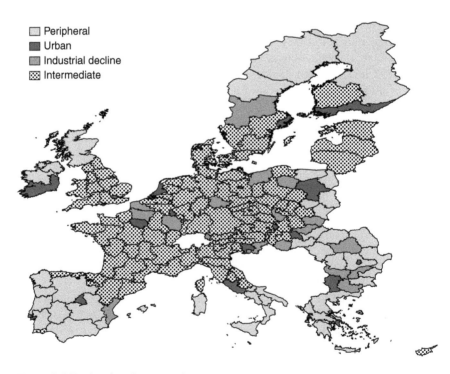

Figure 3.5 Regional socio-economic groups.

Table 3.8 Per capita GDP, labour productivity and employment rate by socio-economic group

Socio-economic groups	Relative per capita GDP		Relative productivity		Relative employment rate	
	2004	*2011*	*2004*	*2011*	*2004*	*2011*
Urban regions	1.538	1.586	1.474	1.504	1.064	1.071
Old industrial regions	0.685	0.705	0.718	0.745	0.939	0.931
Peripheral regions	0.712	0.708	0.780	0.796	0.928	0.911
Intermediate regions	1.053	1.041	1.033	1.015	1.026	1.033

We then ask whether there is some relationship between socio-economic groups and regional levels of per capita GDP, labour productivity and employment rates (see Table 3.8).

Table 3.8 shows that urban areas are by far the richest areas, also presenting above average levels of labour productivity and employment rates. Moreover, over the period 2004–11, they increase their distance from the other groups. Old industrial regions, showing the lowest levels of per capita GDP and labour productivity in 2004, decrease their gap in 2011 in these variables but do not catch up in employment rates. Finally, peripheral regions lag behind in per capita GDP and employment rates, though they slightly improve their position in labour productivity (probably by cutting employment).

Finally, we look at per capita GDP disparities within socio-economic groups on the basis of the ratio between the maximum and the minimum value and between the first and the last quartile (see Table 3.9).

Table 3.9 shows that in 2004 the richest region in the group of peripheral regions (Scotland) had a per capita GDP five times larger than the poorest one (Nord Est in Romania). The ratio reduced to 4.4 in 2011 (when the poorest region was still Nord Est and the richest one Övre Norrland in Sweden). Also, among industrial regions the income gap between the richest region (Vorarlberg in

Table 3.9 Per capita GDP disparities within socio-economic groups

Socio-economic group	min.	max.	p25	med.	p75	max./min.	p75/p25
Peripheral 2004	4.94	25.18	8.43	14.71	18.19	5.10	2.16
Peripheral 2011	7.19	31.46	11.75	16.22	19.65	4.38	1.67
Old industrial 2004	5.77	28.87	8.91	11.66	18.96	5.00	2.13
Old industrial 2011	7.23	34.41	11.23	15.13	21.19	4.76	1.89
Urban 2004	11.03	54.48	22.50	28.88	36.69	4.94	1.63
Urban 2011	19.57	66.75	27.56	34.50	45.39	3.41	1.65
Intermediate 2004	6.96	33.85	18.03	22.00	25.30	4.86	1.40
Intermediate 2011	10.49	37.44	21.06	23.62	27.94	3.57	1.33

Austria) and the poorest one (Severozapaden in Bulgaria) was in the order of five in 2004, decreasing to 4.8 in 2011. Among urban regions the richest region in 2004 (Luxembourg) had a per capita GDP almost four times largest than the poorest one (Yugozapaden in Bulgaria). This gap was reduced in 2011, with a ratio of 3.6. Moreover, if we exclude Luxembourg, the richest urban area is Brussels and the ratio is 4.7 in 2004 and (only) 2.8 in 2011, showing the exceptional performance of capital areas in newcomers. Finally, among intermediate regions the ratio between the maximum and the minimum decreases from 4.9 in 2004 to 3.6 in 2011. When considering disparities measured on the basis of the quartiles, we find the highest ratio between the first and the last quartile for peripheral and old industrial areas (higher than two in 2004 but below two in 2011), while the ratios are smaller for urban areas (1.6) and for intermediate regions (1.4 in 2004 and 1.3 in 2011). Overall, the statistics show some signs of a decrease in disparities within socio-economic groups.

Conclusions

This chapter has discussed the role of specialization, knowledge and socio-economic characteristics for regional economic performance. These elements, largely neglected in the neoclassical theories of economic growth and geography, have been recognized as playing a role in the new neoclassical theories. However, there has been no real effort within the neoclassical tradition to contextualize these elements to the specific characteristics of each territory and to look at their interrelations. In the chapter, we have discussed other streams of literature, each focusing on at least one of these elements and providing interesting insights on the possible causation mechanisms between such features and economic performance. Finally, with the purpose of taking into account simultaneously the role of specialization, knowledge and socio-economic characteristics for the evolution of regional economic disparities (Chapters 4 and 5), we have classified regions on the basis of each of these elements. The descriptive analysis has shown that, although there is some overlap among groupings, each group provides additional information. For instance, while capitals mostly specialize in services (both knowledge intensive and less knowledge intensive ones), few capitals in newcomers specialize in low-tech manufacturing. Moreover, while it is generally true that peripheral regions specialize in agriculture and have low levels of innovation and human capital, a few far-off regions in Sweden and the UK specialize in knowledge intensive services and present high levels of education coupled with high, or medium, innovation. Finally, it appears that there is a relationship between the groups and the levels of per capita GDP, labour productivity and employment rates and that there are large (but generally declining) differences in per capita GDP also within the groups. Disentangling the role of these groups for the evolution of regional disparities in Europe will be the object of the next two chapters.

Appendix 3.1 Regions included in the sample and their classification

NUTS_ID	Name	Specialisation Group 2004	Specialisation Group 2012	Knowl. Gr. 2004	Know. Gr. 2012	Socio-ec. group
AT11	Burgenland (AT)	Less knowl. inten. serv.	Less knowl. inten. serv.	MINMHC	HINMLHC	Intermediate
AT12	Niederösterreich	Agriculture	Agriculture	HINMLHC	HINMLHC	Intermediate
AT13	Wien	Knowl. inten. serv.	Knowl. inten. serv.	HINMLHC	HINMLHC	Urban
AT21	Kärnten	Less knowl. inten. serv.	Agriculture	HINMLHC	HINMLHC	Intermediate
AT22	Steiermark	Med-low tech manuf.	Agriculture	HINMLHC	HINMLHC	Intermediate
AT31	Oberösterreich	Med-low tech manuf.	Med-high tech manuf.	HINMLHC	HINMLHC	Intermediate
AT32	Salzburg	Less knowl. inten. serv.	Less knowl. inten. serv.	HINMLHC	HINMLHC	Intermediate
AT33	Tirol	Less knowl. inten. serv.	Less knowl. inten. serv.	HINMLHC	HINMLHC	Intermediate
AT34	Vorarlberg	Med-low tech manuf.	Med-low tech manuf.	HINMLHC	HINMLHC	Ind. decline
BE1	Région de Bruxelles-Capitale	Knowl. inten. serv.	Less knowl. inten. serv.	HINHHC	HINHHC	Urban
BE2	Vlaams Gewest	Knowl. inten. serv.	Knowl. inten. serv.	HINHHC	HINHHC	Intermediate
BE3	Région wallonne	Knowl. inten. serv.	Knowl. inten. serv.	HINHHC	HINHHC	Intermediate
BG31	Severozapaden (SRE 2005)	Med-low tech manuf.	Med-low tech manuf.	MINMHC		Ind. decline
BG32	Severen tsentralen (SRE 2005)	Agriculture	Med-low tech manuf.	MINMHC	MINMHC	Ind. decline
BG33	Severoiztochen (SRE 2005)	Agriculture	Agriculture	MINMHC		Peripheral
BG34	Yugoiztochen (SRE 2005)	Agriculture	Agriculture	MINMHC	MLINHHC	Peripheral
BG41	Yugozapaden (SRE 2005)	Med-low tech manuf.	Med-low tech manuf.	MLINHHC	MINMHC	Urban
BG42	Yuzhen tsentralen (SRE 2005)	Agriculture	Med-low tech manuf.	LINLHC		Ind. decline
CY	Cyprus	Less knowl. inten. serv.	Less knowl. inten. serv.	MLINHHC	MLINHHC	Intermediate

(Continued)

Appendix 3.1 Regions included in the sample and their classification (Continued)

NUTS_ID	Name	Specialisation Group 2004	Specialisation Group 2012	Knowl. Gr. 2004	Know. Gr. 2012	Socio-ec. group
CZ01	Praha	Knowl. inten. serv.	Knowl. inten. serv.	MLINHHC	MLINHHC	Urban
CZ02	Střední Čechy	Med-high tech manuf.	Med-high tech manuf.	MINMHC	MINMHC	Intermediate
CZ03	Jihozápad	Med-high tech manuf.	Med-high tech manuf.	LINLHC	LINLHC	Intermediate
CZ04	Severozápad	Med-low tech manuf.	Med-high tech manuf.	LINLHC	LINLHC	Intermediate
CZ05	Severovýchod	Med-low tech manuf.	Med-high tech manuf.	MINMHC	MINMHC	Intermediate
CZ06	Jihovýchod	Med-low tech manuf.	Med-low tech manuf.	LINLHC	MINMHC	Intermediate
CZ07	Střední Morava	Med-low tech manuf.	Med-low tech manuf.	LINLHC	LINLHC	Ind. decline
CZ08	Moravskoslezsko	Med-low tech manuf.	Med-low tech manuf.	LINLHC	MINMHC	Intermediate
DE1	Baden-Württemberg	Med-high tech manuf.	Med-high tech manuf.	HINHHC	HINHHC	Intermediate
DE2	Bayern	Med-high tech manuf.	Med-high tech manuf.	HINMLHC	HINMLHC	Intermediate
DE3	Berlin	Knowl. inten. serv.	Knowl. inten. serv.	HINHHC	HINHHC	Urban
DE4	Brandenburg	Less knowl. inten. serv.	Knowl. inten. serv.	HINHHC	HINHHC	Intermediate
DE5	Bremen	Med-high tech manuf.	Med-high tech manuf.	HINMLHC	HINMLHC	Urban
DE6	Hamburg	Knowl. inten. serv.	Knowl. inten. serv.	HINHHC	HINHHC	Urban
DE7	Hessen	Med-high tech manuf.	Med-high tech manuf.	HINHHC	HINMLHC	Intermediate
DE8	Mecklenburg-Vorpommern	Less knowl. inten. serv.	Less knowl. inten. serv.	MLINHHC	MINMHC	Intermediate

DE9	Niedersachsen	Med-high tech manuf.	Med-high tech manuf.	HINMLHC	HINMLHC	Intermediate
DEA	Nordrhein-Westfalen	Med-high tech manuf.	Med-high tech manuf.	HINMLHC	HINMLHC	Intermediate
DEB	Rheinland-Pfalz	Med-high tech manuf.	Med-high tech manuf.	HINMLHC	HINMLHC	Intermediate
DEC	Saarland	Med-high tech manuf.	Med-high tech manuf.	HINMLHC	HINMLHC	Intermediate
DED	Sachsen	Med-high tech manuf.	Med-high tech manuf.	HINNHC	HINNHC	Intermediate
DEE	Sachsen-Anhalt	Less knowl. inten. serv.	Less knowl. inten. serv.	MLINHHC	MINMHC	Intermediate
DEF	Schleswig-Holstein	Less knowl. inten. serv.	Knowl. inten. serv.	HINMLHC	HINMLHC	Intermediate
DEG	Thüringen	Med-high tech manuf.	Med-high tech manuf.	HINNHC	HINMLHC	Ind. decline
DK	Denmark	Knowl. inten. serv.	Knowl. inten. serv.	HINNHC	HINNHC	Intermediate
EE	Estonia	Med-low tech manuf.	Med-low tech manuf.	MLINHHC	MLINHHC	Intermediate
EL1	Voreia Ellada	Agriculture	Agriculture	MINMHC	MINMHC	Peripheral
EL2	Kentriki Ellada	Agriculture	Agriculture	LINLHC	LINLHC	Peripheral
EL3	Attiki	Less knowl. inten. serv.	Less knowl. inten. serv.	MLINHHC	MLINHHC	Urban
EL4	Nisia Aigaiou, Kriti	Agriculture	Agriculture	MINMHC	LINLHC	Peripheral
ES11	Galicia	Agriculture	Agriculture	MLINHHC	MLINHHC	Peripheral
ES12	Principado de Asturias	Less knowl. inten. serv.	Less knowl. inten. serv.	MLINHHC	MLINHHC	Intermediate
ES13	Cantabria	Less knowl. inten. serv.	Less knowl. inten. serv.	MLINHHC	MLINHHC	Intermediate
ES21	Pais Vasco	Med-high tech manuf.	Med-high tech manuf.	MLINHHC	HINHHC	Intermediate

(Continued)

Appendix 3.1 Regions included in the sample and their classification (Continued)

NUTS_ID	Name	Specialisation Group 2004	Specialisation Group 2012	Knowl. Gr. 2004	Know. Gr. 2012	Socio-ec. group
ES22	Comunidad Foral de Navarra	Med-high tech manuf.	Med-high tech manuf.	HINHHC	HINHHC	Intermediate
ES23	La Rioja	Med-low tech manuf.	Med-low tech manuf.	MLINHHC	MLINHHC	Intermediate
ES24	Aragón	Med-high tech manuf.	Med-high tech manuf.	MLINHHC	MLINHHC	Intermediate
ES30	Comunidad de Madrid	Less knowl. inten. serv.	Less knowl. inten. serv.	MLINHHC	MLINHHC	Urban
ES41	Castilla y León	Agriculture	Agriculture	MLINHHC	MLINHHC	Peripheral
ES42	Castilla-la Mancha	Agriculture	Agriculture	MINMHC	MINMHC	Peripheral
ES43	Extremadura	Agriculture	Agriculture	MINMHC	MINMHC	Peripheral
ES51	Cataluña	Med-low tech manuf.	Less knowl. inten. serv.	MLINHHC	MLINHHC	Intermediate
ES52	Comunidad Valenciana	Med-low tech manuf.	Less knowl. inten. serv.	MLINHHC	MINMHC	Ind. decline
ES53	Illes Balears	Less knowl. inten. serv.	Less knowl. inten. serv.	MINMHC	MINMHC	Peripheral
ES61	Andalucía	Agriculture	Agriculture	MINMHC	MINMHC	Peripheral
ES62	Región de Murcia	Agriculture	Agriculture	MINMHC	MINMHC	Peripheral
FI18	Etelä-Suomi (NUTS 2006)	Knowl. inten. serv.	Knowl. inten. serv.	HINHHC	HINHHC	Urban
FI19	Länsi-Suomi	Med-low tech manuf.	Med-low tech manuf.	HINHHC	HINHHC	Intermediate
FI1D	Pohjois-Suomi (NUTS 2006)	Agriculture	Agriculture	HINHHC	HINHHC	Peripheral
FI20	Åland	Knowl. inten. serv.	Knowl. inten. serv.	MINMHC	MINMHC	Intermediate
FR10	Île de France	Knowl. inten. serv.	Knowl. inten. serv.	HINHHC	HINHHC	Urban
FR21	Champagne-Ardenne	Agriculture	Med-low tech manuf.	MINMHC	MINMHC	Intermediate
FR22	Picardie	Med-low tech manuf.	Med-low tech manuf.	HINMLHC	MINMHC	Ind. decline
FR23	Haute-Normandie	Med-high tech manuf.	Med-high tech manuf.	HINMLHC	MINMHC	Intermediate
FR24	Centre (FR)	Med-high tech manuf.	Knowl. inten. serv.	HINMLHC	HINMLHC	Intermediate

FR25	Basse-Normandie	Agriculture	Agriculture	MINMHC	MINMHC	Intermediate
FR26	Bourgogne	Med-high tech manuf.	Agriculture	MINMHC	MINMHC	Intermediate
FR30	Nord - Pas-de-Calais	Knowl. inten. serv.	Med-low tech manuf.	MINMHC	MINMHC	Ind. decline
FR41	Lorraine	Med-high tech manuf.	Med-low tech manuf.	MINMHC	MINMHC	Ind. decline
FR42	Alsace	Med-high tech manuf.	Med-high tech manuf.	HINHHC	HINHHC	Intermediate
FR43	Franche-Comté	Med-high tech manuf.	Med-high tech manuf.	HINMLHC	HINMLHC	Intermediate
FR51	Pays de la Loire	Knowl. inten. serv.	Med-low tech manuf.	MINMHC	HINMLHC	Intermediate
FR52	Bretagne	Med-high tech manuf.	Agriculture	HINHHC	HINMLHC	Intermediate
FR53	Poitou-Charentes	Agriculture	Agriculture	MINMHC	MINMHC	Intermediate
FR61	Aquitaine	Agriculture	Knowl. inten. serv.	MINMHC	MLINHHC	Intermediate
FR62	Midi-Pyrénées	Agriculture	Knowl. inten. serv.	HINHHC	HINHHC	Intermediate
FR63	Limousin	Agriculture	Knowl. inten. serv.	MINMHC	MINMHC	Intermediate
FR71	Rhône-Alpes	Med-high tech manuf.	Knowl. inten. serv.	HINMLHC	HINHHC	Intermediate
FR72	Auvergne	Med-low tech manuf.	Agriculture	HINMLHC	MINMHC	Intermediate
FR81	Languedoc-Roussillon	Knowl. inten. serv.	Less knowl. inten. serv.	MINMHC	MINMHC	Intermediate
FR82	Provence-Alpes-Côte d'Azur	Less knowl. inten. serv.	Knowl. inten. serv.	HINMLHC	HINMLHC	Intermediate
FR83	Corse	Knowl. inten. serv.	Less knowl. inten. serv.	LINLHC	LINLHC	Intermediate
HU10	Közép-Magyarország	Knowl. inten. serv.	Less knowl. inten. serv.	MLINHHC	MLINHHC	Urban
HU21	Közép-Dunántúl	Med-high tech manuf.	Med-high tech manuf.	LINLHC	LINLHC	Intermediate
HU22	Nyugat-Dunántúl	Med-high tech manuf.	Med-high tech manuf.	LINLHC	LINLHC	Intermediate
HU23	Dél-Dunántúl	Agriculture	Agriculture	LINLHC	LINLHC	Ind. decline
HU31	Észak-Magyarország	Med-high tech manuf.	Med-high tech manuf.	LINLHC	LINLHC	Ind. decline

(Continued)

Appendix 3.1 Regions included in the sample and their classification (Continued)

NUTS_ID	Name	Specialisation Group 2004	Specialisation Group 2012	Knowl. Gr. 2004	Know. Gr. 2012	Socio-ec. group
HU32	Észak-Alföld	Med-low tech manuf.	Agriculture	LINLHC	LINLHC	Peripheral
HU33	Dél-Alföld	Agriculture	Agriculture	LINLHC	LINLHC	Peripheral
IE01	Border, Midland and Western	Agriculture	Agriculture	MINMHC	MLINHHC	Peripheral
IE02	Southern and Eastern	Knowl. inten. serv.	Knowl. inten. serv.	MLINHHC	MLINHHC	Urban
ITC1	Piemonte	Med-high tech manuf.	Med-high tech manuf.	HINMLHC	HINMLHC	Intermediate
ITC2	Valle d'Aosta/Vallée d'Aoste	Less knowl. inten. serv.	Less knowl. inten. serv.	MINMHC	MINMHC	Intermediate
ITC3	Liguria	Less knowl. inten. serv.	Less knowl. inten. serv.	MINMHC	HINMLHC	Intermediate
ITC4	Lombardia	Med-low tech manuf.	Med-high tech manuf.	HINMLHC	HINMLHC	Intermediate
ITD1	Provincia Autonoma Bolzano/Bozen (NUTS 2006)	Agriculture	Agriculture	HINMLHC	HINMLHC	Intermediate
ITD2	Provincia Autonoma Trento (NUTS 2006)	Less knowl. inten. serv.	Med-low tech manuf.	MINMHC	MINMHC	Intermediate
ITD3	Veneto (NUTS 2006)	Med-high tech manuf.	Med-low tech manuf.	HINMLHC	HINMLHC	Intermediate
ITD4	Friuli-Venezia Giulia (NUTS 2006)	Med-low tech manuf.	Med-low tech manuf.	HINMLHC	HINMLHC	Intermediate
ITD5	Emilia-Romagna (NUTS 2006)	Med-high tech manuf.	Med-high tech manuf.			Intermediate
ITE1	Toscana (NUTS 2006)	Med-low tech manuf.	Med-low tech manuf.	MINMHC	MINMHC	Intermediate
ITE2	Umbria (NUTS 2006)	Med-low tech manuf.	Med-low tech manuf.	MINMHC	MINMHC	Intermediate
ITE3	Marche (NUTS 2006)	Med-low tech manuf.	Med-low tech manuf.			Intermediate
ITE4	Lazio (NUTS 2006)	Less knowl. inten. serv.	Less knowl. inten. serv.	MINMHC	MINMHC	Urban
ITF1	Abruzzo	Med-high tech manuf.	Med-low tech manuf.	MINMHC	MINMHC	Intermediate

ITF2	Molise	Agriculture	Agriculture	MINMHC	LINLHC	Peripheral
ITF3	Campania	Less knowl. inten. serv.	Less knowl. inten. serv.	MINMHC	LINLHC	Peripheral
ITF4	Puglia	Agriculture	Agriculture	MINMHC	MINMHC	Peripheral
ITF5	Basilicata	Agriculture	Agriculture	MINMHC	LINLHC	Peripheral
ITF6	Calabria	Agriculture	Agriculture	LINLHC	LINLHC	Peripheral
ITG1	Sicilia	Less knowl. inten. serv.	Agriculture	MINMHC	LINLHC	Peripheral
ITG2	Sardegna	Less knowl. inten. serv.	Less knowl. inten. serv.	LINLHC	LINLHC	Peripheral
LT	Lithuania	Agriculture	Agriculture	MLINHHC	MLINHHC	Intermediate
LU	Luxembourg	Knowl. inten. serv.	Knowl. inten. serv.	HINHHC	HINHHC	Urban
LV	Latvia	Agriculture	Agriculture	MINMHC	MINMHC	Intermediate
MT	Malta	Less knowl. inten. serv.	Knowl. inten. serv.	MINMHC	LINLHC	Intermediate
NL1	Noord-Nederland	Knowl. inten. serv.	Knowl. inten. serv.	MLINHHC	MLINHHC	Intermediate
NL2	Oost-Nederland	Knowl. inten. serv.	Knowl. inten. serv.	HINHHC	HINHHC	Intermediate
NL3	West-Nederland	Knowl. inten. serv.	Knowl. inten. serv.	HINHHC	HINHHC	Urban
NL4	Zuid-Nederland	Knowl. inten. serv.	Knowl. inten. serv.	HINHHC	HINMLHC	Intermediate
PL11	Łódzkie	Agriculture	Agriculture	MINMHC	MINMHC	Intermediate
PL12	Mazowieckie	Agriculture	Agriculture	MINMHC	MLINHHC	Urban
PL21	Malopolskie	Agriculture	Agriculture	MINMHC	MINMHC	Intermediate
PL22	Slaskie	Agriculture	Agriculture	LINLHC	MINMHC	Intermediate
PL31	Lubelskie	Agriculture	Agriculture	MINMHC	MINMHC	Peripheral
PL32	Podkarpackie	Agriculture	Agriculture	LINLHC	MINMHC	Peripheral
PL33	Swietokrzyskie	Agriculture	Agriculture	MINMHC	MINMHC	Peripheral
PL34	Podlaskie	Agriculture	Agriculture	MINMHC	MINMHC	Peripheral
PL41	Wielkopolskie	Agriculture	Agriculture	LINLHC	LINLHC	Intermediate
PL42	Zachodniopomorskie	Agriculture	Agriculture	MINMHC	MINMHC	Ind. decline
PL43	Lubuskie	Agriculture	Med-low tech manuf.	LINLHC	LINLHC	Intermediate
PL51	Dolnoslaskie	Agriculture	Agriculture	MINMHC	MINMHC	Peripheral
PL52	Opolskie	Agriculture	Agriculture	LINLHC	LINLHC	Peripheral

(Continued)

Appendix 3.1 Regions included in the sample and their classification (Continued)

NUTS_ID	Name	Specialisation Group 2004	Specialisation Group 2012	Knowl. Gr. 2004	Know. Gr. 2012	Socio-ec. group
PL61	Kujawsko-Pomorskie	Agriculture	Agriculture	LINLHC	LINLHC	Ind. decline
PL62	Warminsko-Mazurskie	Agriculture	Agriculture	LINLHC	MINMHC	Peripheral
PL63	Pomorskie	Agriculture	Agriculture	MINMHC	MINMHC	Intermediate
PT11	Norte	Med-low tech manuf.	Med-low tech manuf.	LINLHC	LINLHC	Peripheral
PT15	Algarve	Less knowl. inten. serv.	Less knowl. inten. serv.	LINLHC	LINLHC	Intermediate
PT16	Centro (PT)	Agriculture	Agriculture	MINMHC	LINLHC	Peripheral
PT17	Lisboa	Less knowl. inten. serv.	Less knowl. inten. serv.	MINMHC	MINMHC	Urban
PT18	Alentejo	Agriculture	Agriculture	LINLHC	LINLHC	Peripheral
RO11	Nord-Vest	Agriculture	Agriculture	LINLHC	LINLHC	Intermediate
RO12	Centru	Agriculture	Agriculture	LINLHC	LINLHC	Ind. decline
RO21	Nord-Est	Agriculture	Agriculture	LINLHC	LINLHC	Peripheral
RO22	Sud-Est	Agriculture	Agriculture	LINLHC		Peripheral
RO31	Sud - Muntenia	Agriculture	Agriculture	LINLHC	LINLHC	Peripheral
RO32	Bucuresti - Ilfov	Med-low tech manuf.	Less knowl. inten. serv.	MLINHHC	MLINHHC	Urban
RO41	Sud-Vest Oltenia	Agriculture	Agriculture	LINLHC	LINLHC	Peripheral
RO42	Vest	Agriculture	Agriculture			Peripheral
SE11	Stockholm	Knowl. inten. serv.	Knowl. inten. serv.	HINHHC	HINHHC	Urban
SE12	Östra Mellansverige	Knowl. inten. serv.	Knowl. inten. serv.	HINHHC	HINHHC	Intermediate
SE21	Småland med öarna	Med-high tech manuf.	Med-low tech manuf.	HINMLHC	HINMLHC	Intermediate
SE22	Sydsverige	Knowl. inten. serv.	Knowl. inten. serv.	HINHHC	HINHHC	Intermediate
SE23	Västsverige	Knowl. inten. serv.	Knowl. inten. serv.	HINHHC	HINHHC	Intermediate
SE31	Norra Mellansverige	Knowl. inten. serv.	Med-low tech manuf.	HINMLHC	HINMLHC	Ind. decline
SE32	Mellersta Norrland	Knowl. inten. serv.	Knowl. inten. serv.	HINHHC	MLINHHC	Peripheral
SE33	Övre Norrland	Knowl. inten. serv.	Knowl. inten. serv.	HINHHC	MLINHHC	Peripheral

SI01	Vzhodna Slovenija	Agriculture	Agriculture	MINMHC	Ind. decline
SI02	Zahodna Slovenija	Med-low tech manuf.	Med-low tech manuf.	MINMHC	Urban
SK01	Bratislavský kraj	Knowl. inten. serv.	Knowl. inten. serv.	MLINHHC	Urban
SK02	Západné Slovensko	Med-high tech manuf.	Med-high tech manuf.	LINLHC	Intermediate
SK03	Stredné Slovensko	Med-low tech manuf.	Med-high tech manuf.	LINLHC	Intermediate
SK04	Východné Slovensko	Med-low tech manuf.	Med-low tech manuf.	LINLHC	Ind. decline
UKC	North East (UK)	Knowl. inten. serv.	Knowl. inten. serv.	MLINHHC	Intermediate
UKD	North West (UK)	Knowl. inten. serv.	Knowl. inten. serv.	MLINHHC	Intermediate
UKE	Yorkshire and The Humber	Knowl. inten. serv.	Knowl. inten. serv.	MLINHHC	Intermediate
UKF	East Midlands (UK)	Knowl. inten. serv.	Knowl. inten. serv.	MLINHHC	Intermediate
UKG	West Midlands (UK)	Med-high tech manuf.	Knowl. inten. serv.	MLINHHC	Intermediate
UKH	East of England	Knowl. inten. serv.	Knowl. inten. serv.	MLINHHC	Intermediate
UKI	London	Knowl. inten. serv.	Knowl. inten. serv.	MLINHHC	Urban
UKJ	South East (UK)	Knowl. inten. serv.	Knowl. inten. serv.	HINHHC	Intermediate
UKK	South West (UK)	Knowl. inten. serv.	Knowl. inten. serv.	MLINHHC	Intermediate
UKL	Wales	Knowl. inten. serv.	Knowl. inten. serv.	MLINHHC	Intermediate
UKM	Scotland	Knowl. inten. serv.	Knowl. inten. serv.	MLINHHC	Peripheral
UKN	Northern Ireland (UK)	Less knowl. inten. serv.	Knowl. inten. serv.	MLINHHC	Peripheral

Note: HINHHC=High patents and high education; HINMLHC=High patents and medium or low education; MLINHHC=Medium or low patents and high education; MINMHC= Medium patents and medium education or medium patents and low education or low education or medium education and low patents; LINLHC=Low patents and education

Notes

1 The Baumol idea of a *structural burden* of services slowing aggregate labour productivity growth is being challenged also empirically (Antonelli, 1998; Peneder *et al.*, 2003; Cainelli *et al.*, 2006; Savona and Lorentz, 2005; Evangelista *et al.*, 2013).
2 KIBS are usually identified in a sub-section of the NACE 74 Business service branch and include the following services activities: legal, accounting, tax consultancy, market research, auditing, opinion polling, management consultancy, architectural, engineering and technical consultancy, technical testing and analyses, advertising, other business activities not elsewhere classified (Muller and Doloreux, 2009).
3 This perspective is also conveyed by Castellacci in its new sectoral taxonomy of innovation integrating service and manufacturing industries (Castellacci, 2008). Also in this contribution the idea is that the emergence of a new set of general purpose technologies (namely those connected to the emergence of the ICTs) has deeply changed the structure of the sectoral linkages fuelling the process of technological accumulation and economic growth.
4 This is especially true for new members whose regions generally lack most of the legal framework, institutional structures and financial means of their western counterparts and have limited administrative powers.
5 Due to geographic remoteness and to the peculiar features that set them apart from EU economies, the following regions are not considered: Ciudad Autonoma de Ceuta, Ciudad Autonoma de Melilla and Canarias (Spain); French Overseas Departments (France); Acores and Regiao Autonoma de Madeira (Portugal).
6 For a discussion on measures of technological innovation see also Archibugi (1988).
7 The seven regions that have been removed are respectively Bremen (Germany), Pais Vasco (Spain), Champagne-Ardenne, Haute-Normandie, Basse Normandie and Lorraine (France) and Liguria (Italy); they have been placed, with the exception of Bremen, in the intermediate group. For two of them (Bremen and Liguria) employment in industry is below the national average, implying that the area is no more predominantly industrial. The others, albeit remaining industrial regions, record unemployment rates below the national average, implying that they are no more problem areas. For similar reasons, the five former DDR *Lander* are not included in the group. In fact, albeit having undergone intense industrialization under central planning, already in the mid-1990s they did not present important features of industrial decline: even if unemployment rates were above the national average, industrial employment was below and growing over the period – so was employment in the service sector, implying diversification away from industry.

References

Abreu, M., H.L.F. de Groot and R.J.G.M. Florax (2004), 'Space and Growth: a Survey of Empirical Evidence and Methods', Tinbergen Institute Working Paper No. TI 04-129/3.

Aghion, P. and P. Howitt (1992), 'A model of growth through creative destruction', *Econometrica*, vol. 60, pp. 323–51.

Antonelli, C. (1998), 'Localized technological change, new information technology and the knowledge-based economy: the European evidence', *Journal of Evolutionary Economics*, vol. 8, pp. 177–98.

Antonietti, R. and G. Cainelli (2008), 'Spatial agglomeration, technology and outsourcing of knowledge intensive business services: empirical insights from Italy', *International Journal of Service Technology and Management*, vol. 10(2–4), pp. 273–98.

Archibugi, D. (1988), 'In search of a useful measure of technological innovation', *Technological Forecasting and Social Change*, vol. 34, pp. 253–77.

Archibugi, D. and A. Coco (2004), 'A new indicator of technological capabilities for developed and developing countries (ArCo)', *World Development*, vol. 32(4), pp. 629–54.

Audretsch, D.B. and M. Feldman (2004), 'Knowledge spillovers and the geography of innovation'. In J.V. Henderson and J.F. Thisse (eds), *Handbook of Urban and Regional Economics, Vol. 4*. Amsterdam: Elsevier, pp. 2713–39.

Bacolod, M., B.S. Blum and W.C. Strange (2009), 'Skills in the city', *Journal of Urban Economics*, vol. 65, pp. 136–53.

Barca, F., F. McCann and Rodríguez-Pose (2012), 'The case for regional development intervention: pace-based versus place-neutral approaches', *Journal of Regional Science*, vol. 52, pp. 134–52.

Baumol, W.J. (1967), 'Macroeconomics of unbalanced growth: the anatomy of an urban crisis', *American Economic Review*, vol. 57, pp. 415–26.

Baumol, W.J. (2001), 'The growth of service industries: the paradox of exploding costs and persistent demand'. In T. ten Raa and R. Schettkat (eds), *Paradox of the Services: Exploding Costs and Persistent Demand*. Cheltenham: E. Elgar.

Baumol, W.J. and W.G. Bowen (1966), *Performing Arts: The Economic Dilemma*. New York: Twentieth Century Found.

Baumol, W.J., Blackman, S.A.B. and E.N. Wolff (1984), 'Unbalanced growth revisited: asymptotic stagnancy and new evidence', Economic Research Reports, CV Starr Center for Applied Economics, New York University.

Baumol, W.J., S.A.B. Blackman and E.N. Wolff (1985), 'Unbalanced growth revisited: asymptotic stagnancy and new evidences', *American Economic Review*, vol. 75, pp. 806–16.

Baumol, W.J., S.A.B. Blackman and E.N. Wolff (1989), *Productivity and American Leadership*. Cambridge, MA: MIT Press.

Boschma, R.A. (2005) 'Proximity and innovation: a critical assessment', *Regional Studies*, vol. 39, pp. 61–74.

Boschma, R.A. and K. Frenken (2011), 'Technological relatedness and regional branching'. In Bathelt H., M.P. Feldman and D.F. Kogler (eds), *Dynamic Geographies of Knowledge Creation and Innovation*. London: Taylor & Francis/Routledge, pp. 64–81.

Boschma, R.A. and S. Iammarino (2009), 'Related variety, trade linkages and regional growth', *Economic Geography*, vol. 85(3), pp. 289–311.

Boschma R.A., A. Minondo and M. Navarro (2012), 'Related variety and regional growth in Spain', *Papers in Regional Science*, vol. 91(2), pp. 241–56.

Cainelli, G., R. Evangelista and M. Savona (2006), 'Innovation and economic performance in services: A firm level analysis', *Cambridge Journal of Economics*, vol. 30, pp. 435–58.

Cantwell, J. and S. Iammarino (2003), *Multinational Corporations and European Regional Systems of Innovation*. London: Routledge.

Castellacci, F. (2008), 'Technological paradigms, regimes and trajectories: manufacturing and service industries in a new taxonomy of sectoral patterns of innovation', *Research Policy*, vol. 37, pp. 978–94.

Castellani, D., V. Meliciani and L. Mirra (2014), 'The determinants of inward foreign direct investment in business services across European regions', *Regional Studies*, 11 July, http://dx.doi.org/10.1080/00343404.2014.928677.

Chapman, S. and V. Meliciani (2012), 'Income disparties in the enlarged EU: socio-economic, specialization and geographical clusters', *Tijdschrift Voor Economische En Sociale Geografie*, vol. 103(3), pp. 293–311.

Cheshire, P. and D. Hay (1989), *Urban Problems in Western Europe: An Economic Analysis*. London: Unwin Hyman.

Ciarli, T., V. Meliciani and M. Savona (2012), 'Knowledge dynamics, structural change and the geography of business services', *Journal of Economic Surveys*, vol. 26, pp. 445–67.

Combes, P.P. (2000), 'Economic structure and local growth: France 1984–1993', *Journal of Urban Economics*, vol. 47, pp. 329–53.

Combes, P.P., G. Duranton and L. Gobillon (2011), 'The identification of agglomeration economies', *Journal of Economic Geography*, Oxford University Press, vol. 11(2), March, pp. 253–66.

Cooke, P. (1997), 'Regions in a global market: the experiences of Wales and Baden-Wurttemberg', *Review of International Political Economy*, vol. 4(2), pp. 13–36.

Crescenzi, R. (2005), 'Innovation and regional growth in the enlarged Europe: the role of local innovative capabilities, peripherality, and education', *Growth and Change*, vol. 36(4), pp. 471–507.

Crescenzi, R. and A. Rodríguez-Pose (2011), *Innovation and Regional Growth in the European Union*. Berlin, Heidelberg and New York: Springer.

Cumbers, A. and K. Birch (2006), 'Divergent pathways in Europe's old industrial regions?', Draft paper for SPIF meeting, 27 October.

David P., D. Foray and B.H. Hall (2009), 'Smart specialization – the concept: knowledge economists policy brief', no. 9, Knowledge for Growth Expert Group.

De Bondt, R. (1996), 'Spillovers and innovation activities', *International Journal of Industrial Organization*, vol. 15, pp. 1–28.

den Hertog, P. (2000), 'Knowledge-intensive business services as co-producers of innovation', *International Journal of Innovation Management*, vol. 4(4), pp. 491–528.

Dosi, G. (1988), 'Sources, procedures, and microeconomic effects of innovation', *Journal of Economic Literature*, vol. 26, pp. 1120–71.

Dosi, G., K. Pavitt and L. Soete (1990), *The Economics of Technical Change and International Trade*. London: Harvester Wheatsheaf.

Dosi, G., C. Freeman, R. Nelson, G. Silveberg and L. Soete (1988), *Technical Change and Economic Theory*. London: Pinter.

Dunford, M. (1993), 'Regional disparities in the European Community: evidence from the REGIO databank', *Regional Studies*, vol. 27, pp. 727–43.

Dunford, M. (1996), 'Disparities in employment, productivity and output in the EU: the roles of labour-market governance and welfare regimes', *Regional Studies*, vol. 30, pp. 339–57.

Duranton, G. and D. Puga (2000), 'Diversity and specialisation in cities: why, where and when does it matter?', *Urban Studies*, vol. 37(3), March, pp. 533–55.

Engelbrecht, H.-J. (1997), 'International R&D spillovers, human capital and productivity in OECD economies: an empirical investigation', *European Economic Review*, vol. 41, pp. 1479–88.

Evangelista, R. (2000), 'Sectoral patterns of technological change in services', *Economics of Innovation and New Technology*, vol. 9, pp. 183–221.

Evangelista, R., M. Lucchese and V. Meliciani (2013), 'Business services, innovation and sectoral growth', *Structural Change and Economic Dynamics*, vol. 25, pp. 119–32.

Fagerberg, J. (1987), 'A technology gap approach to why growth rates differ', *Research Policy*, vol. 16, pp. 87–99.

Foray, D., P. David and B.H. Hall (2009), 'Smart specialisation – the concept', *Knowledge Economists Policy Brief*, no. 9, June. European Commission, Directoral General for Research, Brussels.

Foray, D., P. David and B.H. Hall (2011), 'Smart specialization: from academic idea to political instrument, the surprising career of a concept and the difficulties involved in its implementation', MTEI Working Paper, École Polytechnique Fédérale de Lausanne.

Francois, J.F. (1990), 'Producer services, scale, and the division of labor', *Oxford Economic Papers*, vol. 42, pp. 715–29.

Francois, J. and J. Woerz (2008), 'Producer services, manufacturing linkages, and trade', *Journal of Industry, Competition and Trade*, vol. 8(3), pp. 199–229.

Freeman, C. (1987), *Technology Policy and Economic Performance: Lessons from Japan.* London: Pinter.

Frenken, K. and R.A. Boschma (2007), 'A theoretical framework for evolutionary economic geography: industrial dynamics and urban growth as a branching process', *Journal of Economic Geography*, vol. 7(5), pp. 635–49.

Frenken, K. and J. Hoekman (2006), 'Convergence in an enlarged Europe: the role of network cities', *Journal of Economic and Social Geography*, vol. 97, pp. 321–6.

Frenken K., F.G. van Oort and T. Verburg (2007), 'Related variety, unrelated variety and regional economic growth', *Regional Studies*, vol. 41(5), pp. 685–97.

Friedman, T. (2005), *The World is Flat: A Brief History of the Twenty-First Century.* New York: Farrar, Straus and Giroux.

Fuchs, V.R. (1968), *The Service Economy.* New York: National Bureau of Economic Research.

Fuchs, V.R. (1977), 'The service industries and US economic growth since World War II', NBER Working Paper Series, no. 211, National Bureau of Economic Research.

Gallouj, F. and M. Savona (2009), 'Innovation in services a review of the debate and perspectives for a research agenda', *Journal of Evolutionary Economics*, vol. 19(2), pp. 149–72.

Glaeser, E.L., H.D. Kallal, J. Scheinkman and A. Shleifer (1992), 'Growth in cities', *Journal of Political Economy*, vol. 100, pp. 1126–52.

Grabher, G. (1993), 'The weakness of strong ties: the lock-in of regional development in the Ruhr-area'. In G. Grabher (ed.), *The Embedded Firm: On the Socioeconomics of Industrial Networks.* London: T.J. Press, pp. 255–78.

Gray, A. (1948), *The Development of Economic Doctrine.* London: Longmans, Green.

Grossman, G. and E. Helpman (1991), *Innovation and Growth in the World Economy.* Cambridge, MA: MIT Press.

Guerrieri, P. and V. Meliciani (2005), 'Technology and international competitiveness: the interdependence between manufacturing and producer services', *Structural Change and Economic Dynamics*, vol. 16, pp. 489–502.

Harvey, D. (1985), *The Urbanization of Capital.* Oxford: Basil Blackwell.

Henderson, J.V., A. Kuncoro and M. Turner (1995), 'Industrial development in cities', *Journal of Political Economy*, vol. 103, pp. 1067–90.

Hoekman, B. and C.A. Primo Braga (1997), 'Protection and trade in services', World Bank, Policy Research Working Paper, no. 1747.

Hudson, R. (1994a), 'Institutional change, cultural transformation, and economic regeneration: myths and realities from Europe's old industrial areas'. In A. Amin and N. Thrift (eds), *Globalization, Institutions, and Regional Development in Europe*, Oxford: Oxford University Press.

Hudson, R. (1994b), 'Restructuring production in the West European steel industry', *Tijdschrift voor Economische en Sociale Geografie*, vol. 85, pp. 99–113.

Jacobs, J. (1969), *The Economy of Cities.* New York: Vintage.

Kaldor, N. (1966), *Causes of the Slow Rate of Growth in the United Kingdom.* Cambridge: Cambridge University Press.

Kaldor, N. (1978), *Further Essays on Economic Theory.* London: Duckworth.

Kaldor, N. (1980), *Essays on Economic Stability and Growth*, 2nd edn. London: Duckworth.

Kox, H. and L. Rubalcaba (2007a), 'Analysing the contribution of business services to European economic growth', MPRA Paper no. 2003.

Kox, H. and L. Rubalcaba (2007b), 'Business services and the changing structure of European economic growth', MPRA Paper no. 3570.

Lucas, R.E. (1988), 'On the mechanism of economic development', *Journal of Monetary Economics*, vol. 22, pp. 3–42.

Lundvall, B.A. (1992), *National Systems of Innovation: Towards a Theory of Innovation and Interactive Learning*. London: Pinter.

Martin, R. (1997), 'Regional unemployment disparities and their dynamic', *Regional Studies*, vol. 31, pp. 237–52.

McCann, P. and R. Ortega-Argilés (2013), 'Smart specialization, regional growth, and applications to European Union Cohesion Policy', *Regional Studies*, doi: 10.1080/00343404.2013.799769.

McCann, P. and F.G. van Oort (2009), 'Theories of agglomeration and regional economic growth: a historical review'. In R. Capello and P. Nijkamp, *Handbook of Regional Growth and Development Theories*. London: Edward Elgar.

Meliciani, V. and M. Savona (2014), 'The determinants of regional specialisation in business services: agglomeration economies, vertical linkages and innovation', *Journal of Economic Geography*, pp. 1–30, doi:10.1093/jeg/lbt038, IF=3.26, 5 years IF=5.0.

Miles, I. (2005), 'Innovation in services'. In J. Fagerberg, D. Mowery and R. Nelson (eds), *The Oxford Handbook of Innovation*. Oxford: Oxford University Press, pp. 433–58.

Miles, I.D., B. Tether, K. Blind, N. de Liso and G. Cainelli (2001), 'Analysis of CIS data on innovation in the service sector', Final Report to European Commission by CRIC/IDSE/ISE.

Miozzo, M.and L. Soete (2001), 'Internationalization of services: a technological perspective', *Technological Forecasting and Social Change*, vol. 67, pp. 159–85.

Montresor, S. and G. Vittucci Marzetti (2011), 'The deindustrialization/tertiarisation hypothesis reconsidered: a sub-system application to the OECD7', *Cambridge Journal of Economics*, vol. 35(2), pp. 401–21.

Muller, E. and D. Doloreux (2009), 'What we should know about knowledge-intensive business services', *Technology in Society*, vol. 31, pp. 64–72.

Muller, E. and A. Zenker (2001), 'Business services as actors of knowledge transformation: the role of KIBS in regional and national innovation systems', *Research Policy*, vol. 30, pp. 1501–16.

Nelson, R.R. (1993), *National Innovation Systems: A Comparative Study*. New York: Oxford University Press.

Nelson, R.R. and S. Winter (1982), *An Evolutionary Theory of Economic Change*. Cambridge, MA: Belknap Press.

O'Brien, R. (1992), *Global Financial Integration: The End of Geography*. London: Royal Institute of International Affairs.

Ortega-Argilés, R. (2012), 'The transatlantic productivity gap: a survey of the main causes', *Journal of Economic Surveys*, vol. 26(3), pp. 395–419.

Ottaviano, G. and D. Puga (1998), 'Agglomeration in the global economy: a survey of the "new economic geography"', *The World Economy*, vol. 21, pp. 707–31.

Pasinetti, L. (1981), *Structural Change and Economic Growth*. Cambridge: Cambridge University Press.

Peneder, M., S. Kaniovsky and B. Dachs (2003), 'What follows tertiarisation? Structural change and the role of knowledge-based services', *The Service Industry Journal*, vol. 23, pp. 47–66.

Prager, J.C. and J.F. Thisse (2012), *Economic Geography and the Unequal Development of Regions*. London and New York: Routledge.

Que'vit, M., J. Houard, S. Bodson and A. Dangoisse (1991), *Impact régional 1992: Les régions de tradition industrielle*. Brussels: De Boeck.

Raspe, O. and F.G. van Oort (2007), 'The knowledge economy and urban economic growth', Papers in Evolutionary Economic Geography, June.

Rodríguez-Pose, A. (1994), 'Socioeconomic restructuring and regional change: rethinking growth in the European Community', *Economic Geography*, vol. 70, pp. 325–43.

Rodríguez-Pose, A. (1998a), *The Dynamics of Regional Growth in Europe: Social and Political Factors*. Oxford: Clarendon Press.

Rodríguez-Pose, A. (1998b), 'Social conditions and economic performance: the bond between social structure and regional growth in Western Europe', *International Journal of Urban and Regional Research*, vol. 22, pp. 443–59.

Rodríguez-Pose, A. (1999), 'Convergence or divergence? Types of regional responses to socio-economic change in Western Europe', *Tijdschrift voor Economische en Sociale Geografie*, vol. 90, pp. 365–78.

Rodríguez-Pose, A. and R. Crescenzi (2008), 'Mountains in a flat world: why proximity still matters for the location of economic activity', *Cambridge Journal of Regions, Economy and Society*, Cambridge Political Economy Society, vol. 1(3), pp. 371–88.

Rodrik, D. (2004), 'Industrial policy for the twenty-first century', Paper prepared for UNIDO.

Romer, P.M. (1986), 'Increasing returns and long-run growth', *Journal of Political Economy*, vol. 94, pp. 1002–37.

Rowthorn, R. and R. Ramaswamy (1999), 'Growth, trade and deindustrialisation', *IMF Staff Papers*, vol. 46, pp. 18–41.

Rubalcaba, L. and H. Kox (eds) (2007), *Business Services in European Economic Growth*. New York: Palgrave Macmillan.

Savona, M. and A. Lorentz (2005), 'Demand and technological contribution to structural change and tertiarisation: an input-output structural decomposition analysis', LEM Working Paper Series, 2005/25, December.

Scherer, F.M. (1983), 'The propensity to patent', *International Journal of Industrial Organization*, vol. 1, pp. 107–28.

Scott, A.J. and M. Storper (1992), 'Le développement régional reconsidéré', *Espaces et Sociétés*, vol. 66/67, pp. 7–38.

Shearmur, R. and D. Doloreux (2008), 'Urban hierarchy or local buzz? High-order producer service and (or) knowledge-intensive business service location in Canada, 1991–2001', *Professional Geographer*, vol. 60, pp. 333–55.

Smith, A. (1776), *An Inquiry into the Nature and Causes of the Wealth of Nations*. London.

Solow, R. (1956), 'A contribution to the theory of economic growth', *Quarterly Journal of Economics*, vol. 70, pp. 65–94.

Storper, M. and A.J. Scott (1989), 'The geographical foundations and social regulation of flexible production complexes'. In J. Wolch and M. Dear (eds), *The Power of Geography. How Territory Shapes Social Life*. Boston: Unwin & Hyman.

Ten Raa, T. and E. Wolff (2001), 'Outsourcing of services and the productivity recovery in US manufacturing in the 1980s and 1990s', *Journal of Productivity Analysis*, vol. 16, pp. 149–65.

Tether, B.S. (2005), 'Do services innovate (differently)? Insights from the European Innobarometer Survey', *Industry Innovation*, vol. 12, pp. 153–84.

Tether, B.S. and A. Tajar (2008), 'The organisational-cooperation mode of innovation and its prominence amongst European service firms', *Research Policy*, vol. 37, pp. 720–39.

Todtling, F. and M. Trippl (2005), 'One size fits all? Towards a differentiated regional innovation policy approach', *Research Policy*, vol. 34, pp. 1203–19.

Tomaney, J. (1994), 'Alternative approaches to restructuring in traditional industrial regions: the case of the maritime sector', *Regional Studies*, vol. 28, pp. 544–9.

Tomlinson, M. (2001), 'A new role for business services in economic growth', in D. Archibugi and B. Lundvall, *The Globalizing Learning Economy*, Oxford: Oxford University Press.

Tregenna, F. (2011), 'Manufacturing productivity, deindustrialization, and reindustrialization', Working Paper no. 2011/57, UNU-WIDER (World Institute for Development Economics Research).

van Oort F.G. (2007), 'Spatial and sectoral composition effects of agglomeration economies in the Netherlands', *Papers in Regional Science*, vol. 86(1), pp. 5–30.

Verspagen, B. (1993), *Uneven Growth Between Interdependent Economies*. Avebury: Aldershot.

4 The evolution of income disparities in the enlarged EU and the role of specialization, knowledge and socio-economic groups[1]

Introduction

This chapter assesses the importance of specialization, socio-economic factors and regional capabilities to produce and absorb new knowledge in the evolution of regional income disparities in Europe between 2004 and 2011.

As partly shown in Chapter 2, so far several empirical papers have investigated convergence in the EU-25 (or 27) following different methodologies. Fischer and Stirböck (2005), Debarsy and Ertur (2006), Frenken and Hoekman (2006) and Paas *et al.* (2007) test for convergence across the enlarged EU in the context of regression analysis; Ertur and Koch (2006) use exploratory spatial data analysis; Ezcurra and Rapun (2007) adopt a non-parametric approach; while Chapman *et al.* (2012) and Chapman and Meliciani (2012) use both non-parametric and spatial regimes analyses. Overall they find some evidence of convergence (Fischer and Stirböck, 2005; Frenken and Hoekman, 2006; Ezcurra and Rapun, 2007) but also a new north–west/east polarization pattern which replaces the previous north–south one for the EU-15 (Ertur and Koch, 2006; Chapman *et al.*, 2012). Moreover Frenken and Hoekman (2006) find that network cities, operating in global trade networks and relatively independent from their hinterland, converge more quickly than other areas in the EU-25, while Eczurra and Rapun (2007) empha-size the role of neighbouring regions in explaining the dispersion observed in the distribution of GDP per worker. Finally, Chapman and Meliciani (2012) find, between 1998 and 2005, convergence between countries with increasing disparities within countries. They also find that the result is largely due to the strong diver-gence that is emerging between the regions belonging to newcomer countries, and that partly specialization patterns but, more evidently, socio-economic clusters explain this divergence.

Based on the results of Chapman and Meliciani (2012), we extend the analysis to the post-crisis period and we investigate the explanatory power of countries, specialization, knowledge and socio-economic groups, as defined in Chapter 3, in both old EU members and newcomers.

These factors may produce different effects on agglomeration, growth and convergence. For instance, if, on the one hand, knowledge flows more easily across contiguous areas this would create geographical clusters of innovating and technologically backward regions (Rodríguez-Pose and Crescenzi, 2008) leading to divergence. If, on the other hand, ICTs allow knowledge to spread over distant places, new investments may locate in peripheral areas creating a more homogeneous economic space (Friedman, 2005) and favouring convergence. Specialization patterns may lead to the same results, either creating localized clusters or spreading across far-away regions, depending on the relative strength of agglomeration economies and decreasing transport costs. Socio-economic factors generally interrupt geographic homogeneity: urban areas surrounded by less developed neighbours could experience growth patterns that are more similar to other distant urban areas than to that of their neighbours. Also, national borders could act in the same way, determining different outcomes in areas that are contiguous but belong to different nations, making convergence within countries easier than across countries. Moreover, the relative strength of these factors may vary over time. For example, regions belonging to countries adopting the euro might find it more and more difficult to compete on prices, with an increasing importance of innovation for competitiveness and growth. At the same time, further economic integration, if effective, should reduce the importance of country factors in explaining regional patterns of convergence/divergence.

All these issues are investigated in this chapter, considering, first, all European regions and then focusing on newcomers and on regions of countries belonging to the Eurozone. In fact, the period under study has witnessed some important events with relevant implications for the evolution of regional disparities in Europe. First, in 2004, ten new members, mainly belonging to former centrally planned economies, joined the EU, followed, in 2007, by Romania and Bulgaria. These countries at the onset of integration had income disparities with old members that were far bigger than in previous accessions. At the same time, they shared a record of some 40 years of centralized communist regimes under which regional disparities were often kept artificially low. The integration of these economies in the EU has led to a shift of resources previously devoted especially to Southern European regions towards the east. Moreover, the lower costs of production have facilitated the location of foreign direct investment in the eastern regions, changing regional specialization patterns in Europe. All these elements might have led to a different performance of newcomers with respect to old members.

At the same time, the period under analysis includes one of the strongest crises ever witnessed in Europe: the financial crisis originating in the USA in 2007 and spreading to the EU, starting from 2008. Moreover, for the first time, a group of European countries (those belonging to the European Monetary Union) were confronted with the need to find common responses to the crisis since currency devaluation was no longer possible, monetary policy was centralized and fiscal policy could not be managed freely due to the rules established in the Stability and Growth Path. All these factors should have led to increasing importance of regional characteristics with respect to countries in the capability to overcome the downturn. However, the lack of 'real' integration – that is, the persistence of strong institutional differences across countries in the regulation of the labour market, in taxation rules, in education systems, etc. – might have led to similarities in the impact of the crisis across regions belonging to the same country. The focus on regions from the Eurozone tries to answer these questions by investigating changes in the relative importance of national versus regional characteristics in affecting income distinguishing the period pre- and post-crisis (2004–8 and 2008–11).

The chapter is organized as follows. The next section, 'Descriptive statistics on regional disparities in Europe' looks at some descriptive statistics on regional income disparities across and within countries. Then, 'The role of specialization, knowledge and socio-economic groups for regional income disparities' presents various analyses for the evolution of income disparities in the enlarged Europe, starting with trends in variance, turning, thereafter, to look at entire distributions and, finally, introducing spatial correlation and spatial regression models. 'A closer look at regions from countries joining the EU in 2004 and 2007' focuses on regions belonging to countries that joined the EU after 2004; we then take 'A closer look at the Eurozone' ; followed by 'Conclusions'.

Descriptive statistics on regional disparities in Europe

Before starting analysing the factors contributing to explain regional income disparities, it is useful to have an idea about how large such disparities were at the beginning and at the end of the period under study (2004–11) and to compare regional disparities across Europe with regional disparities within European countries. Table 4.1 reports the minimum, maximum, median and the 10th, 25th, 75th and 90th percentiles of the regional per capita income distribution in 2004, 2008 and 2011.

In 2004 the poorest EU region (Nord-Est Romania) had a per capita income of about 5,000 euros, 11 times smaller than the per capita income of the richest region (Région de Bruxelles Capitale) which was above 54,000 euros. In 2008 the difference was still very large, although in the order of about nine times, rather than 11 times: the poorest region (Severozapaden in Bulgaria) had a per capita income of about 7,000 euros while the richest (Luxembourg) of about 66,000. From 2008–11 there were no major changes: the poorest region (Sud-Est

Table 4.1 Quantiles of the regional per capita GDP distribution in 2004, 2008 and 2011 (thousands of euro)

	min.	*max.*	*p10*	*p25*	*p50*	*p75*	*p90*
GDPPC04	4.94	54.48	8.94	14.2	20.4	24.67	28.87
GDPPC08	7.05	65.82	11.1	17.03	22.77	28.5	33.68
GDPPC11	7.19	66.75	11.81	17.09	22.16	27.88	34.41
	max./min.	*p50/min.*	*max./p50*	*p50/p10*	*p90/p50*	*p50/p25*	*p75/p50*
GDPPC04	11.03	4.13	2.67	2.28	1.42	1.44	1.21
GDPPC08	9.34	3.23	2.89	2.05	1.48	1.34	1.25
GDPPC11	9.28	3.08	3.01	1.88	1.55	1.30	1.26

Romania) showed a per capita income of almost 7,200 euros and the richest (Luxembourg) of almost 67,000.

What is very interesting to observe is that while there are some signs of convergence of the minimum to the median (the difference decreases from a range of four to a range of three), the difference between the richest region and the median increases (from a range of 2.7 to a range of three). The same trend can be observed looking at the 10th and the 90th percentiles: while there is convergence of the 10th percentile to the median (the difference decreases from the order of 2.3 to 1.9), there is divergence of the 90th percentile to the median (the difference increases from the order of 1.4 to the order of 1.5). The same picture emerges when comparing the 25th and the 75th percentiles to the median.

Overall, regional disparities appear to be very high and, although the poorest regions grow more than the average, the income gap between the richest regions and the average also increases. This evidence raises doubts on the existence of a real convergence process by which Europe is becoming a more homogeneous economic area, despite what is auspicated by the European Union.

More detailed information on the behaviour of the single regions can be found in Figure 4.1, reporting the division of the regions in quartiles in 2004 and in 2011.

Figure 4.1 shows a clear spatial pattern in the distribution of regional per capita GDP in Europe in both years, but with some differences. In 2004, almost all regions in the last quartile (the poorest regions) are located in the eastern part of Europe (all but Extremadura in Spain and Centro and Norte in Portugal), while in 2011 we find in the last group also many Southern European regions. More precisely seven regions, all belonging to newcomers, improve their position from the fourth to the third quartile between 2004 and 2011; these are: Yugozapaden, (BG), Moravskoslezsko (CZ), Estonia, Nyugat-Dunántúl (HU), Slaskie (PL), Dolnoslaskie (PL) and Západné Slovensko (SK). At the same time seven regions, all but one belonging to Southern Europe, lose positions moving from the third to the fourth quartile; these are: Severovýchod (CZ), Voreia Ellada (GR), Kentriki Ellada (GR), Campania (IT), Puglia (IT), Calabria (IT) and Sicilia (IT).

The figure also shows that the richest regions are mainly concentrated in Central Europe (Northern Italy, Southern Germany, Luxembourg, Netherlands, Belgium and Austria), in Northern Europe (Sweden, Finland and Denmark) and in capital cities (Lazio, Praha, Madrid, Bucuresti and Bratislavský kraj). Notice that this quartile is very heterogeneous, ranging from a per capita GDP of about 25,000 euros to about 55,000 euros in 2004 and from about 28,000 euros to about 67,000 euros in 2011. Among the richest regions, those losing positions belong mainly to Italy and UK (Piemonte, Toscana, East of England and South-east of England), while those gaining positions belong mainly to Germany (Berlin, Rheinland-Pfalz and Saarland). Finally, it is worth noticing the high growth of Bucuresti, which moves from the third to the first quartile.

Again, the picture emerging from the maps is one in which disparities are persistent with the improvement of newcomer regions at the expense of Southern European regions. Moreover, the map shows a strong spatial association in per capita GDP interrupted by the behaviour of capital cities.

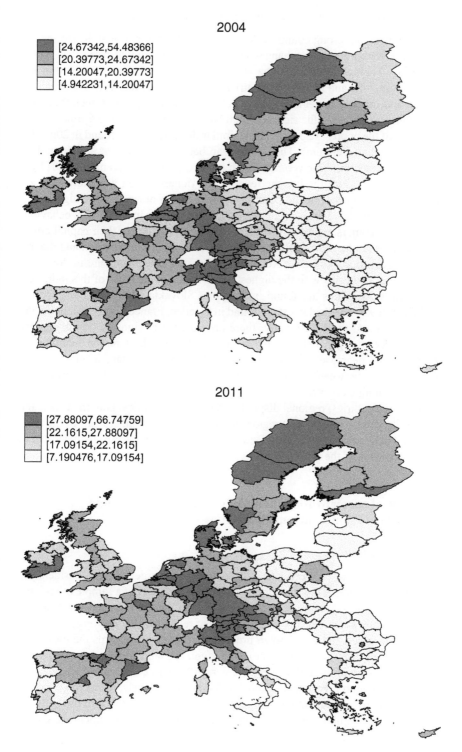

Figure 4.1 Per capita GDP quartiles in 2004 and 2011.

Since there are strong country effects when looking at regional disparities, we might ask how the picture changes when examining regional disparities within countries. Table 4.2 reports some statistics on regional disparities within EU countries in 2004 and in 2011.[2] Countries with the largest disparities between the richest and the poorest regions mainly belong to newcomers (in Czech Republic, Romania and Slovakia the richest region had a per capita GDP 2.5 times higher than that of the poorest region in 2004, similar disparities were found in 2004 also in Germany and Belgium). The income gap between the poorest and the richest region increased in all newcomers (with the exception of Slovenia). In 2011 the only countries where the income level of the richest region was more than 2.5 times higher than that of the poorest region were in newcomers (Bulgaria 2.7, Czech Republic 2.7, Hungary 2.7, Slovakia 3.6 and Romania 4.3). The behaviour of most newcomers appears to be driven by the behaviour of their capital cities: if disparities are measured looking at the difference between the first and the last quartile, countries like Czech Republic, Bulgaria and Romania are no longer in the group of countries with the highest disparities. On the basis of this indicator, the highest disparities are found in Belgium, Slovakia, Hungary, Italy, Ireland and Germany, while the lowest are found in Sweden, France, Czech Republic, the Netherlands and the UK. Finally, there are no general signs of within-country convergence: the gap between the poorest and the richest region increases in 13 countries, decreases in six countries and remains constant in one country, while the gap between the first and last quartile increases in 11 countries and decreases in nine countries.

In many countries, regional disparities have a geographical pattern. This is the case in Italy, where all poorest regions are located in the southern part of the territory, and in Germany and in many newcomers, where they are especially located in the eastern part of the territory.

The role of specialization, knowledge and socio-economic groups for regional income disparities

Analysis of variance

A first approach to convergence is based on σ-convergence that considers the evolution over time of the standard deviation (or variance) of a sample of regions. This approach has come to be extensively used in the literature inasmuch as it is not affected by a number of shortcomings that relate to other convergence measures (for instance, the well-known problem of regression towards the mean that affects widely used β-convergence); moreover, the standard deviation is easily divided into its within- and between-(or across-)groups components. Regions are grouped by country, by human capital and innovation levels, by socio-economic features and by specialization. Total variability is decomposed into the between and the within component for each grouping; results for old members are shown separately from those for newcomers.

Table 4.2 Regional disparities within countries, 2004 and 2011

	n	min.	max.	p25	p50	p75	max./ min.	p75/ p25
Austria 2004	9	19.28	36.69	23.27	26.81	28.87	1.90	1.24
Austria 2011	9	21.71	41.33	27.6	32.52	34.41	1.90	1.25
Belgium 2004	3	18.87	51.87	18.87	26.05	51.87	2.75	2.75
Belgium 2011	3	22.03	55.6	22.03	30.12	55.6	2.52	2.52
Bulgaria 2004	6	5.77	11.03	5.77	6.22	6.88	1.91	1.19
Bulgaria 2011	6	7.23	19.57	7.79	8.77	9.54	2.71	1.22
Czech Republic 2004	8	13.32	35.22	13.8	14.59	15.76	2.64	1.14
Czech Republic 2011	8	15.74	42.9	16.58	17.7	18.3	2.73	1.10
Germany 2004	16	16.54	45.38	17.53	22.46	28.09	2.74	1.60
Germany 2011	16	21.06	50.71	22.19	28.11	34.95	2.41	1.58
Greece 2004	4	17.56	23.95	17.87	19.16	22.05	1.36	1.23
Greece 2011	4	15.42	26.94	15.79	17.33	22.72	1.75	1.44
Spain 2004	16	14.15	28.58	18.19	20.59	25.27	2.02	1.39
Spain 2011	16	16.69	32.5	20.44	23.64	27.78	1.95	1.36
Finland 2004	4	20.32	33.85	21.29	25.57	31.37	1.67	1.47
Finland 2011	4	23.86	34.78	25.06	29.56	33.82	1.46	1.35
France 2004	22	17.93	36.54	19.72	20.82	21.5	2.04	1.09
France 2011	22	20.79	45.59	21.65	22.71	23.98	2.19	1.11
Hungary 2004	7	8.91	21.71	8.94	9.59	14.11	2.44	1.58
Hungary 2011	7	10.02	27.56	10.74	11.23	17.15	2.75	1.60
Ireland 2004	2	21.77	34.13	21.77	27.95	34.13	1.57	1.57
Ireland 2011	2	21.54	36.29	21.54	28.91	36.29	1.68	1.68
Italy 2004	21	14.61	31.78	17.27	24.18	29.88	2.18	1.73
Italy 2011	21	15.71	36.92	19.33	26.65	29.58	2.35	1.53
Netherlands 2004	4	23.22	30.45	24.36	26.2	28.67	1.31	1.18
Netherlands 2011	4	27.23	34.5	29.47	32.05	33.44	1.27	1.13
Poland 2004	16	7.58	16.81	8.44	9.71	10.89	2.22	1.29
Poland 2011	16	11.05	26.73	12	13.67	16.32	2.42	1.36
Portugal 2004	5	13.07	23.59	14.12	15.45	18.52	1.80	1.31
Portugal 2011	5	15.61	26.91	15.96	17.67	19.71	1.72	1.23
Romania 2004	8	4.94	15.43	6.12	6.8	7.75	3.12	1.27
Romania 2011	8	7.19	30.66	9.6	10.26	12.42	4.26	1.29
Sweden 2004	8	23.35	37.57	23.98	24.68	25.6	1.61	1.07
Sweden 2011	8	26.52	43.3	26.92	28.34	30.53	1.63	1.13
Slovenia 2004	2	15.49	22.5	15.49	18.99	22.5	1.45	1.45
Slovenia 2011	2	17.69	25.08	17.69	21.38	25.08	1.42	1.42
Slovakia 2004	4	9.08	27.84	9.57	10.87	19.76	3.07	2.06
Slovakia 2011	4	12.82	46.66	13.82	16.47	32.38	3.64	2.34
United Kingdom 2004	12	19.32	43.61	21.56	23.19	25.26	2.26	1.17
United Kingdom 2011	12	18.6	45.39	20.45	21.9	24.23	2.44	1.18

Table 4.3 shows an overall reduction in disparities across EU regions; variability falls by almost one third from 2004–11.[3] However, the picture is different according to which type of region is considered: old member regions diverge and divergence speeds up in crises-ridden 2008–11; newcomers, instead, converge and it is their performance that dominates that of the whole sample.

Table 4.3 Sum of squares decomposition: EU-27, old members and newcomers by country, knowledge, socio-economic and specialization groups in 2004, 2008 and 2011 (totals, between and within components - absolute values and shares)

	Total	Country groups		Knowledge groups		Socio-economic groups		Specialization groups	
		Between	Within	Between	Within	Between	Within	Between	Within
2004									
EU-27	35.54	26.77	8.78	18.67	16.87	10.97	24.57	14.37	21.17
		0.75	*0.25*	*0.53*	*0.47*	*0.31*	*0.69*	*0.40*	*0.60*
Old members	7.04	2.15	4.90	2.13	4.91	3.36	3.68	1.87	5.17
		0.31	*0.70*	*0.30*	*0.70*	*0.48*	*0.52*	*0.27*	*0.73*
Newcomers	8.60	4.73	3.88	2.34	6.26	5.06	3.54	4.75	3.86
		0.55	*0.45*	*0.27*	*0.73*	*0.59*	*0.41*	*0.55*	*0.45*
2008									
EU-27	28.54	18.70	9.84	15.57	12.97	10.66	17.88	11.03	17.51
		0.66	*0.34*	*0.55*	*0.45*	*0.37*	*0.63*	*0.39*	*0.61*
Old members	7.34	2.34	5.00	2.37	4.97	3.42	3.92	1.71	5.63
		0.32	*0.68*	*0.32*	*0.68*	*0.47*	*0.53*	*0.23*	*0.77*
Newcomers	8.17	3.32	4.85	3.31	4.86	5.61	2.55	4.33	3.84
		0.41	*0.59*	*0.41*	*0.59*	*0.69*	*0.31*	*0.53*	*0.47*
2011									
EU-27	26.24	15.86	10.38	14.54	11.67	10.95	15.29	9.93	16.32
		0.60	*0.40*	*0.55*	*0.44*	*0.42*	*0.58*	*0.38*	*0.62*
Old members	8.17	3.04	5.13	3.15	5.02	3.97	4.20	2.01	6.16
		0.37	*0.63*	*0.39*	*0.61*	*0.49*	*0.51*	*0.25*	*0.75*
Newcomers	7.93	2.68	5.25	3.11	4.82	5.47	2.47	3.79	4.14
		0.34	*0.66*	*0.39*	*0.61*	*0.69*	*0.31*	*0.48*	*0.52*

Coming to the decomposition of total squares in the between- and within-groups components for EU-27 regions, country factors and knowledge groups explain variability better than socio-economic and specialization group. However, over time the explanatory power of countries decreases, while that of knowledge and, more markedly, that of socio-economic groups increases in relative terms. Again, these results hide important differences between old members and newcomers. In fact, for old members socio-economic factors appear to explain variability better than human capital and innovation or specialization patterns. Moreover, over time the explanatory power of countries increases significantly, implying that, notwithstanding 50 years or so of economic integration, disparities are growing country-wise. It is worth observing that also innovation and human capital factors increase their explanatory power considerably, especially between 2008 and 2011, showing their importance as a response to the crisis.

For newcomers, instead, the first evidence is that, notwithstanding overall convergence, there is increasing variability of per capita GDP within countries. Variability between regions is explained mostly by socio-economic and by specialization features. National factors, which are important initially, decline rapidly.

In addition, while newcomer regions become more similar in terms of national and specialization features, they diverge with reference to socio-economic or innovation indicators, particularly between 2004 and 2008. This implies that these elements are becoming increasingly important in shaping economic performance and are contributing to the building of new disparities between these regions. Country factors and specialization patterns are, instead, losing importance.

The evolution of per capita income distributions in the enlarged EU: 2004–11

Although useful to gain a first impression of the underlying phenomenon, the approach considered so far (σ-convergence, comparing standard deviations) provides at best only a view of the *average* behaviour of regions' per capita GDP; in other words, it does not show either the shape of the distribution (its symmetry, tightness, etc.) or the movement of regions across distributions (on this point, see Quah 1996a, 1996b and 1997). An account of the shape of the *entire* cross-section distribution of per capita GDP across EU regions may be obtained by estimating the density function associated with the distribution of regional per capita GDP. The intra-distribution mobility is generally captured by the use of stochastic kernels (see, among others, Quah, 1997, and Bickenbach and Bode, 2003).

In what follows, we calculate the density functions of regional GDP (in logs) normalized both relative to the European average and to each region's national average.[4] For both distributions we compare the situation in the initial and in the final year of observation (2004 and 2011), while the intra-distribution mobility of regions over time is analysed by using the stochastic kernels. In both cases we use Epanechnikov kernel and optimal bandwidth as defined by Silverman (1986).

Figure 4.2 shows the estimated density distribution of EU-relative regional per capita GDP (in logs) in the initial and in the final year of observation and the contour plot of the stochastic kernel. Looking at univariate kernels, it can be observed that the density falls for the lowest per capita GDP levels but grows somewhat for the medium-low ones. Both densities are left-skewed; skewness falls over time (from −0.68 to −0.33) but kurtosis rises (from 3.09 to 3.26). Coherently, the contour plot of the stochastic kernel shows general persistence for regions with above-average per capita GDP levels in 2004 and some convergence for the lower ones.

Figure 4.3 shows again the distribution of per capita GDP, but normalized by the country average. With respect to the previous case, the probability mass appears to be generally tighter and more concentrated around the average, suggesting that country factors account for a considerable part of per capita GDP disparities. However, the density does not show signs of convergence over time. In fact, in 2011 the distribution 1) tends to widen somewhat and 2) presents evidence of a second mode forming for higher per capita GDP levels. Although, according to the Kolmogorov-Smirnov (K-S) test, the two distributions are not statistically significantly different, both skewness and kurtosis grow (respectively

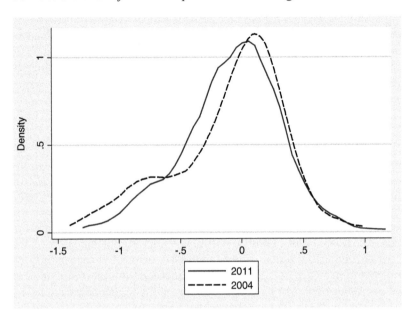

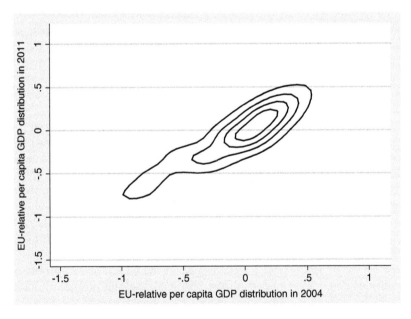

Figure 4.2 EU-relative per capita GDP distributions in 2004 and 2011 and contour plots.

from 0.81 to 0.99 and from 4.31 to 4.81), signalling increasing disparities within countries. The higher kurtosis is coherent with the forming of a group of rich and very rich regions country-relative; this may be also seen in the right tail of the two density functions in Figure 4.3. Analysis of the contour plot confirms the picture, showing persistence throughout the distribution.

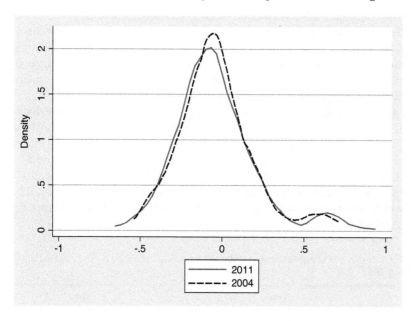

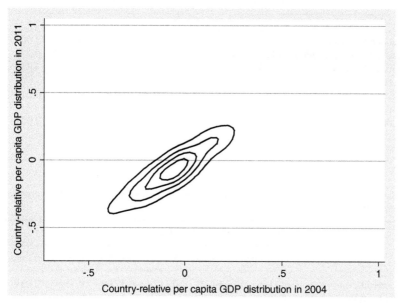

Figure 4.3 Country-relative per capita GDP distributions in 2004 and 2011 and contour plots.

Conditional distributions

We now ask whether the groupings that we proposed in Chapter 3 play a role in explaining EU-relative and country-relative distributions and whether their importance has changed over time. In order to give a preliminary answer to these questions we focus on conditional distributions. These are obtained by, first, regressing per capita GDP (expressed as (log) difference either from the EU or from the country average) on conditioning factors, and then computing the distribution of predicted values plus the vector of residuals when setting to zero the value of the conditioned variable (as in López-Bazo *et al.*, 2002; Meliciani, 2006; Chapman and Meliciani, 2012). Conditioning factors are: countries, socioeconomic groups, specialization groups and knowledge groups.

We also use the K-S test to check whether the original and conditioned distributions are statistically different (the null hypothesis is that they are not). If the test rejects the null hypothesis, the two density functions are significantly different and the conditioning variable explains the distribution of regional income.

Each distribution and each test is carried out both for 2004 and for 2011. Moreover, we consider both EU-relative and country-relative distributions. The results of K-S tests are reported in Tables 4.4 and 4.5, alongside the variance for each distribution.

Table 4.4 Conditioned Europe-relative distribution functions: combined K-S test and variance, 2004 and 2011

	2004	*2011*	*2004*		*2011*	
	Variance	*Variance*	*K-S test*	*p-value*	*K-S test*	*p-value*
Original distribution	0.221	0.163				
Conditioned by country	0.050	0.059	0.2229	0.001	0.2166	0.001
Conditioned by specialization	0.112	0.093	0.1274	0.127	0.1083	0.271
Conditioned by socio-economic groups	0.136	0.085	0.1083	0.316	0.1019	0.339
Conditioned by knowledge groups	0.084	0.060	0.1529	0.039	0.1783	0.014
Conditioned by socio-economic, specialization and knowledge groups	0.058	0.041	0.1847	0.007	0.2166	0.001

Table 4.5 Conditioned country-relative distribution functions: combined K-S test and variance, 2004 and 2011

	2004	*2011*	*2004*		*2011*	
	Variance	*Variance*	*K-S test*	*p-value*	*K-S test*	*p-value*
Conditioned by specialisation	0.044	0.049	0.1274	0.127	0.1529	0.039
Conditioned by socio-economic groups	0.027	0.030	0.1847	0.007	0.2293	0.000
Conditioned by knowledge groups	0.049	0.056	0.1401	0.072	0.1274	0.127
Conditioned by socio-economic, specialization and knowledge groups	0.023	0.025	0.1911	0.004	0.2102	0.001

Table 4.4, referring to EU-relative distributions, shows how countries are becoming less and less important in explaining differences in per capita GDP with respect to specialization, socio-economic and knowledge groups. In fact, while the variance in the per capita GDP distribution conditioned by countries increases between 2004 and 2001, the variance of all other conditioned distributions decreases. Moreover, when conditioning for all factors but countries together, the variance of the conditional distributions in 2011 is lower than the variance of the distribution conditional on countries in the same year (0.041 versus 0.059), while this was not the case in 2004 (when the values were respectively 0.058 and 0.050). However, looking at the K-S test for equality between distributions, we find that in both periods only the distributions conditioned on countries or on knowledge groups are significantly different from the original ones.

A very different picture emerges when looking at country-relative distributions. Here the variance increases over time, pointing to increases in income inequalities within countries. However, conditioning for all explanatory factors strongly reduces the increasing variance, showing again that the groups are becoming more relevant over time also in explaining within-country disparities. Moreover, in the case of country-relative distributions, we find that in both periods the distribution conditioned to socio-economic groups is significantly different from the original one, pointing to the relevance of these groups, especially when trying to explain within-country differences in per capita GDP (as originally suggested by Rodríguez-Pose, 1998a). Specialization appears to matter more in explaining within-country income disparities in 2011, while knowledge groups appeared more important in 2004.

The explanatory power of each factor for EU-relative per capita GDP distributions can be checked visually in Figure 4.4, which compares respectively the original EU-relative with the three conditioned ones in 2011, and in Figure 4.5, which reports the relative contour plots (from original EU-relative distribution to conditional distributions). Curves lying along the main diagonal indicate that the conditioning factor has weak explicative power. Curves that, instead, depart from the diagonal point to a relatively important conditioning factor.

Figure 4.4 shows that conditioning for innovation/human capital groups leads to the most concentrated and symmetric distribution, while specialization and socio-economic groups appear to be less important. All conditioning factors, however, contribute to reduce the skewness (which is 0.07 when conditioning for innovation groups, –0.17 when conditioning for specialization groups and –0.19 when conditioning for socio-economic groups). However, only conditioning for socio-economic groups reduces the kurtosis (to 2.96 from the original value of 3.26).

By and large, these results are confirmed by the contour plots: Figure 4.5 shows that innovation and knowledge groups have a relatively high explanatory power for all regions, while socio-economic and specialization groups appear to be important mainly for the poor and very poor regions EU-relative.

Figure 4.6 shows the explanatory power of the groups with respect to country-relative per capita GDP in 2011, while Figure 4.7 reports the relative contour plots. In this case, the factor which contributes most to reducing the spread of the

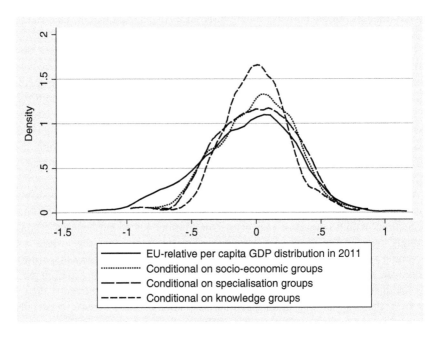

Figure 4.4 Original EU-relative and conditional per capita income distributions in 2011.

distribution and to making it more symmetric is the socio-economic grouping. Again, all factors reduce skeweness (from 0.99 to 0.04 for socio-economic groups; 0.68 for innovation groups and 0.82 for specialization groups). The kurtosis is lowest for socio-economic groups (3.14) followed by innovation groups (4.76) and by specialization ones (4.76). Consideration of the contour plots for the different distributions (Figure 4.7) confirms the results of Figure 4.6: conditioning for socio-economic factors makes the contour lines appear almost entirely horizontal, while curves for specialization and knowledge groups are largely centred around the diagonal, except for the lowest levels of per capita GDP. The figure also shows a second mode forming to the right in the distribution conditioned for socio-economic factors, probably reflecting a cluster of capitals at very high levels of per capita GDP country-relative.

Overall the identified groups appear to matter in explaining income disparities, with knowledge groups being particularly important when explaining disparities across regions and countries, while socio-economic groups are more significant when explaining income disparities within countries. Finally, specialization groups appear to be less important. This contrasts with previous results (Ezcurra *et al.*, 2007; Ezcurra and Rapun, 2007; Chapman and Meliciani, 2012) that found a significant role for specialization before 2005. This could be an effect of consid-erable relocation processes in action, according to which old members have delocalized important portions of the production chain in manufacturing, espe-cially among low-tech products, to newcomers, leading to significant growth in

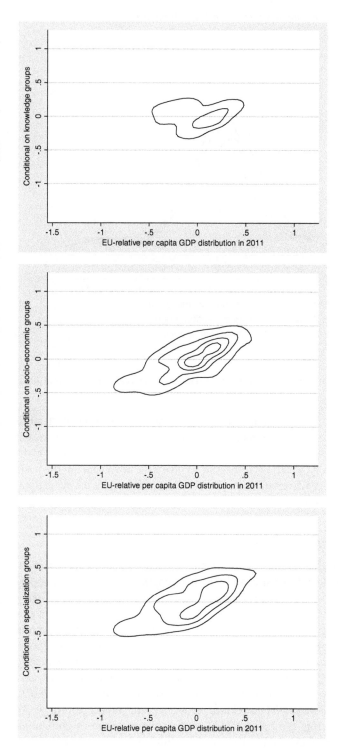

Figure 4.5 Contour plots for EU-relative conditional distributions in 2011.

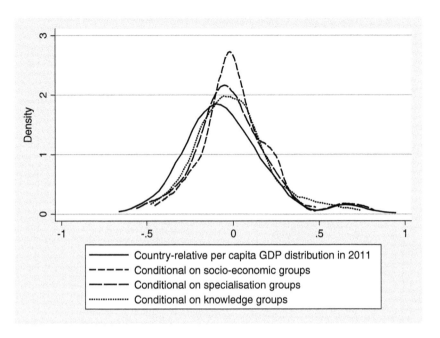

Figure 4.6 Original country-relative and conditional per capita income distributions in 2011.

many CEEC regions. The fact that different types of specialization can lead to different growth patterns in different regions also gives support to the recent literature on smart specialization (McCann and Ortega-Agilés, 2013) that highlights how each territory has its own specific comparative advantage on the basis of which it builds related diversification processes, maximizing, at the same time, local knowledge diffusion and learning networks.

Spatial correlation in per capita GDP

We now turn to consider the question of whether income disparities are somehow linked to a geographical dimension and whether geography increases its importance over time. This means investigating if regional income dynamics is being increasingly affected by the formation of groupings (clusters) where, thanks to spillovers, technology transfers and/or factor mobility, common economic features and trends come to be shared among geographically contiguous regions. Previous literature testing for correlation between neighbouring regions generally finds evidence of high spatial autocorrelation of per capita income levels and dynamics in the EU (see, among others, López-Bazo *et al.*, 1999, and Stirböck, 2004, who find a positive spatial correlation between production sectors as well). Early studies considering the enlarged EU confirm the presence of correlation (see Fischer and Stirböck, 2005; Paas *et al.*, 2007; Chapman *et al.*, 2012; Chapman and Meliciani, 2012).

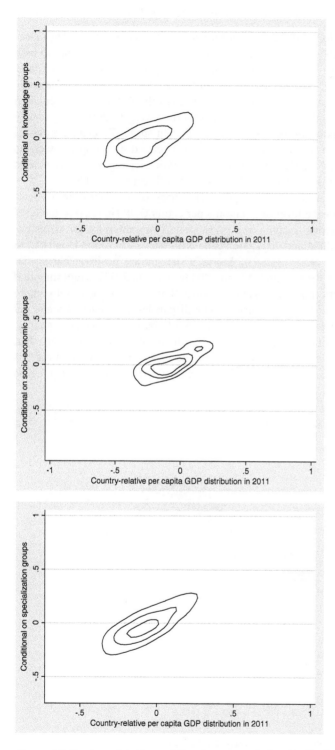

Figure 4.7 Contour plots for conditional country-relative distributions in 2011.

The presence of global spatial dependence across regions may be tested by calculating Moran's I statistic. Positive and significant values of the index point to a high degree of association in the distribution of regions' per capita GDP over space, implying that poor, or rich, regions tend to cluster together. We calculate the index using regions' per capita GDP (in logs) standardized by the EU average. Calculation of the index relies on the definition of an appropriate weight matrix exogenously setting the way regions are related to one another in space. To compute overall spatial correlation we adopt a row standardized inverse distance spatial weights matrix where the bandwidth is chosen in order to allow each region to have at least one neighbour. Results are robust to the choice of different bandwidths.

A useful visual representation of spatial clustering is given by Moran's scatterplot, which relates the level of a region's per capita GDP (in logs) to the level of neighbouring regions' income in a given year. The scatterplot for all neighbours is shown for 2004 and 2011, alongside with the values of the I statistic, in Figures 4.8 and 4.9. Both values of Moran's statistic are positive, but spatial correlation falls over time (from 0.536 in 2004 to 0.412 in 2011), suggesting that the formation of territorial clusters among rich and poor regions does not seem to explain the increasing within-country income disparities. In Figures 4.8 and 4.9 it appears immediately evident that the majority of observations cluster in either the south-west or, more frequently, in the north-east quadrants, meaning that, generally speaking, poor regions tend to have poor neighbours and rich regions to have rich neighbours. Over time the dispersion away from the diagonal is

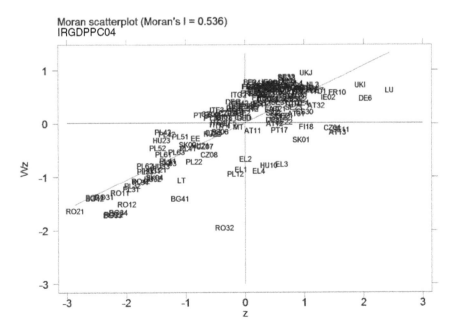

Figure 4.8 Moran scatterplot of EU-relative per capita GDP in 2004.

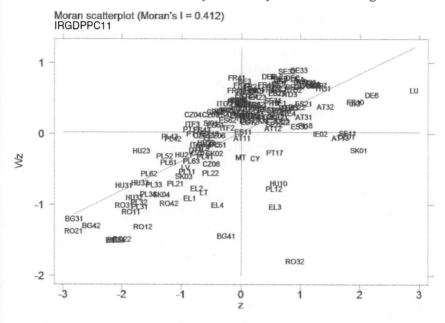

Moran scatterplot (Moran's I = 0.412)
IRGDPPC11

Figure 4.9 Moran scatterplot of EU-relative per capita GDP in 2011.

evident, indicating, as pointed out, a fall in spatial correlation of EU-relative regional income. This occurs especially in the low quadrant to the left, where most CEEC regions are grouped. It is interesting to note that the lower quadrant to the right, which groups regions with higher-than-EU-average incomes and poor neighbours, included only nine regions in 2004 (two of them capitals of newcomer countries: Bratislavský kraj and the Budapest region of Közép-Magyarország), becomes much larger in 2011, with an increase especially in the number of regions from newcomers (together with Bratislavský kraj and Közép-Magyarország also Praha, the Warsaw region of Mazowieckie, and Bucuresti). In other words, most of the regions that manage to be rich despite the fact they are surrounded by poor neighbours are – increasingly – capital areas (together with those of newcomers in 2011, we find also Stockholm, Wien, Lisboa and Attiki).

Spatial regression analysis

Given overall significant spatial correlation in per capita GDP, the evolution of regional disparities is now assessed by means of traditional β-convergence theory, taking into account spatial effects. A well-known problem with traditional cross-sectional growth regressions is that this type of analysis accounts only for a single 'representative' region, being silent on how each region changes its position in the distribution over time. Nevertheless, it can provide complementary information to our non-parametric analysis by formally testing the importance of our groups in explaining per capita GDP growth while taking into account spatial correlation.

The analysis starts from the Spatial Durbin model (SDM), which is a general model that includes among the regressors not only the spatial lagged dependent variable, but also the spatial lagged set of independent variables (see also Chapter 2):

$$Y = WY_\rho + X\beta_1 + WX\beta_2 + \varepsilon$$

where Y denotes a Nx1 vector consisting of one observation for every spatial unit of the dependent variable, X is a NxK matrix of independent variables, with N=number of regions and K=number of explanatory variables, W is an NxN non-negative spatial weights matrix with zeros on the diagonal. A vector or matrix pre-multiplied by W denotes its spatially lagged value, ρ, β_1 and β_2 are response parameters, and ε is a Nx1 vector of residuals with zero mean and variance σ^2.

The SDM nests most models used in the regional literature. In particular, imposing the restriction that $\beta_2 = 0$ leads to a spatial autoregressive (SAR) model that includes a spatial lag of the dependent variable from related regions, but excludes these regions' characteristics. Imposing the restriction that $\beta_2 = -\rho\beta_1$ yields the spatial error model (SEM) that allows only for spatial dependence in the disturbances. Imposing the restriction that $\rho = 0$ leads to a spatially lagged X regression model (SLX) that assumes independence between the regional dependent variables, but includes characteristics from related regions in the form of explanatory variables. Finally, imposing the restriction that $\rho = 0$ and $\beta_2 = 0$ leads to a non-spatial regression model. We choose the appropriate model on the basis of hypotheses testing.[5]

In our spatial regression, which includes a spatial lag of the dependent and independent variables, a change in a single explanatory variable in region *i* has a *direct impact* on region *i* as well as an *indirect impact* on other regions (see LeSage and Fischer, 2008, for a discussion). This result arises from the spatial connectivity relationships that are incorporated in spatial regression models; it raises the difficulty of interpreting the resulting estimates. LeSage and Pace (2009) provide computationally feasible means of calculating scalar summary measures of these two types of impacts that arise from changes in the explanatory variables. Direct and indirect effects are reported in Table 4.6, together with the coefficients. There are two possible (equivalent) interpretations of these effects. One interpretation (the one that we adopt in our discussion) reflects how changing each explanatory variable of all neighbouring regions by some constant amount would affect the dependent variable of a typical region. LeSage and Pace (ibid.) label this as the *average total impact on an observation*. The second interpretation measures the cumulative impact of a change in each explanatory variable in region i over all neighbouring regions, which LeSage and Pace (ibid.) label the *average total impact from an observation* (see also LeSage and Fischer, 2008).

Table 4.6 reports the results of the estimation respectively of the preferred model (chosen on the basis of hypotheses testing) for 1) unconditional growth rates; and for growth rates conditional on: 2) countries, 3) socio-economic groups, 4) innovation–human capital groups, 5) specialization groups and 6) socio-economic, innovation-human capital and specialization groups (conditional convergence).

All regressions show strong evidence of spatial correlation for all models but that conditional on countries. Likelihood ratio (LR) tests suggest that the SDM is preferred to SEM or SAR models in all cases but the model conditional on socio-economic groups. For this model both SEM and SAR are preferred to SDM. However, since robust Lagrange multiplier (LM) tests reject both the SAR and the SEM, we estimate the more general SDM as suggested by LeSage and Pace (2009).

Regression results show the presence of absolute convergence that falls once spatial effects are taken into account. However, once country fixed effects are introduced, the coefficient on the initial level of per capita GDP turns positive and significant, showing within-country divergence. The rate of convergence increases once socio-economic and/or knowledge groups (but not specialization groups) are controlled for indicating that regions are converging to the group average. Finally, for both socio-economic and innovation groups direct effects are significant in explaining differentiated patterns of growth across regions while there is no evidence of significant indirect effects.[6]

Among socio-economic groups, urban areas exhibit significantly higher growth rates with respect to intermediate regions (the base category) while peripheral areas grow significantly less. Among innovation and human capital groups, regions with high levels of both education and patents or with high levels of either education or patents experience growth rates that are significantly higher than those of regions with low education and patents (the base category).

Interestingly, and differently from previous studies (Ezcurra *et al.*, 2007; Ezcurra and Rapun, 2007), in the period under analysis (2004–11) specialization groups are no longer significant in explaining regional growth rates.

Finally, results are robust to including all groups together in the regression, showing that socio-economic and innovation and human capital groups capture different ingredients of the growth process as discussed in Chapter 3. In the more general model, we have positive and significant direct effects for urban areas, for regions with high levels of both innovation and human capital or either innovation or human capital and significant negative direct effects for peripheral and old industrial regions. Moreover, being surrounded by regions with high levels of human capital and medium or low levels of innovation has a displacing effect (the indirect effect is negative and significant at 10 per cent). All other indirect effects are not significant at conventional levels.

A closer look at regions from countries joining the EU in 2004 and 2007

This section focuses on regions belonging to countries that joined the European Union in 2004 and 2007 (newcomers). We will come back to this sample of regions again in Chapter 6, which is fully dedicated to investigating the reasons

Table 4.6 Regression results for β-convergence models

	Unconditional convergence				Conditional on countries	Conditional on socio-economic groups			
	OLS	Spatial Durbin			OLS	OLS	Spatial Durbin		
	Coef.	Coef.	Direct	Indirect	Coef.	Coef.	Coef.	Direct	Indirect
Intercept	0.099	0.052			−0.010	0.132	0.042		
	0.000	0.001			0.522	0.000	0.085		
Per capita GDP in 2004 (in ln)	−0.026	−0.005	−0.006	−0.055	0.010	−0.037	−0.022	−0.023	−0.038
	0.000	0.153	0.066	0.022	0.013	0.000	0.000	0.000	0.574
Urban						0.021	0.013	0.010	−0.144
						0.000	0.002	0.055	0.572
Peripheral						−0.012	−0.007	−0.007	−0.013
						0.000	0.015	0.017	0.892
Industrial decline						−0.010	−0.008	−0.008	0.042
						0.000	0.014	0.129	0.858
High innovation high human capital									
High innovation medium or low human capital									
Medium or low innovation high human capital									
Medium innovation and medium or low human capital or medium human capital and medium or low innovation									
Agriculture									
Knowledge intensive services									
High-tech manufacturing									
Less knowledge intensive services									
R-squared	0.335	0.420			0.890	0.501	0.538		
Rho		0.734					0.777		
		0.000					0.000		
LM(error)		107.963			1.750		97.951		
		0.000			0.186		0.000		
R-LM(error)		8.602			0.429		25.752		
		0.003			0.513		0.000		
LM(lag)		129.851			2.025		83.227		
		0.000			0.155		0.000		
R-LM(lag)		30.490			0.703		11.029		
		0.000			0.401		0.001		
LR(lag)		2.771					4.307		
		0.060					0.125		
LR(error)		9.755					3.471		
		0.000					0.153		

Notes: 174 observations; probabilities in italics; all estimations are heteroscedasticity consistent; in the regression with socio-economic groups the base category is intermediate; in the regression with innovation groups the base category is

| Conditional on knowledge groups | | | | Conditional on specialization groups | | | | Conditional on all groups | | | |
| OLS | Spatial Durbin | | | OLS | Spatial Durbin | | | OLS | Spatial Durbin | | |
Coef.	Coef.	Direct	Indirect	Coef.	Coef.	Direct	Indirect	Coef.	Coef.	Direct	Indirect
0.120	0.069			0.103	0.058			0.143	0.075	0.073	0.070
0.000	*0.006*			*0.000*	*0.018*			*0.000*	*0.039*	*0.000*	*0.000*
−0.035	−0.016	−0.016	−0.030	−0.026	−0.006	−0.007	−0.047	−0.043	−0.032	−0.032	0.006
0.000	*0.000*	*0.000*	*0.264*	*0.000*	*0.013*	*0.080*	*0.393*	*0.000*	*0.000*	*0.000*	*0.831*
								0.024	0.013	0.012	−0.067
								0.000	*0.001*	*0.009*	*0.440*
								−0.010	−0.005	−0.005	0.023
								0.000	*0.078*	*0.102*	*0.562*
								−0.009	−0.010	−0.011	−0.079
								0.011	*0.002*	*0.002*	*0.498*
0.014	0.011	0.010	−0.012					0.016	0.011	0.011	−0.009
0.005	*0.016*	*0.020*	*0.749*					*0.001*	*0.009*	*0.010*	*0.776*
0.013	0.007	0.007	−0.008					0.017	0.009	0.009	−0.012
0.011	*0.077*	*0.093*	*0.881*					*0.000*	*0.019*	*0.020*	*0.789*
0.012	0.018	0.017	−0.066					0.009	0.015	0.013	−0.079
0.054	*0.000*	*0.000*	*0.128*					*0.040*	*0.000*	*0.000*	*0.103*
−0.001	0.003	0.002	−0.034					0.000	0.000	−0.001	−0.080
0.817	*0.329*	*0.474*	*0.382*					*0.957*	*0.872*	*0.777*	*0.109*
				−0.003	0.001	0.002	0.016	0.003	0.005	0.005	0.006
				0.514	*0.671*	*0.635*	*0.884*	*0.317*	*0.084*	*0.091*	*0.927*
				−0.001	0.004	0.004	−0.025	−0.005	0.000	0.001	−0.025
				0.913	*0.311*	*0.356*	*0.707*	*0.241*	*0.960*	*0.845*	*0.619*
				−0.003	0.002	0.003	0.093	−0.002	−0.001	−0.001	0.006
				0.567	*0.651*	*0.414*	*0.630*	*0.498*	*0.682*	*0.743*	*0.918*
				−0.004	0.002	0.000	−0.091	−0.002	−0.003	−0.004	0.087
				0.000	*0.575*	*0.919*	*0.333*	*0.551*	*0.330*	*0.297*	*0.758*
0.403	0.556			0.339	0.516			0.578	0.710		
	0.607				0.647				0.489	0.604	0.644
	0.000				*0.000*				*0.002*	*0.000*	*0.000*
	89.133				103.713				56.236		
	0.000				*0.000*				*0.000*		
	8.975				6.880				16.259		
	0.003				*0.009*				*0.000*		
	31.278				128.415				49.651		
	0.000				*0.000*				*0.000*		
	31.278				103.713				16.259		
	0.000				*0.000*				*0.000*		
	19.677				14.145				32.672		
	0.000				*0.006*				*0.000*		
	18.250				21.225				21.790		
	0.001				*0.000*				*0.012*		

Low patents/Low human capital; in the regressions with specialization groups the base category is low and medium low-tech manufacturing. LR(lag) and LR(error) test respectively the spatial lag and the spatial error model versus the spatial Durbin behind the increase in regional disparities within newcomers over a longer time span (1991–2011).

Table 4.7 reports average levels of income for countries joining the EU after 2004 with respect to the EU average in 2004, 2008 and 2011 and their standard deviation. What emerges clearly from Table 4.7 is, for all countries (with the exception of Slovenia), a trend of convergence towards the EU average at the expense of growing inter-country disparities across regions. At the beginning of the period disparities were very large for the majority of countries and particularly for Romania and Bulgaria (see also Artelaris *et al.*, 2010). As a consequence, due to lower production costs, integration was accompanied by a delocalization process from the mature economies towards new accession countries (Breuss *et al.*, 2010). In particular, old members delocalized important portions of the production chain in manufacturing, especially among low-tech products, to the New Europe, with positive effects on total factor productivity (Marrocu *et al.*, 2013). This process, matched with EU structural funds, has favoured a process of convergence of newcomers towards levels of development of (some) old members, at the expense of those countries/regions with lower levels of innovation and specialized in traditional sectors.

At the same time, before integration, income disparities in former centrally planned economies were kept artificially low. Integration and liberalization appear to have increased these disparities in all countries. This trend is particularly strong in the two countries joining the EU later (Romania, where the standard deviation increases from 0.16 in 2004 to 0.32 in 2011, and Bulgaria, where it increases from 0.10 in 2004 to 0.19 in 2011), but is sizeable also in Poland (from 0.11 to 0.17) and in Slovakia (from 0.44 to 0.68). Moreover, it is interesting to observe that there appears to be a positive relationship between countries' growth and the increase in income disparities. This is consistent with Artelaris *et al.* (2010), showing the

Table 4.7 Average and standard deviation of EU-relative per capita GDP

	Average			*Standard deviation*		
	2004	*2008*	*2011*	*2004*	*2008*	*2011*
Bulgaria	0.347	0.419	0.439	0.101	0.180	0.198
Czech Republic	0.851	0.873	0.874	0.367	0.406	0.389
Hungary	0.609	0.600	0.626	0.231	0.251	0.267
Poland	0.501	0.552	0.631	0.113	0.131	0.168
Romania	0.384	0.528	0.547	0.162	0.300	0.317
Slovenia	0.945	0.984	0.913	0.247	0.253	0.223
Slovakia	0.730	0.928	0.986	0.440	0.580	0.677
Cyprus	0.976	1.066	1.009			
Estonia	0.617	0.739	0.742			
Lithuania	0.555	0.690	0.723			
Latvia	0.501	0.626	0.642			
Malta	0.858	0.872	0.919			

Note: unweighted averages across regions

heterogeneous spatial impact of the EU economic integration process across regions through the formation of different convergence clubs in new members.

Figure 4.10 shows the country-relative per capita GDP distribution (keeping only countries that have more than one region) in newcomers in 2004 and in 2011. It is clear that the increase in variance (from 0.08 in 2004 to 0.11 in 2011) is associated with an increase in the weight of the upper tail of the distribution. In fact, while the skewness of the distribution stays almost constant (1.21 in 2004 and 1.22 in 2011), the kurtosis increases from 3.95 to 4.03.

Figures 4.11 and 4.12 report Moran scatterplots of EU-relative per capita GDP in regions from newcomer countries, respectively in 2004 and in 2011. They show a significant decrease in spatial correlation over time to the extent that, in 2011, spatial correlation is no longer significant (the value of the Moran decreases from 0.380, significantly different from 0 at 1 per cent, to 0.076 not significantly different from zero).

This is partly due to the behaviour of regions with capital cities of Romania and Bulgaria moving away from their neighbouring regions, and to the decrease in the importance of countries in explaining differences in per capita GDP in newcomers.

This evidence is confirmed by regression analysis showing that urban regions converge to higher levels of per capita GDP with respect to intermediate regions while the opposite occurs for regions in industrial decline (see Table 4.8). Table 4.8 also shows that regions with high levels of education grow more, while specialization

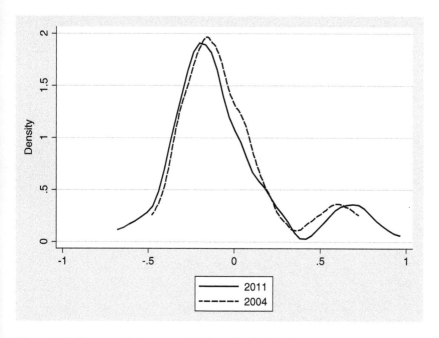

Figure 4.10 Country-relative per capita GDP distributions in newcomers, 2004 and 2011.

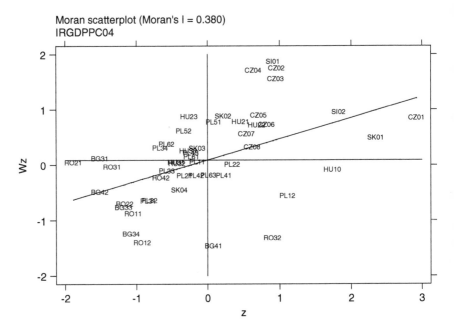

Figure 4.11 Moran scatterplot of EU-relative per capita GDP in 2004 for newcomers.

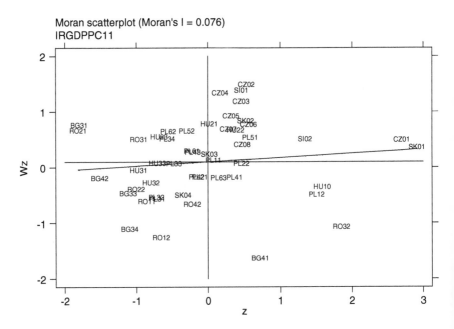

Figure 4.12 Moran scatterplot of EU-relative per capita GDP in 2011 for newcomers.

Table 4.8 Regression results for β-convergence models in newcomers

Newcomers: $n=49$	(1)	(2)	(3)	(4)	(5)
Constant	0.074 (0.000)	0.135 (0.000)	0.109 (0.000)	0.064 (0.008)	0.090 (0.001)
Per capita GDP in 2004 (logs)	−0.012 (0.096)	−0.038 (0.000)	−0.029 (0.000)	−0.009 (0.349)	−0.022 (0.027)
Urban		0.036 (0.001)			0.009 (0.504)
Peripheral		−0.005 (0.451)			−0.008 (0.220)
Industrial decline		−0.014 (0.013)			−0.013 (0.024)
High human capital medium-low innovation			0.042 (0.000)		0.048 (0.005)
Medium innovation and medium or low human capital or medium human capital and medium or low innovation			0.005 (0.352)		−0.001 (0.835)
Agriculture				0.007 (0.358)	0.016 (0.004)
High-tech manufacturing				−0.013 (0.204)	−0.004 (0.586)
Knowledge intensive services				0.011 (0.509)	−0.028 (0.122)
R-squared	0.064	0.395	0.356	0.198	0.582

Notes: p-values in brackets. For socio-economic groups the base category is intermediate; for knowledge groups it is low innovation low human capital; for specialization it is low-tech manufacturing. Less knowledge intensive services have not been included since no region was specialized in that category.

groups do not help in explaining differentiated patters of growth. Finally, in newcomers, when controlling for knowledge groups, urban areas do not exhibit significantly higher growth rates compared to intermediate regions. This result probably is due to the relatively low number of observations and the fact that there is a high degree of overlap between capital regions and regions with high levels of human capital.

A closer look at the Eurozone

Finally, we focus the attention on those countries that, at the beginning of the period under study, were part of the Eurozone. For this group of countries, factors affecting economic convergence may be partly different with respect to those contributing to convergence for the whole European Union. Having a common currency should, on the one hand, make regions more independent from the countries they belong to. In fact, movements in exchange rates affecting simultaneously the international competitiveness of all regions belonging to the same country are no longer possible. Moreover, for each region, there is only one common central monetary policy rather than different national policies. On the basis of these arguments we should find a decreasing importance of countries in explaining differences in per capita income across regions.

On the other hand, while countries have undertaken monetary integration, they are still characterized by heterogeneous labour markets, taxation rules, education systems, etc. All these differences can lead to different national responses to common shocks, with countries still significantly affecting regional dynamics in per capita GDP. Finally, Krugman (1991b), contrary to the prevailing thesis of the European Commission (1990), suggests that further economic integration in a monetary union can lead to an increase in the spatial concentration of production, thus increasing the probability of the occurrence of asymmetric shocks.

Since Europe was hit by the financial crisis originating in the USA in 2008, we look at patterns of convergence/divergence among European regions belonging to the Eurozone, distinguishing between the periods 2004–8 and 2008–11. Table 4.9 reports average levels of income for countries belonging to the Eurozone (at the beginning of the period) with respect to the EU average in 2004, 2008 and 2011 and their standard deviation across regions.

From Table 4.9 we can observe that all countries with below-average levels of per capita GDP increase their distance with the average of the Eurozone from 2004–11. Moreover, divergence is more marked after 2008, so that also those countries that had reduced their distance to the average between 2004 and 2008 (Spain and Portugal) end up being more distant from the average in 2011 with respect to their initial position in 2004. However, there appears to be no clear trend in income variability across regions within each country. In particular, within-country disparities decrease in Belgium, Germany, Finland, the Netherlands and Portugal, increase in Austria, Greece, France and Ireland and stay almost constant in Spain and Italy.

Not only does the variance among regions belonging to the Eurozone increase after the crisis, but, as shown in Figures 4.13 and 4.14, there is also an increase

Table 4.9 Average and standard deviation of Eurozone-relative per capita GDP

	Average			Standard deviation		
	2004	*2008*	*2011*	*2004*	*2008*	*2011*
Austria	1.145	1.130	1.181	0.223	0.222	0.227
Belgium	1.377	1.301	1.348	0.740	0.647	0.658
Germany	1.040	1.056	1.116	0.332	0.313	0.305
Greece	0.852	0.837	0.723	0.123	0.208	0.199
Spain	0.921	0.972	0.915	0.183	0.182	0.183
Finland	1.123	1.112	1.105	0.265	0.186	0.196
France	0.911	0.878	0.897	0.157	0.180	0.193
Ireland	1.193	1.112	1.085	0.373	0.366	0.392
Italy	0.971	0.960	0.942	0.248	0.239	0.244
Netherlands	1.132	1.211	1.181	0.129	0.123	0.115
Portugal	0.723	0.735	0.720	0.181	0.183	0.174
Luxembourg	2.325	2.465	2.505			

Note: unweighted averages across regions

in spatial correlation of regional per capita GDP showing a further clustering of rich and poor regions after the economic crisis.

Finally, we assess by means of spatial regression analysis the explanatory power of socio-economic, specialization and knowledge groups in explaining divergence across regions belonging to the Eurozone. For the sake of simplicity,

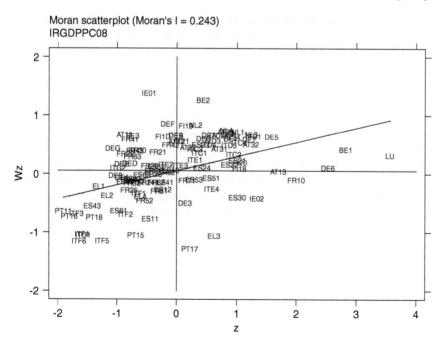

Figure 4.13 Moran scatterplot of Eurozone-relative per capita GDP in 2008.

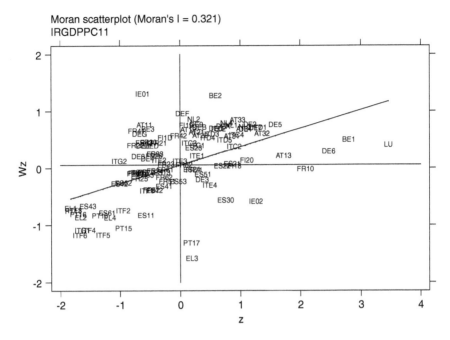

Figure 4.14 Moran scatterplot of Eurozone-relative per capita GDP in 2011.

considering the similarity in the results when using the spatial lag or the more general SDM, in Table 4.10 we report results based on the spatial lag model.

Differently from the case of newcomers and for the whole sample of European Union's regions, in the case of Eurozone's regions, there is no evidence of absolute convergence. Moreover, urban regions do not exhibit significantly higher growth rates, while specialization groups appear to matter. In particular, among socio-economic groups only peripheral regions have below-average performance while urban areas and regions in industrial decline do not behave differently from intermediate regions. Among knowledge groups, regions with high levels of either education or patents perform better than regions with low or medium levels of both variables, with human capital appearing to be more important than patents (the highest coefficient is found for regions with high levels of human capital and intermediate or low levels of patents). Between specialization groups regions specialized in knowledge intensive services, in less knowledge intensive services and in high-tech manufacturing perform better than regions specialized in agriculture, while the growth performance of regions specialized in low- and medium-low-tech manufacturing does not differ significantly from that of regions specialized in agriculture. Finally, when all groups are introduced simultaneously in the regression, only knowledge groups and specialization in services remain significant. This can be due to some overlapping between the knowledge categories (particularly patents) and high-tech manufacturing specialization and between peripheral regions and regions specialized in agriculture.

Table 4.10 Regression results for β-convergence models in the Eurozone

Eurozone: n=99	(1)	(2)	(3)	(4)	(5)
Constant	-0.003 (0.712)	0.022 (0.127)	0.015 (0.179)	0.007 (0.461)	0.028 (0.045)
Per capita GDP in 2004 (logs)	0.003 (0.377)	-0.005 (0.252)	-0.004 (0.196)	-0.002 (0.598)	-0.009 (0.045)
Urban		0.002 (0.440)			0.000 (0.825)
Peripheral		-0.006 (0.016)			-0.002 (0.242)
Industrial decline		-0.003 (0.407)			-0.002 (0.537)
High innovation high human capital			0.008 (0.000)		0.007 (0.001)
High innovation medium or low human capital			0.007 (0.001)		0.007 (0.001)
High human capital medium or low innovation			0.010 (0.000)		0.009 (0.000)
Low innovation low human capital			0.001 (0.881)		0.002 (0.709)
Low-tech manufacturing				0.002 (0.327)	-0.000 (0.763)
High-tech manufacturing				0.006 (0.019)	0.002 (0.304)
Knowledge intensive services				0.006 (0.002)	0.004 (0.036)
Less knowledge intensive services				0.005 (0.040)	0.003 (0.033)
Autoregressive coefficient	0.723 (0.000)	0.689 (0.000)	0.650 (0.000)	0.689 (0.000)	0.630 (0.000)
Squared correlation	0.477	0.498	0.558	0.504	0.589

Notes: p-values in brackets. For socio-economic groups the base category is intermediate; for knowledge groups it is medium innovation and medium or low human capital or medium human capital and medium or low innovation; for specialization it is agriculture

Overall these results show that, among the factors identified in this book, it is innovation and human capital together with related patterns of specialization (knowledge intensive activities offering more opportunities than low-tech manufacturing or agriculture) which better explain the increase in income and employment disparities in the Eurozone. This shows the importance of investing in innovation as a response to the crisis in the absence of other compensating mechanisms. However, relying on these mechanisms alone appears to be dangerous for European cohesion since, in the absence of appropriate industrial and technology policies, they appear to strengthen pre-existing technology and economic gaps. Our results are consistent with the hypothesis that increasing gaps between the core of Europe (particularly northern countries and Germany) and Southern Europe in innovation and human capital are responsible for divergence in per capita GDP after the crisis.

The European Commission rightly recognizes the importance of devoting more resources for 'growth-enhancing activities' such as education, R&D and innovation and includes them in the goals of Europe 2020. However, these goals are often difficult to reach in the presence of stringent rules for fiscal consolidation and debt reduction so that expenditure cuts in the context of fiscal consolidation strategies in Southern European countries have happened mainly at the cost of public investment, including investment in education and in R&D. The European Commission and EU governments should, therefore, look for mechanisms allowing reconciliation of the goals of Europe 2020 with the rules governing public deficits in the Eurozone.

Conclusions

This chapter has assessed the impact of different factors in explaining regional disparities in per capita GDP in the EU and their evolution over the period 2004–11. It has been shown that the general trend of falling variability in per capita income across EU–27 regions actually conceals different and diverse phenomena: 1) income disparities increase among regions of old EU member countries, in particular after the 2008 crisis, while 2) regions belonging to newcomers reduce their distance from the EU average at the expense of increasing inequalities within countries.

Coming to the determinants of these phenomena, for the EU as a whole country factors lose importance in explaining regional income disparities. However, this does not hold for older members alone, where country factors regain importance especially after the crisis. This result runs counter to current wisdom concerning the most likely outcome of 50 years or so of economic integration and raises the question of what determines different reactions to exogenous shocks across countries, most of which share full monetary integration but only partial real integration.

For all regions (within either old or new EU members), innovation and socioeconomic groups gain importance over time. In particular, innovation groups explain differences in EU-relative per capita GDP better, while socio-economic groups do so with respect to differences within countries. The increasing importance of innovation is hardly surprising in the case of the older members, in view of the growing difficulties faced by advanced countries in competing in global markets on the basis of cost/price elements. Interestingly, the same conclusion applies also to newcomers, where innovation and especially human capital appear to set a dividing line between catching up and lagging behind.

Among the different groupings examined in this chapter, that based on specialization shows the lowest explanatory power. This contrasts with previous findings according to which specialization had a significant role, at least up to 2005 (Ezcurra *et al.*, 2007; Ezcurra and Rapun, 2007; Chapman and Meliciani, 2012). The falling importance of specialization could be an effect of considerable relocation processes in action, whereby old members have delocalized important portions of the production chain in manufacturing, especially among low-tech products, to newcomers, leading to significant growth in many CEECs regions (Marrocu *et al.*, 2013). This interpretation is supported by the fact that, in the Eurozone, specialization continues to play a significant role in affecting growth with services and high-tech manufacturing offering better opportunities as compared to agriculture and low-tech manufacturing. The fact that different types of specialization can lead to different growth patterns in different regions gives support to the recent literature on smart specialization (McCann and Ortega-Agilés, 2013) highlighting how each territory has its own specific comparative advantage on the basis of which it builds related diversification processes, maximizing, at the same time, local knowledge diffusion and learning networks.

Notes

1 Part of this chapter draws on the paper 'Behind the Pan-European convergence path: the role of innovation, specialization and socio-economic factors' jointly written with Sheila Chapman and forthcoming in Growth and Change. I would like to thank my co-author Sheila Chapman for her contribution.
2 Here we use quantiles; later on in the chapter we will also look at disparities measured by the variance.
3 The fall is even bigger if year 2000 is considered as the starting point.
4 Density functions depend on the bandwidth that has been chosen, very narrow values leading to undersmoothed (i.e., spiky) functions and large values determining oversmoothed (i.e., exceedingly flat) ones. In this chapter we have adopted the data-based automatic bandwidth suggested by Silverman (1986).
5 Lagrange Multiplier tests and their robust versions are used to test the OLS versus the SAR and SEM; likelihood ratio (LR) tests are used for testing the SAR and SEM versus the SDM, while the test of the SLX versus the SDM is a t-test on the coefficient of the spatial lag of the dependent variable in the SDM. If the (robust) LM tests point to another model than the LR tests, then the Spatial Durbin model is adopted. This is because this model generalizes both the spatial lag and the spatial error model.
6 The fact that LR tests in most cases favour the SDM model indicate that, although no single indirect effect is statistically significant, accounting for all of them simultaneously improves the likelihood of the model.

References

Artelaris, P., D. Kallioras and G. Petrakos (2010), 'Regional inequalities and convergence clubs in the European Union new member-states', *Eastern Journal of European Studies*, vol. 1, pp. 113–33.

Bickenbach, F. and E. Bode (2003), 'Evaluating the Markov property in studies of economic convergence', *International Regional Science Review*, vol. 26, pp. 363–92.

Breuss, F., P. Egger and M. Pfaffermayr (2010), 'Structural funds, EU enlargement and the redistribution of FDI in Europe', *Review of World Economics*, vol. 146, pp. 469–94.

Chapman, S. and V. Meliciani (2012), 'Income disparties in the enlarged EU: socio-economic, specialization and geographical clusters', *Tijdschrift Voor Economische En Sociale Geografie*, vol. 103(3), pp. 293–311.

Chapman, S., S. Cosci and L. Mirra (2012), 'Income dynamics in an enlarged Europe: the role of capital regions', *The Annals of Regional Science*, vol. 48, pp. 663–93.

Debarsy, N. and C. Ertur (2006), 'The European enlargement process and regional convergence revisited: spatial effects still matter', ERSA Conference Papers.

Ertur, C. and W. Koch (2006), 'Regional disparities in the European Union and the enlargement process: an exploratory spatial data analysis, 1995–2000', *The Annals of Regional Science*, vol. 40, pp. 721–65.

European Commission (1990), 'One market, one money', *European Economy*, vol. 44.

Ezcurra, R., P. Pascual and M. Rapun (2007), 'The dynamics of regional disparities in Central and Eastern Europe during transition', *European Planning Studies*, vol. 15, pp. 1397–421.

Ezcurra, R., C. Gil, P. Pascual and M. Rapun (2005), 'Regional inequality in the European Union: does industry mix matter?', *Regional Studies*, vol. 39(6), pp. 679–97.

Fischer, M.M. and C. Stirböck (2005), 'Pan-European regional income growth and club-convergence: insights from a spatial econometric perspective', *The Annals of Regional Science*, vol. 40, pp. 693–721.

Frenken, K. and J. Hoekman (2006), 'Convergence in an enlarged Europe: the role of network cities', *Journal of Economic and Social Geography*, vol. 97, pp. 321–6.

Friedman, T. (2005), *The World is Flat: A Brief History of the Twenty-First Century*. New York: Farrar, Straus and Giroux.

Krugman, P. (1991b), *Geography and Trade*. Cambridge, MA: MIT Press.

LeSage, J.P. and M.M. Fischer (2008), 'Spatial growth regressions: model specification, estimation and interpretation', *Spatial Economic Analysis*, vol. 3, pp. 275–304.

LeSage J.P. and R.K. Pace (2009), *Introduction to Spatial Econometrics*. Boca Raton: Taylor & Francis CRC Press.

López-Bazo, E., T. Del Barrio and M. Artís (2002), 'The regional distribution of Spanish unemployment: a spatial analysis', *Papers in Regional Science*, vol. 81, pp. 365–89.

López-Bazo, E., E. Vayá, A. Mora and J. Surinach (1999), 'Regional economic dynamics and convergence in the European Union', *Annals of Regional Science*, vol. 33, pp. 343–70.

Marrocu, E., R. Paci and S. Usai (2013), 'Productivity growth in the old and new Europe: the role of agglomeration externalities', *Journal of Regional Science*, vol. 53(3), pp. 418–42.

McCann, P. and R. Ortega-Argilés (2013), 'Smart specialization, regional growth, and applications to European Union Cohesion Policy', *Regional Studies*, doi: 10.1080/00343404.2013.799769.

Meliciani, V. (2006), 'Income and employment disparities across European regions: the role of national and spatial factors', *Regional Studies*, vol. 40, pp. 75–91.

Paas, T., A. Kuusk, F. Schlitte and A. Vork (2007), 'econometric analysis of income convergence in selected EU countries and their NUTS 3 level regions', Working Paper Series 60, University of Tartu, Faculty of Economics and Business Administration.

Quah, D.T. (1996a), 'Empirics for economic growth and convergence', CEPR Discussion Papers 1140.

Quah, D.T. (1996b), 'Regional convergence clusters across Europe', *European Economic Review*, vol. 40, pp. 951–8.

Quah, D.T. (1997), 'Empirics for growth and distribution: stratifcation, polarization, and convergence clubs', *Journal of Economic Growth*, vol. 2, pp. 27–59.

Rodríguez-Pose, A. (1998a), *The Dynamics of Regional Growth in Europe: Social and Political Factors*. Oxford: Clarendon Press.

Rodríguez-Pose, A. and R. Crescenzi (2008), 'Mountains in a flat world: why proximity still matters for the location of economic activity', *Cambridge Journal of Regions, Economy and Society*, Cambridge Political Economy Society, vol. 1(3), pp. 371–88.

Silverman, B.W. (1986), *Density Estimation for Statistics and Data Analysis*. London: Chapman & Hall.

Stirböck, C. (2004), 'What determines relative sectoral investment patterns in EU regions?'. In J. Bradley, G. Petrakos and I. Traistaru (eds), *Integration, Growth and Cohesion in an Enlarged European Union*. Berlin: Springer-Verlag, pp. 87–130.

5 The evolution of regional disparities in labour productivity and employment rates in the EU

The role of specialization, knowledge and socio-economic groups

Introduction

This chapter assesses the importance of specialization, socio-economic factors and regional capabilities in producing and absorbing new knowledge for the evolution of EU regional disparities in labour productivity and employment rates between 2004 and 2011.

We start from the observation that disparities in per capita GDP can be decomposed into two main components: disparities in labour productivity and disparities in the ratio of employees to total population:

$$\frac{GDP}{POPULATION} = \frac{GDP}{EMPLOYEES} \times \frac{EMPLOYEES}{POPULATION}$$

In Chapter 4, we have focused the attention on per capita GDP, showing that EU regions have witnessed a process of convergence between 2004 and 2011 mostly due to the behaviour of regions from newcomers. We have also shown that per capita GDP in old members has diverged, with regions with high levels of innovation and human capital, which were already richer than the average in 2004, experiencing above-average growth rates while technology laggard regions fall behind. Moreover, also within newcomers, disparities in per capita income levels have increased within countries, especially due to the divergent behaviour of regions with capital cities, which have grown above the average after the EU enlargement.

We now ask whether trends in per capita GDP reflect similar trends in labour productivity and employment or, rather, whether these variables experience differentiated patterns across regions and over time. In particular, in this chapter we focus on the distinct behaviour of labour productivity (the ratio of GDP to total employees) and the ratio of total employees to population that, for simplicity, we call the employment rate.[1]

There are several reasons for expecting that labour productivity and employment rates might follow different paths across regions and over time. First, we can expect that further economic integration and trade liberalization by increasing competition lead to convergence in labour productivity. Regions lagging behind in productivity levels, in order to catch up with leading regions, are pushed to adopt new technologies and to increase their investments (either domestically or attracting foreign direct investment). However, in the absence of sufficient absorption capacity and financial resources devoted to new investment or of capabilities to attract FDI, they will be able to increase labour productivity only by cutting employment. If regions with low productivity levels also experience low employment rates and are pushed to cut employment in order to decrease their disparities in labour productivity, we might observe convergence in labour productivity accompanied by divergence in employment rates. Second, we can expect country factors to be particularly important in affecting employment rates. The ratio of employment to population depends on both participation in the labour market and on unemployment rates. It is well known that southern countries lag behind Nordic ones in participation rates, especially when referring to females and older workers. Moreover, regulation of the labour market still occurs at the national level. Differences across countries in the difficulty of hiring and firing workers, power of the unions, labour taxation, minimum wages, unemployment benefits, etc. can lead to differences across countries in unemployment rates and to a different response of employment to variations in output. When hit by negative shocks, unemployment might rise more in countries where the labour market is less flexible. Although migration can work as a counterbalancing force, its impact may be limited due to differences in languages and education across countries.

But how do we expect specialization, socio-economic characteristics and knowledge to affect patterns of convergence/divergence in labour productivity and employment rates across regions?

In the case of specialization (as broadly defined in Chapter 3), several studies[2] have documented an increasing share of services in total employment while in the case of labour productivity the evidence is less strong. We may, therefore, expect the sectoral classification to be more relevant in the case of employment than in the case of labour productivity. The classification of regions according to socio-economic groups (urban areas, peripheral areas and areas in industrial decline) may matter in explaining differences in both labour productivity and employment rates. In fact, large urban areas due to the agglomeration of economic activity and human capital may favour both higher employment rates and higher levels of labour productivity. Areas in industrial decline may suffer especially in terms of employment opportunities, while peripheral areas may suffer from their distance to the core making it more difficult to adopt new technologies and to attract investment, causing problems in both labour productivity and employment rates. Finally, the literature is unanimous in recognising the positive impact of innovation and human capital on labour productivity. In contrast, the effects of innovation on employment are less clear cut since, on the one hand innovation, by increasing labour productivity, may have a displacing effect on employment, but, on the other, the introduction of new products can lead to increases in demand counterbalancing the displacing effect.[3] Finally, high levels of human capital are expected to positively affect both labour productivity and employment rates. Overall, high innovation and human capital regions are expected to differ from technologically backward regions both in labour productivity and employment rates but the explanatory power of knowledge groups is expected to be higher in the case of labour productivity.

The evolution of regional disparities in labour productivity and employment rates: descriptive statistics

Before looking at the role of our groups in explaining labour productivity and employment rate disparities, we present some descriptive statistics on such disparities in Europe and within each country. In particular, we look at the minimum, the maximum and some quantiles of the labour productivity and the employment rate distributions.

Table 5.1 shows very high disparities, although decreasing, between the region with the highest and the lowest level of labour productivity. The region with the highest productivity level in 2004 (Bruxelles) had a productivity level 13 times larger than the least productive one (Nord Est in Romania). In 2011 (when the most productive region was Luxembourg followed by Bruxelles) the difference was still of ten times. As in the case of per capita GDP (see Chapter 4), the decrease in the ratio between the maximum and the minimum value is mainly due to a process of catching up of the least productive region towards the median. The same picture emerges when looking at the ratio between percentiles: while both the ratio between the median and the 10th percentile and between the median and the 25th percentiles decrease, the ratio between the 90th percentile and the median and between the 75th percentile and the median increase.

Overall, the data show some signs of catching up of the least productive regions towards the median of the distribution (mostly due to the behaviour of regions from newcomers), while there are no signs of overall convergence since the most productive regions appear to forge ahead, increasing their distance with the median region.

Looking at the employment rate, the region with the highest level in 2004 (Centro in Portugal) had a level twice as large as the lowest region (Corse in

Table 5.1 Regional disparities in labour productivity and in employment rates

	min.	max.	p10	p25	p50	p75	p90
lprod04	10.65	144.42	25.56	33.4	50.21	55.51	63.75
lprod11	15.35	153.96	31.28	41.56	56.05	65.41	71.76
empr04	0.23	0.52	0.35	0.38	0.42	0.46	0.48
empr11	0.27	0.57	0.36	0.39	0.43	0.47	0.49

	max./min.	p50/min.	max./p50	p50/p10	p90/p50	p50/p25	p75/p50
lprod04	13.56	4.71	2.88	1.96	1.27	1.50	1.11
lprod11	10.03	3.65	2.75	1.79	1.28	1.35	1.17
empr04	2.26	1.83	1.24	1.20	1.14	1.11	1.10
empr11	2.11	1.59	1.33	1.19	1.14	1.10	1.09

France). In 2011, the difference was slightly reduced, with a change in the ranking of the regions: the first region was Aland in Finland (Centro in Portugal lost many positions with a reduction of the employment rate from 0.52 to 0.46) and the last region was Campania in Italy. Also, in the case of employment, there is evidence of catching up of the minimum to the median but there is an increasing gap between the maximum and the median. Finally, when looking at the ratio between percentiles, we find a high degree of stability, with no evident signs of catching up.

Examining the dynamics of regional disparities within countries, Table 5.2 reports the within-country mean and standard deviation of the labour productivity and employment rate distribution, while Tables 5.3 and 5.4 look at minimum, maximum and some percentiles.

Table 5.2 EU-relative labour productivity and employment rates: mean and standard deviation across countries

Country	Averages				Standard deviations			
	Labour productivity		Employment rate		Labour productivity		Employment rate	
	2004	2011	2004	2011	2004	2011	2004	2011
Austria	1.252	1.169	1.076	1.157	0.236	0.221	0.051	0.042
Belgium	1.804	1.716	0.913	0.919	1.062	0.948	0.091	0.089
Bulgaria	**0.398**	**0.489**	**0.901**	**0.923**	**0.086**	**0.164**	**0.085**	**0.099**
Cyprus	**0.895**	**0.936**	**1.101**	**1.085**				
Czech Republic	**0.770**	**0.794**	**1.100**	**1.092**	**0.273**	**0.290**	**0.070**	**0.062**
Germany	1.206	1.137	1.012	1.124	0.365	0.300	0.053	0.044
Denmark	1.121	1.193	1.217	1.135				
Estonia	**0.590**	**0.703**	**1.056**	**1.063**				
Greece	1.067	0.981	0.937	0.840	0.112	0.228	0.042	0.042
Spain	1.078	1.120	0.999	0.929	0.133	0.143	0.098	0.075
Finland	1.178	1.125	1.111	1.123	0.160	0.088	0.114	0.155
France	1.140	1.104	0.947	0.931	0.187	0.205	0.101	0.064
Hungary	**0.662**	**0.703**	**0.911**	**0.880**	**0.183**	**0.238**	**0.098**	**0.087**
Ireland	1.313	1.335	1.063	0.923	0.353	0.401	0.048	0.059
Italy	1.209	1.188	0.917	0.882	0.162	0.151	0.137	0.143
Lithuania	**0.549**	**0.752**	**1.020**	**0.969**				
Luxembourg	2.781	2.832	0.984	1.014				
Latvia	**0.467**	**0.660**	**1.082**	**0.979**				
Malta	**0.992**	**0.980**	**0.873**	**0.944**				
Netherlands	1.124	1.163	1.184	1.164	0.118	0.121	0.024	0.023
Poland	**0.602**	**0.666**	**0.845**	**0.961**	**0.138**	**0.161**	**0.084**	**0.113**
Portugal	0.748	0.798	1.144	1.038	0.199	0.210	0.063	0.034
Romania	**0.397**	**0.571**	**1.011**	**0.990**	**0.171**	**0.295**	**0.056**	**0.085**
Sweden	1.152	1.144	1.137	1.130	0.160	0.161	0.049	0.046
Slovenia	**0.841**	**0.864**	**1.131**	**1.062**	**0.201**	**0.189**	**0.026**	**0.028**
Slovakia	**0.712**	**0.887**	**0.989**	**1.058**	**0.305**	**0.444**	**0.157**	**0.177**
United Kingdom	1.120	0.963	1.115	1.072	0.265	0.264	0.059	0.041

Notes: newcomers in bold. Average denotes the unweighted average across regions

Table 5.3 Minimum, maximum and percentiles of the labour productivity distribution

	N	min.	max.	p25	p50	p75	max./ min.	p75/ p25
Austria 2004	9	45.07	84.83	55.3	59.4	61.4	1.88	1.11
Austria 2011	9	45.5	87.63	56.51	64.32	67.73	1.93	1.20
Belgium 2004	3	52.56	144.42	52.56	61.36	144.42	2.75	2.75
Belgium 2011	3	58.36	152.47	58.36	69.08	152.47	2.61	2.61
Bulgaria 2004	**6**	**14.91**	**25.93**	**16.2**	**17.79**	**18.49**	**1.74**	**1.14**
Bulgaria 2011	**6**	**20.75**	**42.27**	**20.85**	**22.73**	**24.32**	**2.04**	**1.17**
Czech Republic 2004	**8**	**30.15**	**68.84**	**30.96**	**33.14**	**33.4**	**2.28**	**1.08**
Czech Republic 2011	**8**	**34.95**	**81.96**	**36.58**	**37.39**	**40.26**	**2.35**	**1.10**
Germany 2004	16	38.42	101.84	43.24	53.44	61.51	2.65	1.42
Germany 2011	16	42.87	100.87	46.45	59.56	68.42	2.35	1.47
Greece 2004	4	46.33	58.59	47.51	49.38	54.33	1.26	1.14
Greece 2011	4	43.95	70.92	44.7	49.18	61.91	1.61	1.39
Spain 2004	16	41.17	61.35	46.18	51.06	55.58	1.49	1.20
Spain 2011	16	48.86	74.28	54.78	60.11	66.69	1.52	1.22
Finland 2004	4	49.77	65.55	50	62.49	65.55	1.32	1.31
Finland 2011	4	56.41	67.76	57.99	60.23	64.32	1.20	1.11
France 2004	22	46.87	83.6	50.27	51.79	53.25	1.78	1.06
France 2011	22	51.68	104.4	54.94	56.95	59.74	2.02	1.09
Hungary 2004	**7**	**26.36**	**50.44**	**26.56**	**26.63**	**33.14**	**1.91**	**1.25**
Hungary 2011	**7**	**30.16**	**66.03**	**30.79**	**31.5**	**41.38**	**2.19**	**1.34**
Ireland 2004	2	50.75	74.58	50.75	62.67	74.58	1.47	1.47
Ireland 2011	2	57.17	88.02	57.17	72.6	88.02	1.54	1.54
Italy 2004	21	47.48	69.86	50.9	60.01	63.57	1.47	1.25
Italy 2011	21	53.96	78.78	57.43	66.27	70.3	1.46	1.22
Netherlands 2004	4	47.1	60.82	50.13	53.4	57.23	1.29	1.14
Netherlands 2011	4	53.89	68.57	58.73	65.26	67.77	1.27	1.15
Poland 2004	**16**	**18.97**	**45.49**	**23.9**	**26.93**	**32.86**	**2.40**	**1.37**
Poland 2011	**16**	**24.22**	**56.57**	**29.48**	**35.61**	**41.84**	**2.34**	**1.42**
Portugal 2004	5	27.23	50.2	27.47	34.71	38.86	1.84	1.41
Portugal 2011	5	34.37	62.15	34.42	41.16	44.88	1.81	1.30
Romania 2004	**8**	**10.65**	**36.14**	**13.73**	**16.44**	**19.41**	**3.39**	**1.41**
Romania 2011	**8**	**15.35**	**65.32**	**22.32**	**24.96**	**31.14**	**4.26**	**1.40**
Sweden 2004	8	49.75	73.37	50.99	53.46	54.06	1.47	1.06
Sweden 2011	8	56.32	82.28	56.82	58.64	64.04	1.46	1.13
Slovenia 2004	**2**	**33.37**	**46.92**	**33.37**	**40.15**	**46.92**	**1.41**	**1.41**
Slovenia 2011	**2**	**39.7**	**54.24**	**39.7**	**46.97**	**54.24**	**1.37**	**1.37**
Slovakia 2004	**4**	**26.05**	**55.8**	**26.35**	**27.07**	**41.64**	**2.14**	**1.58**
Slovakia 2011	**4**	**33.93**	**84.24**	**34.7**	**37.39**	**61.78**	**2.48**	**1.78**
United Kingdom 2004	12	43.16	91.83	48.08	50.74	52.15	2.13	1.08
United Kingdom 2011	12	42.74	95.9	45.42	49.16	51.44	2.24	1.13

Note: newcomers in bold

Looking at standard deviations, we observe increasing disparities within newcomers: the standard deviation of labour productivity increases in all newcomers but Slovenia, and the standard deviation of the employment rate also increases for the majority of them (this is the case for Bulgaria, Poland, Romania,

Table 5.4 Minimum, maximum and percentiles of the employment rate distribution

	n	min.	max.	p25	p50	p75	max.– min. %	p75– p25 %
Austria 2004	9	0.42	0.48	0.43	0.45	0.46	6	3
Austria 2011	9	0.47	0.52	0.48	0.50	0.51	5	3
Belgium 2004	3	0.36	0.42	0.36	0.36	0.42	6	6
Belgium 2011	3	0.36	0.44	0.36	0.38	0.44	8	8
Bulgaria 2004	**6**	**0.33**	**0.42**	**0.36**	**0.37**	**0.39**	**9**	**3**
Bulgaria 2011	**6**	**0.35**	**0.46**	**0.37**	**0.39**	**0.39**	**11**	**2**
Czech Republic 2004	**8**	**0.41**	**0.51**	**0.45**	**0.46**	**0.47**	**10**	**3**
Czech Republic 2011	**8**	**0.44**	**0.52**	**0.45**	**0.46**	**0.48**	**8**	**3**
Germany 2004	16	0.39	0.46	0.40	0.42	0.44	7	3
Germany 2011	16	0.45	0.51	0.47	0.48	0.49	6	3
Greece 2004	4	0.37	0.41	0.38	0.39	0.41	4	3
Greece 2011	4	0.34	0.38	0.34	0.36	0.37	4	3
Spain 2004	16	0.34	0.48	0.38	0.43	0.44	14	6
Spain 2011	16	0.33	0.44	0.38	0.40	0.42	11	5
Finland 2004	4	0.41	0.52	0.43	0.46	0.50	11	8
Finland 2011	4	0.42	0.57	0.43	0.46	0.53	15	10
France 2004	22	0.23	0.44	0.38	0.41	0.42	21	4
France 2011	22	0.31	0.45	0.39	0.40	0.41	14	2
Hungary 2004	**7**	**0.34**	**0.43**	**0.34**	**0.36**	**0.43**	**9**	**9**
Hungary 2011	**7**	**0.32**	**0.42**	**0.34**	**0.37**	**0.41**	**10**	**7**
Ireland 2004	2	0.43	0.46	0.43	0.44	0.46	3	3
Ireland 2011	2	0.38	0.41	0.38	0.39	0.41	3	4
Italy 2004	21	0.29	0.46	0.35	0.41	0.43	17	9
Italy 2011	21	0.27	0.47	0.34	0.40	0.43	20	9
Netherlands 2004	4	0.48	0.5	0.49	0.50	0.50	2	1
Netherlands 2011	4	0.48	0.5	0.49	0.50	0.50	2	1
Poland 2004	**16**	**0.3**	**0.41**	**0.32**	**0.36**	**0.37**	**11**	**5**
Poland 2011	**16**	**0.33**	**0.5**	**0.37**	**0.40**	**0.44**	**17**	**7**
Portugal 2004	5	0.44	0.52	0.47	0.48	0.48	8	1
Portugal 2011	5	0.43	0.46	0.43	0.44	0.45	3	2
Romania 2004	**8**	**0.39**	**0.46**	**0.41**	**0.42**	**0.45**	**7**	**4**
Romania 2011	**8**	**0.37**	**0.47**	**0.40**	**0.43**	**0.46**	**10**	**7**
Sweden 2004	8	0.45	0.51	0.46	0.46	0.49	6	3
Sweden 2011	8	0.47	0.53	0.47	0.48	0.49	6	2
Slovenia 2004	**2**	**0.46**	**0.48**	**0.46**	**0.47**	**0.48**	**2**	**2**
Slovenia 2011	**2**	**0.44**	**0.46**	**0.45**	**0.45**	**0.46**	**2**	**2**
Slovakia 2004	**4**	**0.35**	**0.5**	**0.36**	**0.40**	**0.46**	**15**	**10**
Slovakia 2011	**4**	**0.38**	**0.55**	**0.40**	**0.44**	**0.51**	**17**	**11**
United Kingdom 2004	12	0.41	0.49	0.45	0.47	0.48	8	3
United Kingdom 2011	12	0.43	0.48	0.44	0.46	0.47	5	3

Slovenia and Slovakia). In old members the picture is more mixed, with a prevalence of increases in the standard deviation of labour productivity within countries and a prevalence of decreases in the standard deviation of the employment rate.

When measuring disparities in the ratio between the maximum and minimum value, we observe that countries with the largest disparities between the most productive and the least productive region are mainly among newcomers. Romania, Czech Republic, Bulgaria, Hungary, Poland and Slovakia all have a ratio above two in 2011; similar ratios are found also in Belgium, Germany and the UK. Moreover, the ratio increases in all newcomers but Slovenia and Poland. Overall, the ratio of the maximum to the minimum value of labour productivity increases in 11 countries and decreases in nine countries, showing no signs of a general convergence trend. When looking at the ratio between the 75th and the 25th percentile, the trend is towards an increase in labour productivity disparities: the ratio increases in 14 countries and decreases only in six countries. The ratio is higher in Belgium, Ireland, Slovakia, Germany, Poland and Romania and is lower in France, Netherlands, Sweden, the UK, Bulgaria and Czech Republic.

Table 5.4 reports the same indicators of disparities computed for employment rates; rather than reporting the ratio between the maximum and the minimum value and between the 75th and the 25th percentiles, Table 5.4 reports differences (in percentages). This is because employment rates vary between zero and one and it is more intuitive to compare differences in percentage points. If we look at the difference between the maximum and the minimum value, for all newcomers but Slovenia we find differences in the order of ten percentage points or more. Very high differences (higher than ten percentage points) are also found in Spain, Finland, France and Italy (which, in 2011, has the highest difference of 20 points). The smaller values (below five percentage points in 2011) are found in Greece, Ireland, the Netherlands, Portugal and Slovenia. When looking at differences between the 75th and the 25th percentile, the higher differences are found in Slovakia, Italy, Hungary, Finland and Belgium (all above five points) and the lowest (less than three points in 2011) in the Netherlands, Portugal, Sweden, France, Slovenia and Bulgaria. Finally, looking at trends there are no common patterns across countries: the difference between the maximum and the minimum increases in eight countries, decreases in seven countries and stays constant in five countries, while the difference between the 75th and the 25th percentile increases in seven countries, decreases in five countries and stays constant in eight countries. However, when looking at extreme values (the minimum and the maximum) there is a high prevalence of polarization in newcomers (the difference in employment rates increases in all of them but Slovenia and Czech Republic).

The evolution of regional disparities in labour productivity and employment rates: the role of specialization, knowledge and socio-economic groups

Analysis of variance

A first and simple way to assess the role of our groups in the evolution of regional disparities in labour productivity and employment rates is through the analysis of variance. The decomposition of total squares in the between- and within-groups component allows assessment of the changing importance of country, knowledge, socio-economic and specialization groups in explaining total variability. The analysis is performed for the whole sample of 27 European Union countries and separately for old members and for newcomers (countries joining the EU after 2004). Due to some missing data for employment in 2008, we consider the following years: 2004; 2007 and 2011.

The results of the decomposition for labour productivity and employment rates are reported respectively in Tables 5.5 and 5.6.

The following trends for the European Union can be observed:

1   The decrease in income disparities for the whole sample documented in Chapter 4 is due to a decrease in disparities in labour productivity while disparities in employment rates grow after the crisis;
2   Distinguishing the within- and between-country components, disparities in labour productivity decrease between countries but increase within countries;

Table 5.5 Sum of squares decomposition of labour productivity: EU-27, EU-15 and newcomers by country, knowledge, socio-economic and specialization groups, 2004, 2007 and 2011 (totals, between and within components – absolute values and shares)

		Country groups		Knowledge groups		Socio-economic groups		Specialization groups	
	Total	*Between*	*Within*	*Between*	*Within*	*Between*	*Within*	*Between*	*Within*
2004									
EU-27	29.79	22.98	6.8	13.38	16.4	7.79	21.99	7.84	21.94
		0.77	*0.23*	*0.45*	*0.55*	*0.26*	*0.74*	*0.26*	*0.74*
Old members	6.17	2.42	3.75	0.99	5.18	2.68	3.48	0.32	5.85
		0.39	*0.61*	*0.16*	*0.84*	*0.43*	*0.57*	*0.05*	*0.95*
Newcomers	6.64	3.59	3.05	1.3	5.33	3.07	3.57	2.97	3.66
		0.54	*0.46*	*0.2*	*0.8*	*0.46*	*0.54*	*0.45*	*0.55*
2007									
EU-27	26.7	19.08	7.62	11.67	15.02	8.2	18.5	7.16	19.54
		0.71	*0.29*	*0.44*	*0.56*	*0.31*	*0.69*	*0.27*	*0.73*
Old members	6.15	2.24	3.92	0.84	5.31	2.79	3.36	0.36	5.79
		0.36	*0.64*	*0.14*	*0.86*	*0.45*	*0.55*	*0.06*	*0.94*
Newcomers	6.48	2.77	3.7	1.84	4.64	3.82	2.65	3.21	3.27
		0.43	*0.57*	*0.28*	*0.72*	*0.59*	*0.41*	*0.5*	*0.5*
2011									
EU-27	21.74	13.96	7.78	9.34	12.4	7.24	14.5	4.94	16.8
		0.64	*0.36*	*0.43*	*0.57*	*0.33*	*0.67*	*0.23*	*0.77*
Old members	6.26	2.41	3.85	0.88	5.38	2.69	3.57	0.23	6.03
		0.39	*0.61*	*0.14*	*0.86*	*0.43*	*0.57*	*0.04*	*0.96*
Newcomers	5.69	1.75	3.94	1.96	3.73	3.42	2.27	2.58	3.11
		0.31	*0.69*	*0.34*	*0.66*	*0.6*	*0.4*	*0.45*	*0.55*

Table 5.6 Sum of squares decomposition of employment rates: EU-27, EU-15 and new-comers by country, knowledge, socio-economic and specialization groups, 2004, 2007 and 2011 (totals, between and within components – absolute values and shares)

	Total	Country groups		Knowledge groups		Socio-economic groups		Specialization groups	
		Between	Within	Between	Within	Between	Within	Between	Within
2004									
EU-27	2.73	1.6	1.13	0.64	2.09	0.53	2.2	0.77	1.97
		0.58	*0.42*	*0.24*	*0.76*	*0.19*	*0.81*	*0.28*	*0.72*
Old members	1.6	0.84	0.76	0.33	1.28	0.23	1.37	0.41	1.19
		0.53	*0.47*	*0.2*	*0.8*	*0.15*	*0.85*	*0.26*	*0.74*
Newcomers	0.96	0.59	0.38	0.16	0.8	0.26	0.71	0.23	0.73
		0.61	*0.39*	*0.17*	*0.83*	*0.27*	*0.73*	*0.24*	*0.76*
2007									
EU-27	2.56	1.49	1.06	0.63	1.93	0.45	2.11	0.47	2.09
		0.58	*0.42*	*0.25*	*0.75*	*0.18*	*0.82*	*0.18*	*0.82*
Old members	1.69	1.02	0.67	0.43	1.26	0.22	1.47	0.29	1.4
		0.6	*0.4*	*0.25*	*0.75*	*0.13*	*0.87*	*0.17*	*0.83*
Newcomers	0.82	0.42	0.4	0.19	0.63	0.27	0.55	0.14	0.68
		0.51	*0.49*	*0.23*	*0.77*	*0.33*	*0.67*	*0.17*	*0.83*
2011									
EU-27	2.9	1.7	1.2	0.82	2.09	0.73	2.18	0.63	2.28
		0.59	*0.41*	*0.28*	*0.72*	*0.25*	*0.75*	*0.22*	*0.78*
Old members	2.18	1.43	0.75	0.83	1.35	0.58	1.61	0.58	1.61
		0.66	*0.34*	*0.38*	*0.62*	*0.26*	*0.74*	*0.26*	*0.74*
Newcomers	0.71	0.26	0.45	0.13	0.58	0.31	0.41	0.12	0.59
		0.37	*0.63*	*0.18*	*0.82*	*0.43*	*0.57*	*0.17*	*0.83*

3.   In the case of employment, disparities, after declining in 2007, increase after the crisis, both within and between countries.

There are strong differences in the behaviour of old members and newcomers. For old members we observe that:

1.   Both disparities in labour productivity and in employment rates increase;
2.   In the case of employment this is due to an increase in disparities across countries while disparities are stable within countries (at the end of the period more than 60 per cent of the total variance in employment rates is explained by countries while the share is 40 per cent for labour productivity);
3.   In the case of labour productivity, disparities increase especially within countries while they are stable across countries.

For newcomers labour productivity and employment disparities decrease across countries while they increase within countries.

Overall, only for newcomers this evidence is consistent with the prediction that further European integration should lead to a decrease in the importance of country factors in explaining disparities across regions. In contrast, for old members, further integration and the adoption of a single currency have been accompanied by a sharp increase in disparities in the employment rate, especially across countries. At the same time, disparities in labour productivity have increased, especially within countries. The increase in employment disparities across countries is not so surprising considering the lack of a common policy regulating the labour market in Europe. Market forces operating via migration and wage flexibility have so far proved insufficient to solve the problem. The fact that disparities in labour productivity have not increased between countries can be due to competition effects, whereby countries have responded to increasing competition from newcomers by cutting employment. If, in most countries, national policies have led to a certain degree of homogeneity across regions in changes in employment, this might have favoured more those regions in the country with the higher levels of labour productivity (competing in international markets) leading to within-country divergence in labour productivity.

Finally, looking at the importance of our groupings, we find that:

1. Knowledge groups are more relevant for labour productivity in the whole sample, while socio-economic groups are more relevant for old members and newcomers separately (innovation explains better differences in labour productivity between old members and newcomers);
2. Over time the importance of knowledge groups and socio-economic groups in explaining disparities in the employment rate (but not in labour productivity) increases for the whole sample;
3. The importance of knowledge increases especially in old members while the importance of socio-economic groups increases especially in newcomers;
4. The importance of specialization groups does not change much over the sample period.

Overall, the analysis of variance highlights how, similarly to the case of income disparities, Europe is confronted with two major problems relating to increases in disparities: on the one hand, the increase in productivity and employment disparities across countries in old members and, on the other, the increase in disparities across regions within countries in newcomers.

Distribution dynamics

As in the case of per capita GDP, in order to have a broader view of the evolution of disparities in labour productivity and employment rates, we look at changes in the shape of kernel distributions between 2004 and 2011. In particular, Figure 5.1 reports the EU-relative and country-relative labour productivity distributions in 2004 and 2011, while Figure 5.2 reports the employment rate distributions.

Figure 5.1 shows that the EU-relative labour productivity distribution becomes more concentrated around a single mode in 2011 with respect to 2004, with

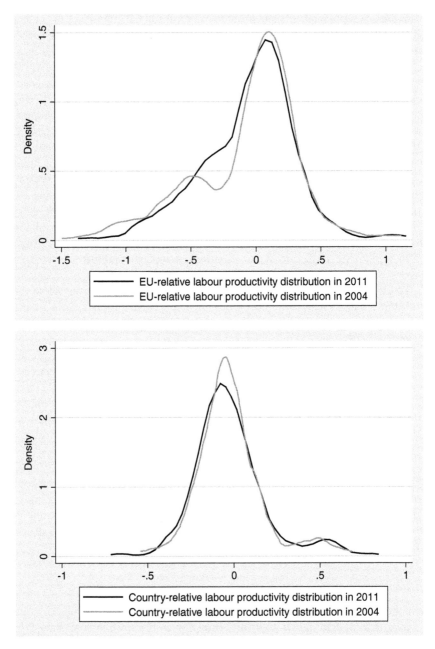

Figure 5.1 EU and country-relative labour productivity distributions in 2004 and 2011.

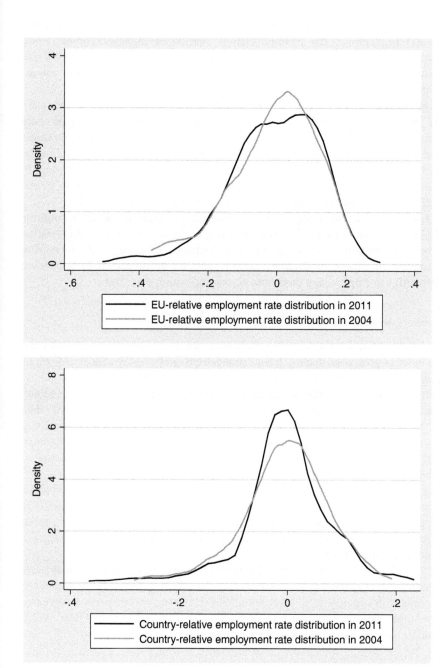

Figure 5.2 EU and country-relative employment rate distributions in 2004 and 2011.

apparent signs of convergence, especially for regions with low initial productivity levels. In contrast, the country-relative distribution appears slightly more dispersed in 2011 when compared to 2004. Moreover, skewness and kurtosis also grow (respectively from 0.92 to 0.98 and from 5.00 to 5.24), pointing to within-country divergence in labour productivity.

In the case of the EU-relative employment rate distribution (Figure 5.2) there are no signs of convergence; on the contrary, the distribution appears to be more dispersed, especially for medium levels of the employment rate. Moreover, skewness and kurtosis grow (respectively from –0.66 to –0.74 and from 3.10 to 3.72). Finally, in the case of the country-relative employment rate distribution, although it seems to tighten, it also becomes more skewed (skewness increases from –0.52 to –0.70) and with weight in both tails increasing (kurtosis increases from 3.88 to 5.57).

Overall, while conveying richer information, the study of densities confirms the results of the analysis of variance pointing to convergence only in EU-relative labour productivity, due to convergence between countries, with increasing disparities in labour productivity within countries accompanied by increasing disparities in employment rates both across and within countries.

Spatial correlation

Before investigating the role of specialization, socio-economic characteristics and knowledge groups in shaping labour productivity and employment rate distributions, we examine the degree of spatial correlation of these distributions in 2004 and 2011 by means of the Moran statistics and the Moran scatterplot. The Moran statistics points to a higher degree of spatial correlation in labour productivity than in employment rates. However, while spatial correlation in labour productivity decreases between 2004 and 2011 from 0.532 to 0.426, it increases in employment rates from 0.255 to 0.322. A visual inspection of patterns of spatial correlation in labour productivity and employment rates is given in Figures 5.3 and 5.4

From Figure 5.3 we can observe that regions contributing mostly to reduce spatial correlation are those with high levels of labour productivity surrounded by neighbours with low levels. This group of regions, including mainly capital regions from newcomers, increases its distance from the diagonal, contributing to reduce spatial correlation.

From Figure 5.4 it is apparent that regional employment rates are much more dispersed over space than regional labour productivities, with a larger number of regions with negative local Moran statistics. However, this dispersion decreases over time, especially for regions with medium levels of employment rates, which tend to become more similar to their neighbours.

Conditional distributions

Similarly to the case of per capita GDP, we assess the contribution of our groupings to regional disparities in labour productivity and in the employment rate by looking at the shape of conditional distributions and by computing the

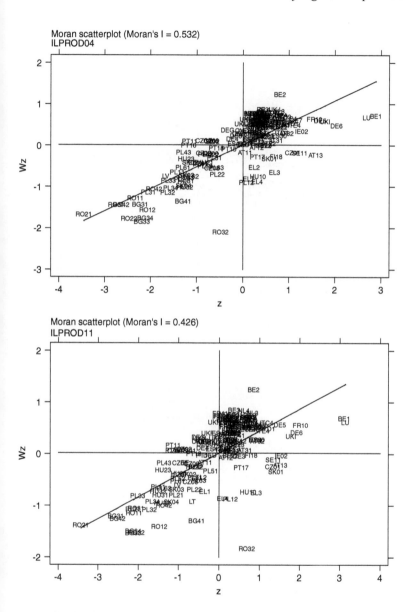

Figure 5.3 Spatial correlation in labour productivity in 2004 and 2011.

Kolmogorov-Smirnov (K-S) test to check whether the original and conditioned distributions are statistically different (the null hypothesis is that they are not). If the test rejects the null hypothesis, the two density functions are significantly different and the conditioning variable explains the distribution of regional income. We consider both EU-relative and country-relative distributions. The results of

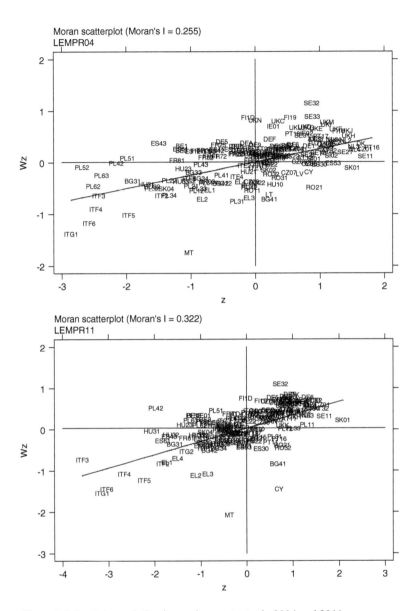

Figure 5.4 Spatial correlation in employment rates in 2004 and 2011.

K-S tests are reported in Tables 5.7 and 5.8 below, alongside with the variance for each distribution. Table 5.7 reports results for the labour productivity distribution while Table 5.8 focuses on the employment rate distribution.

Looking at the first part of Table 5.7 (EU-relative distributions), we can notice that, similarly to the case of the per capita GDP distribution, the importance of

Table 5.7 Conditioned labour productivity distribution functions: combined K-S test and variance, 2004 and 2011

	EU-relative labour productivity distribution					
	2004	2011	2004		2011	
	Variance	Variance	K-S test	p-value	K-S test	p-value
Original distribution	0.161	0.117				
Conditioned by country	0.036	0.042	0.256	0.000	0.261	0.000
Conditioned by specialization	0.109	0.089	0.132	0.073	0.120	0.141
Conditioned by socio-economic groups	0.123	0.081	0.117	0.142	0.161	0.014
Conditioned by knowledge groups	0.087	0.065	0.161	0.014	0.172	0.007
Conditioned by socio-economic, specialization and knowledge groups	0.068	0.048	0.173	0.007	0.207	0.001

	Country-relative labour productivity distribution					
	2004	2011	2004		2011	
	Variance	Variance	K-S test	p-value	K-S test	p-value
Conditioned by specialization	0.034	0.039	0.172	0.007	0.194	0.001
Conditioned by socio-economic groups	0.020	0.022	0.206	0.001	0.239	0.000
Conditioned by knowledge groups	0.032	0.037	0.157	0.018	0.179	0.006
Conditioned by socio-economic, specialization and knowledge groups	0.018	0.020	0.202	0.001	0.238	0.000

socio-economic factors, knowledge and specialization increases over time with respect to the relevance of country factors. In fact, while the variance of country-relative labour productivity distribution increases between 2004 and 2011, that of the other conditional distributions decreases over the same time span. Also K-S tests highlight the important and increasing role of our groupings in explaining regional differences in EU-relative labour productivity: while in 2004 only the distributions conditional on countries and knowledge groups were highly significantly different from the original one, in 2011 also the distribution conditional on socio-economic groups becomes significantly different from the original one.

When looking at country-relative distributions (second part of Table 5.7), we observe an increase in the variance showing within-country divergence also in labour productivity (the same was found for per capita GDP). Again (as in the case of per capita GDP), the increase in variance is smaller for conditional distributions (particularly that conditional on socio-economic groups); moreover, all groupings are highly significant, with significance increasing over time (p-values decrease over time).

Table 5.8 Conditioned employment rate distribution functions: combined K-S test and variance, 2004 and 2011

	EU-relative employment rate distribution					
	2004	*2011*	*2004*		*2011*	
	Variance	*Variance*	*K-S test*	*p-value*	*K-S test*	*p-value*
Original distribution	0.015	0.017				
Conditioned by country	0.007	0.007	0.1333	0.064	0.1889	0.002
Conditioned by specialization	0.011	0.013	0.1008	0.286	0.0954	0.367
Conditioned by socio-economic groups	0.012	0.012	0.0667	0.784	0.0778	0.600
Conditioned by knowledge groups	0.011	0.011	0.0889	0.426	0.1000	0.285
Conditioned by socio-economic, specialization and knowledge groups	0.009	0.009	0.1349	0.063	0.1274	0.091

	Country-relative employment rate distribution					
	2004	*2011*	*2004*		*2011*	
	Variance	*Variance*	*K-S test*	*p-value*	*K-S test*	*p-value*
Conditioned by specialization	0.006	0.007	0.0611	0.865		
Conditioned by socio-economic Groups	0.005	0.005	0.0556	0.928	0.0667	0.784
Conditioned by knowledge groups	0.006	0.006	0.0680	0.772	0.0698	0.760
Conditioned by socio-economic, specialization and knowledge groups	0.005	0.005	0.0648	0.821	0.0697	0.744

Table 5.8 focuses on the employment rate.

Here the picture is different from that emerging from per capita GDP and labour productivity: first, we notice overall divergence; second, K-S tests show an increase in importance of countries in explaining variations in the employment rate; third, only when conditioning for all factors is the EU-relative conditional distribution significantly (not highly) different from the original one; fourth, conditional country-relative distributions are not significantly different from the original ones. All these observations point to the strong and increasing importance of country factors in explaining differences across regions in the employment rate.

The explanatory power of each factor at the end of the period (2011) for EU-relative and country-relative distributions can be checked visually in Figures 5.5, 5.6, 5.7 and 5.8, the first two referring to labour productivity

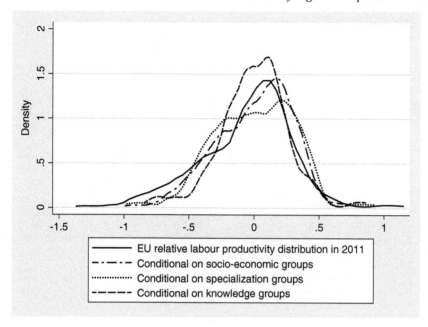

Figure 5.5 EU-relative original and conditional labour productivity distributions in 2011.

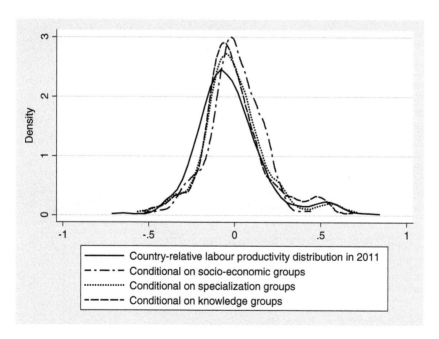

Figure 5.6 Country-relative original and conditional labour productivity distributions in 2011.

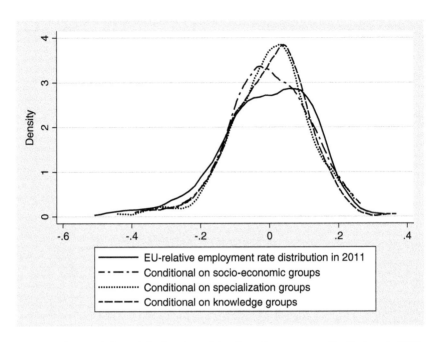

Figure 5.7 EU-relative original and conditional employment rate distributions in 2011.

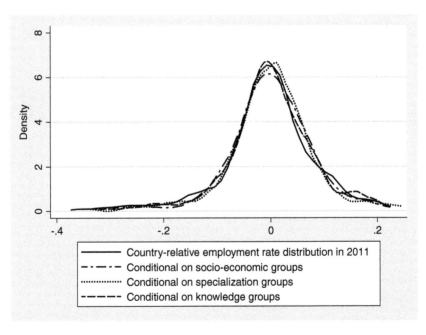

Figure 5.8 Country-relative original and conditional employment rate distributions in 2011.

(EU-relative and country-relative) and the last two to the employment rate. In the case of EU-relative labour productivity (Figure 5.5), we can notice that, similarly to the case of per capita GDP, the classification contributing mostly to reducing the spread of the EU-relative distribution is knowledge group. Moreover, knowledge groups contribute also to make the distribution more symmetric (skewness decreases from –0.55 to –0.41). However, only conditioning for socio-economic groups and specialization groups reduces the kurtosis (from 3.86 to respectively 3.06 and 3.20).

Looking at country-relative distributions (Figure 5.6), the most relevant factor appears to be socio-economic groups; however, all factors contribute to reduce variance, skewness and kurtosis.

When focusing on EU-relative employment rate distributions, we can observe that, although K-S tests do not reject equality between original and conditional distributions, the visual inspection of the figure suggests that specialization and knowledge groups contribute to tightening the distribution; moreover, all factors reduce skewness (Figure 5.7). Finally, in the case of country-relative employment rate distributions (Figure 5.8), visual inspection also shows that conditional distributions are very similar to the original one, suggesting little explanatory power of conditioning factors once the country factor has been accounted for.

Conclusions

This chapter has investigated the evolution of regional disparities in labour productivity and employment rate in the EU-27, distinguishing between old members and newcomers. The results point to an overall process of convergence only in labour productivity consistent with increasing competition across EU regions, but accompanied by increasing regional disparities in the employment rate. Moreover, when old members are separated from newcomers, they are found to experience divergence in both labour productivity and employment rates. At the same time, the overall convergence in newcomers hides growing disparities in both productivity and employment at the regional level.

Coming to the factors that are responsible for these disparities, countries explain a great (and increasing) share of regional disparities in employment rates, especially in old members. This runs counter to the wisdom that the impact of further integration in the EU and the adoption of a single currency should lead to a reduction in the explanatory power of national factors. The result suggests that competition from new members and the economic downturn following the financial crisis have hit particularly the weaker economies of the old Europe, while wage flexibility and migration have proved ineffective response mechanisms. However, as expected, countries lose importance in explaining disparities in regional labour productivity: convergence in labour productivity occurs within knowledge, socio-economic and specialization groups but not within countries.

Finally, in newcomers within-country disparities in both labour productivity and employment are increasingly explained by innovation and socio-economic groups, with innovation increasing in importance, especially for explaining disparities in labour productivity, and socio-economic groups in explaining disparities in both labour productivity and employment.

Notes

1 In the Eurostat statistics the employment rate is computed as the ratio of employees to population of age 15–64. Here, in order to decompose per capita GDP into only two components, we take the ratio of employees to total population.
2 For a review see D'Agostino *et al.* (2006).
3 For a discussion of this issue, see Mario Pianta, 'Innovation and employment'. In J. Fagerberg *et al.* (eds), *The Oxford Handbook of Innovation*. Oxford: Oxford University Press, 2005. 568–98.

References

D'Agostino, A., R. Serafini and M. Ward-Warmedinger (2006), 'Sectoral explanations of employment in Europe: the role of services', European Central Bank, Working Paper Series, no. 625.

Pianta, M. (2005), 'Innovation and employment'. In J. Fagerberg, D. Mowery and R. Nelson (eds), *The Oxford Handbook of Innovation*. Oxford: Oxford University Press, pp. 568–98.

6 A closer look at the evolution of regional disparities in Central and Eastern Europe after the transition

Introduction

After ten years or so of often painful transition following the fall of the Iron Curtain, since the turn of the century the former centrally planned economies of Central and Eastern Europe (CEECs) have been heading towards a virtuous path of steady economic growth and productivity gains. By general consent, this is the result of a 'distinctive model of development',[1] based on integration with the West, eventually leading to membership in the EU and envisaging economic reforms, privatizations, trade and financial liberalization and labour mobility. However, it has also imposed plant closures, industrial restructuring and the reconversion of whole lines of production, changing and often redefining the whole economic geography of CEECs. This was in order for at least five reasons: 1) socialism had forced on most regions a strongly specialized (mono-industry) development blueprint generally concentrated on heavy industry and based on obsolete, large-scale, capital- and labour-intensive technology, often leading to serious environmental problems. All this imposed radical restructuring throughout the area when moving from central planning to a market economy; 2) the end of central planning changed the area's geopolitical framework, redirecting trade flows away from the former Soviet Union towards the West; 3) capital regions, being the centres of political power and hosting the head-quarters of banks, companies, universities and research centres, were far more rich than other areas already in the early 1990s and forged ahead after transition; 4) all CEECs lie at the eastern borders of the EU; however, some regions are closer to the West and appear to benefit from this closeness, having grown more than regions located far east; 5) in addition, sometimes a different location entails a different historical background and also different regional culture and traditions. For example, until World War I Poland was divided among centralized Prussia and Russia and the relatively decentralized Hapsburg Empire, that granted some degree of local self-government. The Banat region in Romania was under the highly centralized Hungarian Crown up to 1918, and so on.[2] The end of the strongly centralized socialist regimes opened the way to regional development paths that may differ also in relation to history, local traditions and culture.

All in all, while indicators point to restructuring processes generally ending in the early 2000s, CEECs have since increasingly presented a two-fold character: on one side, aggregate growth rates, labour productivity and employment rates are constantly above those of their western counterparts, marking catching up – or convergence – *at the country level*.[3] At the same time, growing disparities are building up *within countries* (divergence), signalling that some regions jump ahead while others lag behind, sharply changing one of the main features of socialism – that of a relatively egalitarian society, at least by western standards.[4] In other words, some CEEC regions, including capitals, managed to direct restructuring processes strategically, specializing in new, increasing returns to scale, sectors and benefiting from agglomeration economies and from proximity to the West.[5] Others, instead, simply lost their industrial base to international competition.

This chapter investigates the role of structural change on the growing disparities among newcomer regions. Its main focus is on the spatial patterns of development prevailing in CEEC regions once the hardest phase of transition was over and growth picked up at the aggregate level. Put differently, where and why did restructuring eventually lead to growth and to specialization in more advanced sectors and where and why did it simply amount in plant closures?

To this end, the chapter classifies CEECs regions according to new criteria, adapting the traditional subdivision suggested by Rodríguez-Pose (1998a) for old members. According to that classification, EU regions could be divided among urban/capital areas, old industrialized, peripheral and intermediate regions. We add to these groups another one that captures the performance of areas where old lines of production have been successfully restructured or reconverted, or where these processes, although still under way, appear likely to bring recovery. Given that successful structural change and growth in newcomer regions is often found to be linked to the inflow of foreign direct investment (FDI),[6] the group is built to include regions where both specialization (country-relative) in industry or services grew over the 2000s and the share in national FDI is relatively high. It is, accordingly, named the FDI-based restructuring group. In turn, the peripheral group includes regions that share borders with at least one non-EU member;[7] they often present a strong specialization in agriculture (country-relative).

The chapter is organized as follows. The first section, 'The recent empirical evidence', reviews the recent literature on regional income disparities in CEECs. 'Regional disparities within CEECs' reports some descriptive statistics on the evolution of regional GDP disparities in CEECs between 1991 and 2011. 'Old and new patterns of industrialization in CEECs' discusses how the interplay between old and new patterns of industrialization, the geographical location of the regions and their ability in attracting FDI might be related to regional growth in each country. 'Explaining increasing regional disparities in CEECs', after having classified CEEC regions in different socio-economic groups, tests the relevance of such groups in explaining regional disparities in per capita GDP by means of both non-parametric methodologies (analysis of variance and kernel densities) and regression analysis. Finally, the chapter concludes.

The recent empirical evidence

A growing literature analyses processes of convergence/divergence within CEECs. These countries represent a particularly interesting case for the study of convergence inasmuch as they all share, to differing extents, the following features: 1) before integration regional disparities had been kept artificially low by socialist regimes; also, the average levels of per capita GDP were far below western ones; 2) starting from the 1990s the sudden process of integration into Europe led to the redirection of the main axes of development away from the Soviet Union, causing massive restructuring; 3) finally, while all CEECs are located in the eastern part of Europe, regions within them are more or less distant from the core of Europe and provide an interesting sample to assess how geography might affect convergence.

Weise *et al.* (2001) identify the following four types of regions in new member states: 1) capital cities and major urban agglomerations; 2) EU border regions; 3) peripheral regions; and 4) old industrial regions. Urban areas present the highest growth rates, are mostly specialized in services and attract the highest shares (country-relative) of FDIs. In most new members the only relevant urban areas are the capital cities (exceptions are in Poland and Lithuania). EU border regions, which before the transition suffered due to their unfavourable location, later benefited from EU membership more than other regions. Due to their closeness to old EU regions, their relatively developed infrastructure and low wages coupled with a relatively highly skilled workforce, they managed to attract considerable FDI flows from western regions. Other benefits deriving from closeness to the West came in the form of cross-border education, technological cooperation and tourism. This seemed to be the case especially for Hungarian, Polish and Slovak regions (Boeri *et al.*, 2001).

Peripheral areas tend to be the poorest ones. The reorientation of the main economic and political ties away from the East towards the West left the regions at far eastern borders of the area outside the main axes of industrialization and development. Boeri *et al.* (ibid.) and Gorzelak (1996) identify a belt of backward, depressed regions bordering the former Soviet Union from north-eastern Poland to the Moldavian districts of Romania. These regions are mostly specialized in agriculture; moreover, poor infrastructures coupled with low factor mobility did not favour industrial development. Finally, old industrial regions were the focus of planned development and were based on heavy industry. The shift from planned to market economy led to large-scale declines in heavy industry, causing huge unemployment. In some cases old industries were kept artificially alive to avoid excessive job losses. These regions are currently facing the challenge of restructuring by introducing new technology and new products and by investing in new skills.

These results are confirmed by Petrakos (2001) and by Artelaris *et al.* (2010). Both papers address the question of disparities in newcomers. The first one analyses four countries (Poland, Hungary, Romania and Bulgaria, all at the NUTS3 level) during the mid-1990s. Various indicators (gross regional product per capita, average wages, industrial production per capita, investment per capita and FDI per capita) point to growing regional disparities for all countries. In particular, urban areas jump ahead while regions sharing common borders with old EU members (particularly in Poland and in Hungary) benefit more from integration than regions that do not. The second paper analyses the evolution of per capita GDP in each new member state at the NUTS3 level in the period 1990–2005. As a general pattern, descriptive statistics show that urban regions and western regions perform better than the country average, confirming the importance of agglomeration economies and of geography for economic development. Estimating non-linear equations for the evolution of per capita GDP, the authors also find evidence of the existence of convergence clubs within each country (with the exception of Poland and Slovakia, where all regions diverge from the richest one).

Also, Ezcurra *et al.* (2007) find evidence of strong within-country divergence, coupled with between-country convergence in CEECs from 1990–2001 (the NUTS2 level breakdown is considered, leading, in all, to 39 regions). Their analysis is based on different inequality measures (the Gini coefficient, the Theil index) as well as on the distribution dynamics of regional per capita income. They show that the density becomes somewhat less polarized over time, although not uniformly, while the stochastic kernels show relative stability in the distribution, with some signs of convergence for the poorer regions. However, the ergodic distribution highlights that convergence will not persist in the long run. Finally, using conditional distributions, they study the role of various factors – the national component, a region's location in space, its productive structure, agglomeration economies (employment density) and the percentage of GDP devoted to investment – in explaining the distribution dynamics. They find that all these factors matter, but that the productive structure is the only variable with a uniform effect on the whole distribution.

Finally, Kallioras and Petrakos (2010) focus on structural change in the regions of five new member states (Hungary, Estonia, Slovenia, Bulgaria and Romania) over the transition period (1991–2000). They estimate the determinants of the rate of growth (decline) of industrial employment and find a negative effect of economic integration and a positive effect of productive diversification, of high shares in capital intensive industries, of average firm size and of geographic centrality.

Regional disparities within CEECs

The recent literature on convergence in new member states shows that while these countries have reduced their distance from the EU average, at the same time they have raised the disparities within countries. Before integration, these had been kept artificially low by socialist regimes, but they started to grow rapidly once integration and liberalization was under way, leading to a marked – and sometimes overwhelming – polarization of income within countries. Table 6.1 reports some measures of within-country regional disparities in 1991 and in 2011 for CEECs.

In all these countries, regional disparities in per capita GDP increase significantly between 1991 and 2011. In particular, the standard deviation of the per

Table 6.1 Standard deviation and percentiles of country-relative distributions in CEECs

	Standard deviation		Poorest region		25th percentile		75th percentile		Richest region	
	1991	2011	1991	2011	1991	2011	1991	2011	1991	2011
Bulgaria	0.114	0.510	0.828	0.667	0.932	0.729	1.080	0.914	1.148	2.024
Czech Republic	0.301	0.473	0.795	0.791	0.849	0.796	0.985	0.894	1.727	2.167
Hungary	0.229	0.455	0.795	0.699	0.830	0.747	1.124	1.072	1.459	1.986
Poland	0.155	0.264	0.785	0.726	0.847	0.833	1.106	1.115	1.278	1.821
Romania	0.165	0.568	0.774	0.579	0.880	0.726	1.054	0.978	1.321	2.362
Slovenia	0.232	0.266	0.836	0.811					1.164	1.188
Slovakia	0.519	0.696	0.670	0.544	0.721	0.594	1.279	1.405	1.775	2.034

capita GDP distribution grows in all countries, the highest increases being in Romania and in Bulgaria. The share of per capita GDP of the poorest regions over the country average falls in all countries. For instance, in the initial year (1991) only Slovakia presented a share below 70 per cent, while in 2011 this occurred also in Bulgaria, Hungary and Romania. In 1991 a larger group of regions (the 25th percentile) had a share of national per capita GDP over 80 per cent in all countries but Slovakia; in 2011 the same group was below 80 per cent in all countries but Poland. The richest regions (the ones including the capital cities) leap ahead, marking a growing gap with the rest of the country: in 2011, in all countries but Slovenia, the per capita GDP of the richest region is almost twice the national average. The differences were much smaller in 1991. Finally, as far as the 75th percentile is concerned, there are some signs of convergence towards the average in Bulgaria, Hungary and Romania, while Poland and Slovakia show divergence. In the Czech Republic – where Prague, already in 1991, had a per capita GDP over one and half times the country average – the 75th percentile was below the average in 1991 and fell even more behind in 2011.

Figure 6.1 shows the country-relative per capita GDP distribution (including only countries with more than one region) in CEECs in 1991 and in 2011 and the contour plot.

Figure 6.1 shows clear signs of divergence, in particular for the upper tail of the distribution where a second mode, probably due to the behaviour of capital regions, appears to be emerging in 2011. Divergence is also confirmed by the large growth in the variance (from 0.039 in 1991 to 0.113 in 2011), and by the increase in skewness (from 0.988 to 1.338) and kurtosis (from 4.225 to 4.264). Finally, the Kolmogornov-Smirnov (K-S) test indicates that the two distributions are significantly different at 1 per cent (see Table 6.3).

Old and new patterns of industrialization in CEECs

Before attempting to identify the main factors explaining increasing regional disparities in CEECs, it is worth considering the interplay between industrialization

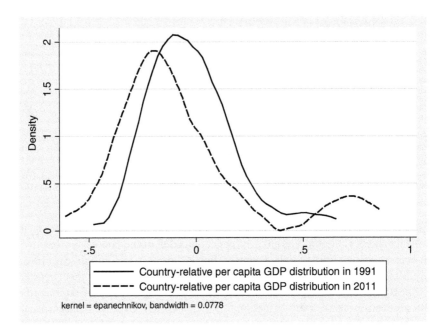

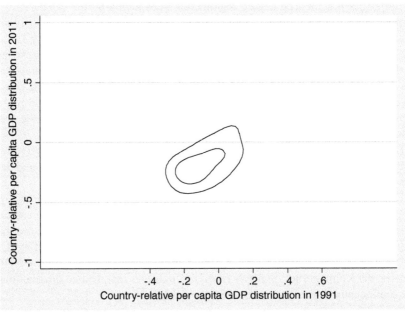

Figure 6.1 Country-relative per capita GDP distributions in 1991 and 2011 and contour plots.

and regional development within each country. This entails considering how regions within each country have changed their position with respect to the country average, starting from the initial year (1991), going to an intermediate date (2000) and ending in the final year (2011). In so doing, special attention is given to the question of whether such changes are linked to the evolution of regional specialization, to the geographical position of a region and/or to its ability to attract FDI.

Specialization is measured by the revealed comparative advantage index on gross value added. This is computed as the share of gross value added (*GVA*) in sector *s* over total gross value added in region *i* divided by the share of sector *s* in total country gross value added:

$$RCA_s = \frac{GVA_{i,s} / \sum_s GVA_{i,s}}{\sum_{i=1}^{n_C} GVA_{i,s} / \sum_s \sum_{i=1}^{n_C} GVA_{i,s}}$$

where n_C is the number of regions within each country. We refer each value to the country's total in order to capture regional disparities within countries.[8] The sectors considered are agriculture, industry, construction and services. Finally, differently from the previous chapters where specialization groups were defined referring to employment, we use GVA since it provides better information on the economic value of each sector.[9]

Hungary

Research on the economic consequences of transition in Hungary (between the end of the 1990s and mid-2000s) finds evidence of a new spatial pattern of regional development: economic growth concentrates in a small number of metropolitan and western areas, whereas a large number of regions, mainly in eastern and north-eastern areas, witness economic decline (Lackenbauer, 2004).

The interplay of a series of factors contributes to the success of Budapest and of the western regions bordering Austria. These include good infrastructure links, a dynamically growing private sector and a great number of international joint ventures acting as connections to international networks (Bachtler *et al.*, 1999; Horváth, 2002). The main difference between the Budapest area and western regions arises from their productive structure: Budapest is specialized in services, while the counties of Győr-Moson-Sopron and Vas (in Nyugat-Dunántúl) become centres of specialized industrial mass-production (Rechnitzer, 2000). The most significant factors of economic growth were thus the external activating effects of the relatively close, economically powerful south German, Austrian and north Italian regions (Nemes-Nagy, 2001). The fact that the far western regions had been relatively left out of the socialist drive towards heavy industrialization on account of their distance from the Soviet Union allowed them to start from a more flexible economic structure in transition.

For instance, the city of Győr, situated exactly halfway between Vienna and Budapest along excellent rail and road links, opened Hungary's first greenfield industrial site, the local business park, in 1991. Ever since, the city has attracted big international investors such as Audi, Philips and Amoco Fabrics (Lackenbauer, 2004). Later, when multinational investment started to decline, Györ began developing home-grown companies that recruited a highly educated labour force, while big manufacturing companies upgraded production lines and added R&D units. Like Györ, western Hungary in general is striving to 'move up the value chain' (Condon, 2004).

On the whole, the eastern, north-eastern and southern regions are the losers of transition (Visy *et al.*, 2005). In general, these regions have a comparatively poor infrastructure, small numbers of joint ventures and a very weak private sector (Bachtler *et al.*, 1999). In particular, the eastern periphery (e.g., the counties of Szabolcs-Szatmár-Bereg and Hajdú-Bihar in Észak-Alföld) suffers from a regional crisis in both manufacturing and food industry, which used to supply the Soviet market. The southern border counties like Bác-Kiskun in Dél-Alföld were negatively affected by the Balkan crisis, which discouraged foreign investment. However, in former locations of heavy industry (coal and uranium mining) like Pécs (in Dél-Dunántúl) commercial, administrative and cultural services, formerly playing a subsidiary role, are now the primary focus of development (Visy *et al.*, 2005). Finally, Hungary's northern counties (e.g., Nograd and Borsod-Abauj-Zemplen in Észak-Magyarország) struggle with their obsolete heavy industrial base. In some cases, like in the towns of Miskolc and Salgotarjan, thanks to monuments and natural resources, future growth prospects could be linked to services and tourism. Moreover, proximity to the national border with Slovakia gives these areas access to funds in support of cross-border cooperation (Visy *et al.*, 2005).

In 1991 per capita GDP country-relative was highest in the capital region, followed by the industrial western regions of Nyugat-Dunántúl (Western Transdanubia, HU22) and of Közép-Dunántúl (Central Transdanubia, HU21). This changes somewhat over time: while the distance between the capital and other regions increases, development seemingly concentrates in the western areas spreading also to Dél-Dunántúl (Southern Transdanubia, HU23), creating an internal divide between regions to the west and the east of the Danube. In the eastern part of the country, the poorest regions lag behind. In particular, the old industrialized area of Észak-Magyarország (Northern Hungary, HU31) becomes the poorest region in the country, averaging less than 70 per cent of the country level, whereas it averaged over 80 per cent in 1991 (see Figure 6.2).

Data on specialization (measured by the RCA index relative to the country average) show services already prevailing in the capital region in 1991 and growing in the following years. In the two western regions (Western and Central Transdanubia) industrial specialization grows, while the old industrial area of Észak-Magyarország loses its specialization in industry and, by 2011, becomes mainly specialized in agriculture. Specialization in agriculture grows in the two regions of the Great Plain (Észak-Alföld and Dél-Alföld) as well, while per capita GDP lags behind (see Figure 6.3).[10]

Together with industry, also FDI concentrates, apart from the capital region, in the regions of Western and Central Transdanubia.[11]

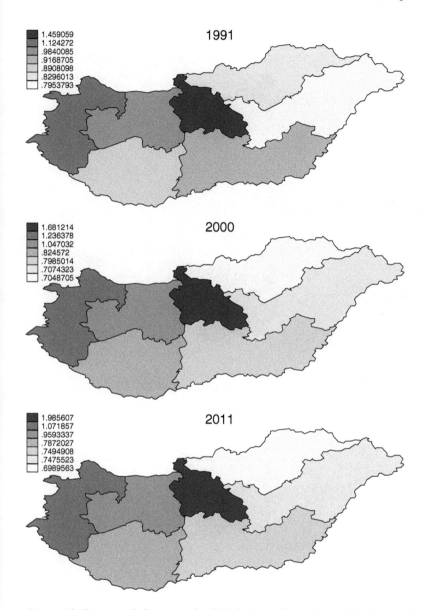

Figure 6.2 Country-relative per capita GDP in Hungarian regions, 1991, 2000 and 2011.

Romania

In Romania the socialist regime forced a typical, centrally planned industrial pattern on all regions of the country (Nadejde *et al.*, 2005). The scheme envisaged six macro-zones, each one with a specific industrial specialization (Cucu, 1996). The Southern Peri-Carpathian area included centres of extraction (oil and coal),

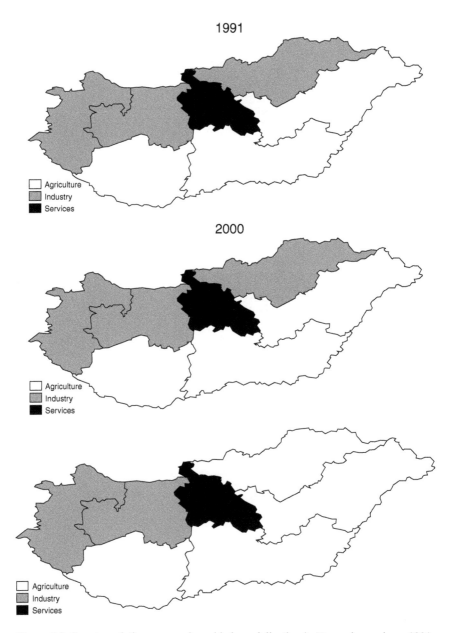

Figure 6.3 Country-relative gross value added specialization in Hungarian regions, 1991, 2000 and 2011.

petrochemical industries, iron production, drilling equipment and engineering plants, shipyards and chemicals. The South-Western Banat area was devoted to mining, metal processing and engineering. The Crisana-Maramures area contained several extractive, metal- and wood-processing centres, as well as engineering industries. The Eastern Peri-Carpathian area developed a young industry based on energy generation plants, metallurgy and engineering and chemistry. Also the south-eastern area dominantly had new industry, including centres of metallurgy, chemistry and shipyards. The Central Transilvania area, where old industrial centres prevailed, had extensive manufacturing in engineering, chemistry and in construction materials (Nadejde *et al.*, 2005). Overall, industry appeared to spread all over Romania. By and large, these industrial poles carried on into the early phase of transition: in 1995, 135 'industrial centres' defined as 'administrative-territorial units where the share of industrial employment in regard to total employment is dominant' were identified (ibid., p. 183). The majority (35) was located in the Central region followed by the South (24) and the West (18). Among the 135 industrial centres, 75 (grouped mainly in the centre and in the north-west of the country) had a longer pre-socialist tradition.

To a large extent, industrialization patterns determined economic development both under socialism and in early transitions years. In 1991 the richest areas of the country were the capital region, followed by South-east (RO22 – the region on the Black Sea including the town of Constanta that ranked first in terms of per capita investment received in that year, see Petrakos, 2001) and South (RO31) (see Figure 6.4). The ranking changed significantly in 2011 as the eastern regions (North-east and South-east – RO21 and RO22) lagged behind, becoming among the poorest in the country, while the richest (apart from the capital) included West (RO 42 – the Banat area bordering Hungary) and Centre (RO12).

Both fast-growing regions are specialized (country-relative) in industry in 2011 but not in 1991, when industry was mostly concentrated in the south. This points to the creation of new industrial centres. In contrast, the (currently) poorest regions in the east specialize in agriculture. As usual, in the capital region the service sector prevails (Figure 6.5).

Overall, the post-socialist industrialization patterns appear to determine regional development as well as creating a new west–east divide. Territories formerly belonging to Hungary (the Banat and Crisana regions) are more rich now (country-relative) than they were in 1991, when the richest areas were located in the South-east. An important role for development seems to be played by infrastructure. In fact, the infrastructure index is highest in the Bucharest-Ilfov region, by far the richest area in the country, while the lowest index belongs to the South-eastern part of the country, which is also the poorest (Miron *et al.*, 2009). Also, FDI seems to correlate with industrialization and development: the capital region attracts by far the largest share in FDI (60.6 per cent of total FDI in 2001 according to data of the National Bank of Romania, 2013) followed by the relatively rich areas of Centre and West (respectively 7.8 and 7.6 per cent). In this respect, the case of the Banat region (West) is particularly interesting. The region, which borders Hungary and was Hungarian until 1918, witnesses the localization of groups of firms,

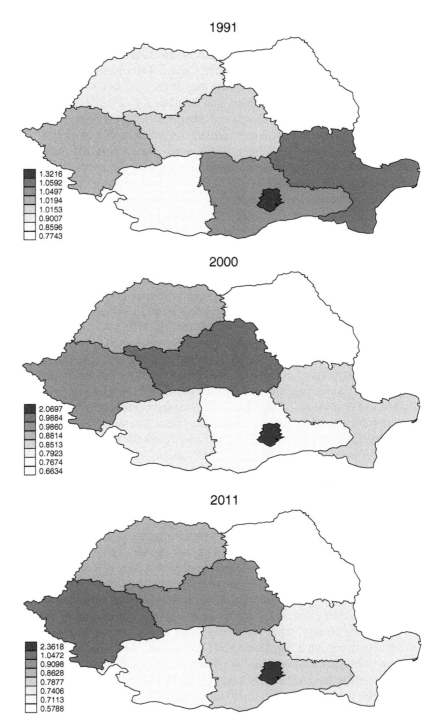

Figure 6.4 Country-relative per capita GDP in Romanian regions, 1991, 2000 and 2011.

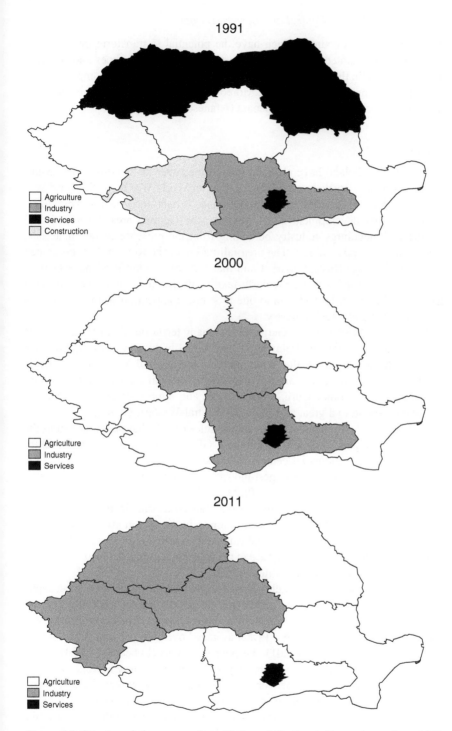

Figure 6.5 Country-relative gross value added specialization in Romanian regions, 1991, 2000 and 2011.

especially in Timis county, which have the potential to transform into clusters. These are concentrated in the wood industry and in textiles, shoes and software and electronics. In this last sector a number of well-known foreign companies such as Alcatel, Siemens, etc. are present. Moreover, promising links are being set with the Polytechnic University of Timisoara (Isfanescu, 2010).

Poland

The borders of Poland have changed many times over the centuries. The country's existing borders were established only after World War II. Until World War I, the country was divided between Germany, Russia and Austria. This determined unequal development across regions: the German area developed coal mining and metallurgy industry benefiting from the presence of raw materials, particularly in Upper Silesia. The area falling under the Russian Empire gained access to the huge Russian market and managed to develop local manufacture, privileging light industry (particularly textiles in the Lodz area). The Austrian territories, however, lagged behind due to strong competition from more developed Austrian and Czech industry.

After World Wars I and II, Germany lost many territories that are now part of Poland. The territories lost following World War I include most of the Province of Posen (now Poznań in the Wielkopolskie region) and West Prussia, while further territories were lost after World War II including East Prussia, Farther Pomerania, East Brandenburg, Upper Silesia and almost all of Lower Silesia. These correspond to a great part of actual Central-Western Poland.

In Poland, industrialization followed the rules of socialist planning and in the 1960s industry provided half of Poland's GDP. Under socialism the country presented 32 large industrial centres (Okraska, 2005); these carried on into the early years of transition. The largest industrial agglomeration is around the coal-mining district of Upper Silesia (PL22 – Slaskie); the area presents power stations, metallurgy plants, machine works, transportation, electric and chemical industries. The second largest concentration is in the region around Warszawa, dominated by machine and metal industries (with also a high share of high-tech industry). Further agglomerations are in the Lódzkie region (PL11) and are based on light industry and mainly textiles (ibid.).

In 1991, as in the rest of centrally planned economies, the distribution of per capita GDP across regions was fairly egalitarian: the poorest region, Podlaskie (PL34), achieved almost 80 per cent of the country average while the richest ones (Slaskie and the capital region Mazowieckie – PL12) averaged over 120 per cent. These differences widened over time: in 2011 the poorest regions (Lubelskie – PL31 – and Podkarpasckie – PL32) were beneath 75 per cent of the country average while the capital region was above 180 per cent. In 1991, the country presented a broad east–west divide, the poorest regions clustering around north-eastern borders. In 2011 the pattern was largely confirmed, eastern regions remaining among the poorest in the country notwithstanding some intra-group shifts (the northern area of Podlaskie – bordering Lithuania – improved its relative position with respect to eastern regions

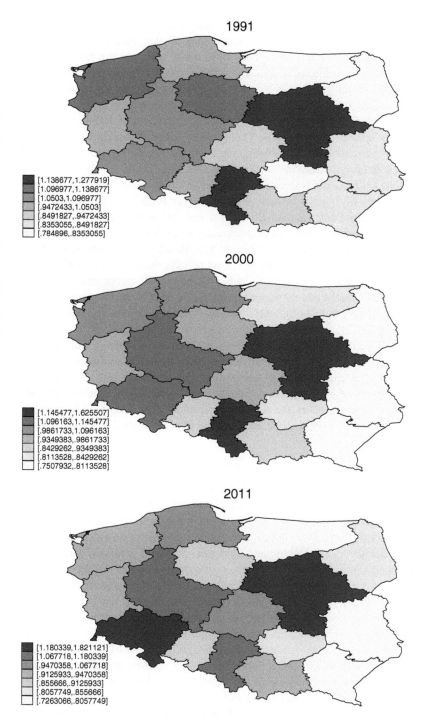

Figure 6.6 Country-relative per capita GDP in Polish regions, 1991, 2000 and 2011.

Lubelskie and Podkarpackie). At the same time, in the west Dolnoslaskie (PL51) became the second richest area in the country while Slaskie fell behind (Figure 6.6).

As far as specialization is concerned, in the initial year only two regions (out of 16) appear to be specialized in industry, country-relative: Slaskie and Kujawsko-Pomorskie. Careful analysis of the data reveals that only the first one actually qualifies as industrial, while in the second relative specialization is the outcome of a strong diversification in many sectors. Four other regions, including the capital, appear to be specialized in services. This could be linked to the country's tradition, even before the end of the socialist regime, to allow private business, which, over time, became fairly widespread (Aslund and Orlowski, 2014). Finally, two southern regions are specialized in construction.[12] The situation changes over time as a larger number of regions specialize in industry: in 2000 these include also Dolnoslaskie and Podkarpackie. By 2011 a vast industrial belt appears to have formed in the south-western area of the country spreading from the western region of Lubuskie to Dolnoslaskie, Opolskie (PL52), Slaskie and Podkarpaskie. These, with the exception of Opolskie, are industrial regions also relative to the EU average. In 2011 there are three regions, including the capital, specialized in services, the other two being the coastal regions on the Baltic Sea (Zachodniopomorskie and Pomorskie – PL42 and PL63), where tourism is developing. Finally, the region of Malopolskie (PL21), where Cracow, the country's second largest city is located, is specialized in construction and keeps its specialization over time (Figure 6.7).

The east–west divide is confirmed also by data on foreign investors: almost 70 per cent of total employment in companies with foreign capital occurs in the western regions of Wielkopolskie, Slaskie and Dolnoslaskie, together with the capital region Mazowieckie. Relatively high values are also found in Malopolskie, Zachodniopomorskie, Pomorskie and Lódzkie (Central Statistical Office, 2014).

Slovakia

The Czechoslovak Republic was created after World War I following the collapse of the Hapsburg Empire. In that period Slovakia's industry stood as one of the most developed examples of the whole Empire but it declined considerably in the interwar period (Finka *et al.*, 2005). Industrialization picked up again after World War II under socialism. The biggest and most successful industrial centres were concentrated along the Vah river (in the north-western part of the territory along the (present) border with the Czech Republic), in Bratislava and in the far East, around the city of Kosice. The end of central planning left the country with a non-competitive industry by Western (EU) standards, heavily dependent on the import of raw materials and, essentially, directed towards the Soviet market. The share of industry (including construction) in GDP fell from 61 per cent in 1986 to 26.6 per cent in 1998 (ibid.). Some regions, particularly that around Kosice, also suffered from the break-up of the Warsaw Pact and from the halt of arms exports (a sector of high specialization).

At the onset of transition the Slovak Republic presented a sharp east–west divide, per capita GDP falling systematically upon moving from the capital

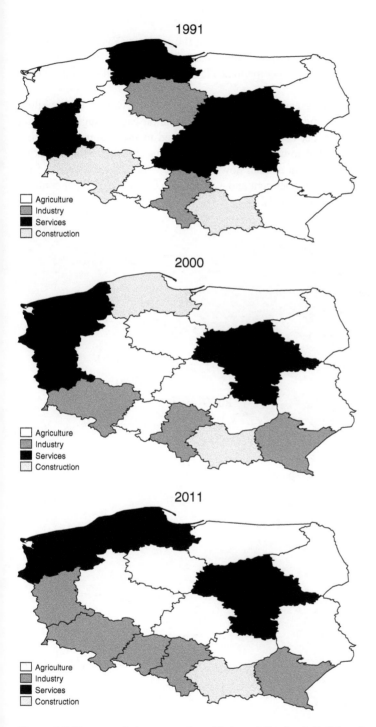

Figure 6.7 Country-relative gross value added specialization in Polish regions, 1991, 2000 and 2011.

region Bratislavský at the Austrian border to the far East (Východné – SK04). Over time this feature deepens: the capital passes from 1.77 in 1991 to twice the country's average per capita income in 2011, the poorest one falling from 0.67 to 0.54 (Figure 6.8).

The acceleration of the east–west divide may be partly driven by FDI: while in 2001 important investments were still present in the far eastern region (the area of Kosice totalled 16 per cent of total FDI directed to the country), over time projects were redirected towards the western regions (in 2010 Bratislavský – SK01– absorbed 62 per cent of total flows, Západné – SK02 – averaged 19.5 per cent, Stredné – SK03 – 9.5 per cent and Východné – SK04 – only 9 per cent, see Sochulakova and Igazova, 2013).

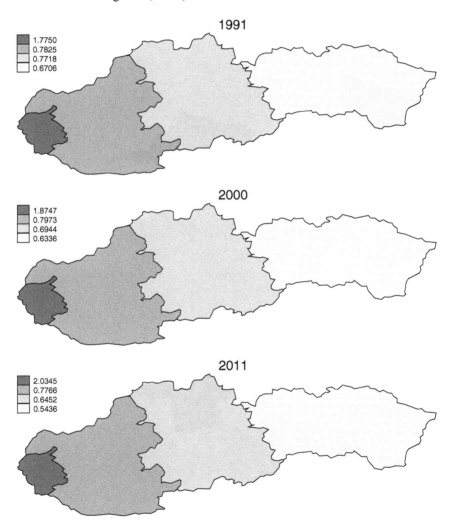

Figure 6.8 Country-relative per capita GDP in Slovak regions, 1991, 2000 and 2011.

As far as specialization is concerned (country-relative), the 1991 pattern is fairly predictable: the capital specialized in services, its closest neighbour in industry and the two eastern regions in agriculture. The picture remains largely unchanged until 2000, with only the western region next to the capital (Západné) changing its main sector of specialization into agriculture. This can be interpreted as a sign of restructuring, given that in 2011 the prevalent sector is industry once again. At the same time the two regions located more to the east (Stredné and Východné), although keeping a strong specialization in agriculture, become relatively more specialized in construction (Figure 6.9).

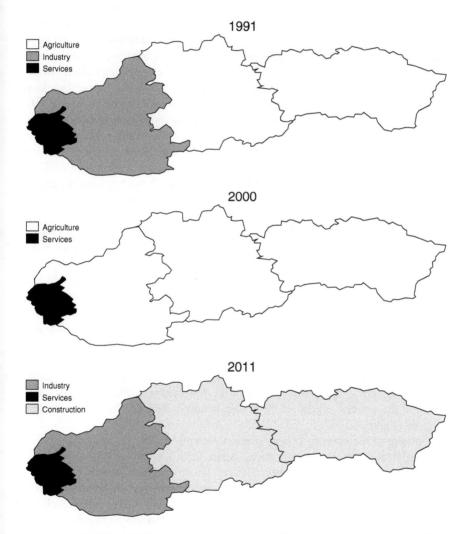

Figure 6.9 Country-relative gross value added specialization in Slovak regions, 1991, 2000 and 2011.

As for most CEECs, in 1991 EU-relative specialization shows a prevalence of services in the capital and agriculture in the rest of the country, although industry is relatively high in the western region of Západné. There is no sign of change over time even though industry strengthens in all regions, and especially in western Západné.

Czech Republic

The Czech Republic is formed by the two historical regions of Bohemia and Moravia. Under the socialist regime industry was mainly concentrated at the north-western border with Germany (Severozápad – CZ04) and in the eastern region of Moravia-Silesia (Moravskoslezsko – CZ08). Past industrial development in Severozápad was based on easily available raw materials, especially large deposits of brown coal that lay close to the surface. Therefore, the region was strong in the energy industry, coal mining, mechanical engineering and the chemical and glass industries. The Moravian-Silesian region was the former heartland of Czechoslovakia's coal, steel and heavy engineering industries (Skokan, 2009). During the transition both regions suffered from a significant decline in heavy industry's production and employment. Also the areas in the north-east of the country (around Pardubice), in Central Moravia (Střední Morava – CZ07 – around Zlín) and the south-east (Highlands), where light industry was present, suffered from the decline in the clothing and footwear sectors. A marked loss of agricultural workforce occurred in the traditionally agrarian regions (the south-east and in Central Moravia).[13]

Notwithstanding the uneven distribution of industry, at the onset of transition the country presented a fairly egalitarian distribution of income. Apart from the capital region Praha, which, in 1991, reached 1.7 times the country average per capita income, the other regions fell between 79 per cent (Střední Morava) and 99 per cent (Severozápad) of the country average. Over time the relatively egalitarian trait of the country has been sustained (with the notable exception of the capital region): in 2011 no region achieved less than 79 per cent of the national average. However, the geographical pattern of development changed markedly, favouring the region around the capital and the southern ones bordering Austria and Germany. The previously relatively rich north-western region of Severozápad underwent serious problems of industrial restructuring (Stejskal, 2005) and became the poorest region in the whole country, followed by the far eastern regions (Figure 6.10).

Coming to the country's specialization pattern, in 1991 it presented a rather unusual (for CEECs) diversification. Apart from the strong specialization of Praha in services (EU and country-relative), the other regions mostly presented a comparative advantage in three out of four sectors, construction being the prevalent area of activity with respect to the EU average. In terms of country-relativity, three regions (Severozápad, Střední Cechy – CZ02 and Moravskoslezsko – CZ08) scored the highest RCA in industry while in the rest of the country agriculture prevailed. Over time, the country becomes prevalently industrial (in 2011 all

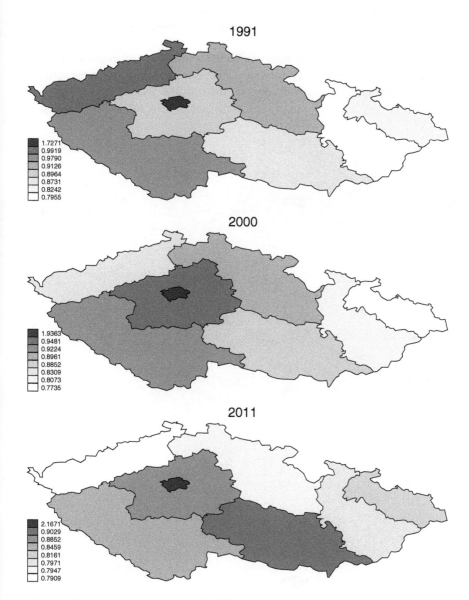

Figure 6.10 Country-relative per capita GDP in Czech regions, 1991, 2000 and 2011.

regions but the capital present an index of specialization above two EU-relative), with two regions presenting specialization also in services (Praha and its surrounding region Strední Cechy), suggesting the formation of a virtuous cluster of tertiary activities. From a country-relative perspective, industry is stronger in old industrialized Severozápad and in Moravskoslezsko (according to the regional policy of the Czech government introduced in the year 2000 these two regions are undergoing structural change and are defined as problem regions, see Stejskal, 2005), and in Strední Morava which, however, lags behind in terms of per capita GDP (Figure 6.11).

Data on FDI reveals strong inflows after the approval of FDI incentives in 1998 (Czech National Bank, 2013). Flows are directed especially towards the automotive industry and services (software, IT and financial services). The major EU

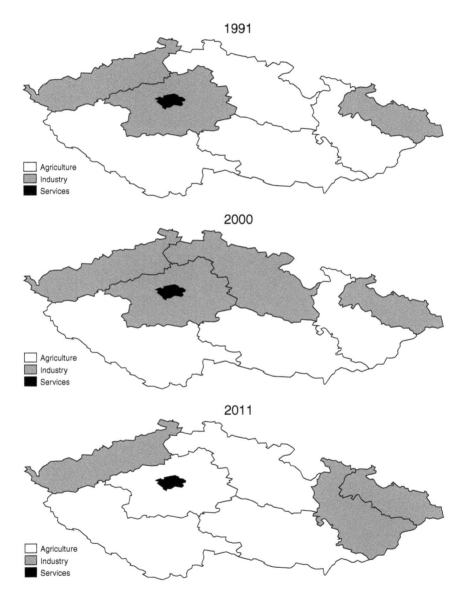

Figure 6.11 Country-relative gross value added specialization in Czech regions, 1991, 2000 and 2011.

investors are Germany and Austria. In 2011 the richest regions are the ones that attract the overwhelming portion of national FDI: Praha obtains by far the largest percentage (52.3 per cent) followed by Střední Cechy (10.6 per cent) and Jihovýchod (8.7 per cent). These flows concentrate mainly in southern Moravia around Brno.

Bulgaria

In Bulgaria central planning succeeded in transforming the country's economy, changing the longstanding rural tradition into a network of powerful industrial regions. However, the country lacked the necessary resources and markets for sustainable industrial development to the point that in the 1980s Bulgaria entered a stage of over-industrialization (Spiridonova and Novakova, 2005). Development took place along two parallel infrastructure corridors, one in the north and one in the south, crossing the country from the west, where the capital Sofia stands, to the Black Sea. Specialization was consistent with the Council for Mutual Economic Cooperation (CMEA) scheme; when it disintegrated this had strongly negative consequences for Bulgarian industrial regions. During the transition the whole country suffered from industrial decline; deindustrialization was matched by growing unemployment and negative growth.

Even more than other CEECs Bulgaria initially had a strongly egalitarian distribution of per capita GDP: the poorest region (southern Yuzhen tsentralen – BG42) achieved over 80 per cent of the country average while the richest one (Yugozapaden – BG41), which includes the capital, was just above 100 per cent. A completely different picture emerges 20 years later: in 2011 income is strongly polarized between the capital region that scores above 200 per cent of the country average and the remaining regions, among which the poorest lie in the north (Severozapaden – BG31– and Severen tsentralen – BG32) and fall below 75 per cent. Together, there is a marked redirection of development away from the northern regions at the border with Romania towards the south. Without considering the southern capital region Yugozapaden, which always scores first, in 2000 the two eastern regions on the Black Sea switch places: Southern Yugoiztochen (BG34) gaining the second place at the expense of Northern Severoiztochen (BG33), which ranks third. Both regions keep these positions well into the 2000s. As far as the other regions are concerned the far north-western region of Severozapaden (BG31), which ranks fourth until 2000, falls to the last place in 2011; at the same time southern Yuzhen tsentralen (BG42), which was last until 2000, becomes fourth (Figure 6.12).

As far as specialization is concerned, similarly to Romania (which shares with Bulgaria the role of poorest country in the EU), throughout the period all regions are specialized mainly in agriculture. The only exception is the capital region, which, in 2011, obtains relative specialization in services. However, in 1991 all regions have an index of comparative advantage above one also in industry, indicating a relatively high specialization in the sector. The regions with a still stronger specialization in industry (index above 1.5) were

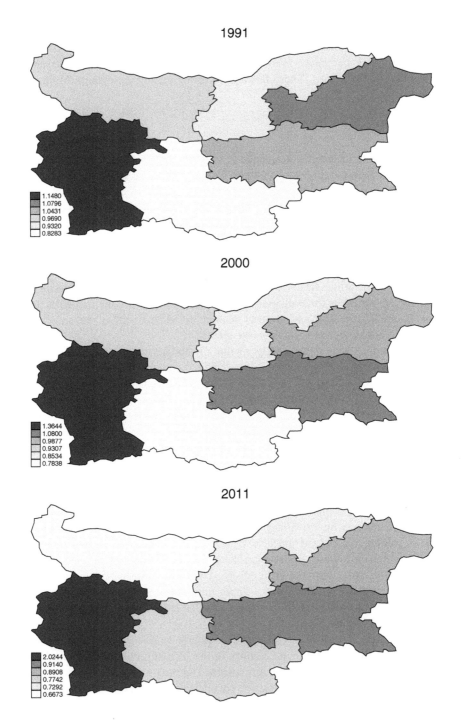

Figure 6.12 Country-relative per capita GDP in Bulgarian regions, 1991, 2000 and 2011.

south-eastern Yugoiztochen followed by north-western Severozapaden and Severen tsentralen. In 2011 only four regions have a value above one: the three quoted above plus Yuzhen tsentralen, which scores the highest index in the country, possibly reflecting a process of new industrialization occurring in the region coupled with deindustrialization going on in the others. This is indicated also in relative growth in the first region coupled with relative impoverishment in the other two.

Country-relative in 1991 industry concentrated in the northern regions of Severozapaden and Severen tsentralen while all other ones (with the exception of the capital region) specialized mainly in agriculture. In 2000, the pattern of industrialization changes completely: industry concentrates in Yugoiztochen, while all other regions except the capital become relatively specialized in agriculture. In 2011 Yugoiztochen gains a relative specialization in construction, while the capital region (formerly specialized, country-relative, in construction) becomes specialized in services. The other regions keep their relative specialization in agriculture (Figure 6.13).

In 2011 the regions that absorb the highest values of national FDI[14] are, as expected, the capital region (62 per cent) followed by the two regions on the Black Sea (Yugoiztochen with 13.6 per cent and Severoiztochen with 9.3 per cent) and Yuzhen tsentralen (8.8 per cent). However, while the southern regions of Yuzhen tsentralen and Yugoiztochen see a marked increase of FDI from the early 2000s (when the shares were respectively 2 per cent and 3.8 per cent), northern Severoiztochen loses position (its share in 2000 was 14 per cent) and the same occurs also to another northern region (Severen tsentralen, for which FDI falls from 12.5 per cent in 2000 to 3.7 per cent in 2011).

Slovenia

After World War I, with the partition of the Austro-Hungarian Empire, Slovenia became part of the newly established state of Yugoslavia. In this period, being part of a relatively large and protected market, industry shifted from raw materials and intermediate products to final goods. Starting from the 1930s, the country specialized in heavy industry, even if some light industry sectors were present (textiles and food industry) (Plostajner, 2005). After World War II, industrialization continued being part of the socialist development blueprint and was aimed mainly at satisfying domestic demand. The decline in industrial production and employment started with the oil crisis before the partition of Yugoslavia and the transition to a market economy. However, problems linked to the transition were less severe in Slovenia than in other CEECs since the country had the advantage of earlier experience in self-management, quasi-market economic rules and free trade and labour mobility, especially with Italy and Austria (ibid.).

Being a two-region country, the analysis for Slovenia is fairly simple and less informative than in other cases. The old industrial areas are spread evenly in both regions, in Zahodna Slovenija (SI02 – around the Gorenjska area) and in Vzhodna Slovenija (SI01 – in Savinjska and Podravje).[15]

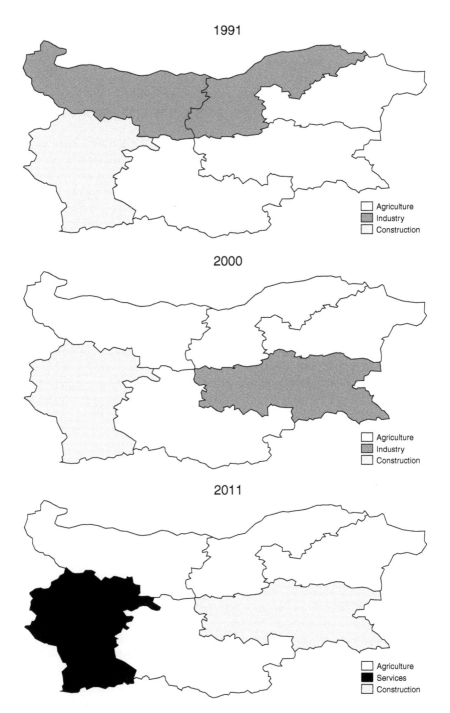

Figure 6.13 Country-relative gross value added specialization in Bulgarian regions, 1991, 2000 and 2011.

As expected, the capital region (Zahodna Slovenija) is richer than the rest of the country even though differentials are rather low and grow only slightly over time as the capital region passes from 1.16 times the country per capita GDP average in 1991 to 1.19 in 2011 (Figure 6.14).

As far as specialization is concerned, in 1991 EU-relative the country was divided between industry prevailing in the capital and agriculture in the other region. This changed as of 2000 with the capital becoming specialized in services (this feature carries on in 2011). The other region remains mainly specialized in agriculture although industry grows over time. A similar pattern emerges when considering specialization country-relative, the only difference being that in the initial year the capital region was already relatively specialized in services (Figure 6.15).

Classifying regions

The previous paragraphs underline some of the most important features and development paths of post-socialist Eastern European regions. These may be briefly summarized as follows: regional economic disparities grow rapidly and considerably. While capital regions jump ahead everywhere, other areas lag behind. At the same time, an east–west divide forms in many CEECs, development mainly occurring in regions lying at the borders of rich western countries, where direct investments from abroad tend to concentrate. In contrast, regions at the eastern borders that, under socialism, had benefited from closeness to the Soviet Union, are often left out of growth paths and face considerable problems linked to the conversion and restructuring of obsolete, materials- and labour-intensive lines of production.

On the basis of these findings, we put forward a classification of regions in CEECs that is similar to that of Rodríguez-Pose, but adds a new category – that of 'successful FDI-based restructuring'. This is done in order to capture regions that, often through considerable FDI, have managed to reconvert the old industrial base and recover in terms of per capita GDP and employment. Therefore, CEEC regions are classified into the following five groups: 1) peripheral regions; 2) capital regions; 3) old industrial regions; 4) FDI-based restructuring regions; 5) other regions. The list of the regions and the indicators used for the classification are reported in Appendix 6.1. Figure 6.16 shows the classification in a map.

Peripheral regions are located at the periphery of each respective country, far away from the centre of Europe. In particular, in Hungary the peripheral region lies in the far eastern part of the country and borders Ukraine. In Romania the peripheral regions are the three north-eastern ones bordering Ukraine and Moldavia. In Poland, four peripheral regions in the eastern and northern areas border respectively Ukraine, Belarus, Russia and the Baltic Sea. In Slovakia we have the far eastern peripheral region bordering Ukraine; in Bulgaria the two eastern ones are on the Black Sea. Finally, no region qualifies as peripheral in the Czech Republic and in Slovenia. This leads in all to 11 regions. It is worth noting that all peripheral regions are specialized (country-relative) in agriculture both in

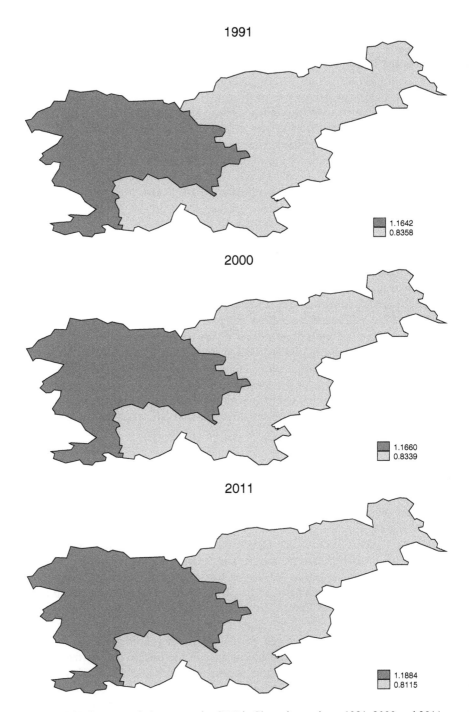

Figure 6.14 Country-relative per capita GDP in Slovenian regions, 1991, 2000 and 2011.

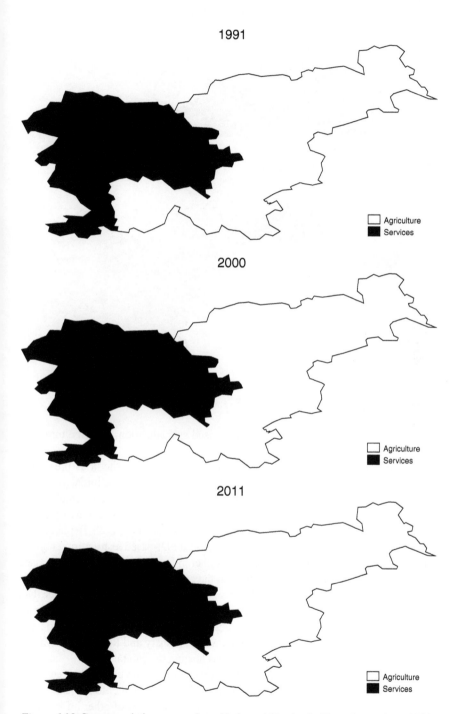

Figure 6.15 Country-relative gross value added specialization in Slovenian regions, 1991, 2000 and 2011.

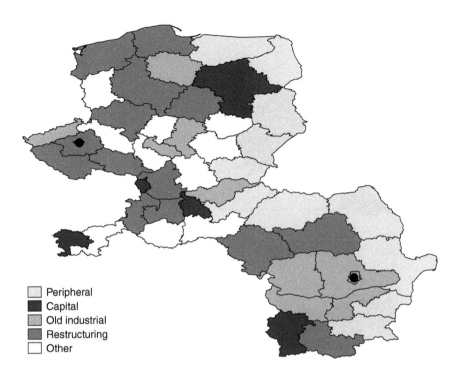

Peripheral
Capital
Old industrial
Restructuring
Other

Figure 6.16 Typologies of regions in CEECs.

1991 and in 2011, most of them having raised specialization in agriculture over time (see Appendix 6.1).

Old industrial regions are defined with reference to EU criteria as presenting relatively high (country-relative) specialization in industry in the initial year, falling over time (between 1991 and 2000) and with a rate of decline of employment in industry above the country average. In the sample, nine regions classify as old industrialized, two respectively in Bulgaria, Romania, the Czech Republic and Poland and one in Hungary. In contrast, successful FDI-based restructuring regions are specialized country-relative in 2011 in either industry or services, having raised their specialization over 2000 and 2011 (in the case of services excluding the capital regions) and having attracted a large share of FDI (that is, a share higher than the country average excluding the capital region). On the basis of these criteria 14 areas are identified as successfully restructuring, one respectively in Bulgaria and in Slovakia, three in the Czech Republic, two in Hungary and Romania and five in Poland. Finally, capital regions are the areas hosting the capital city.

Whenever it is not possible to assign a region to one group univocally because it presents the features of more than one group, it is assigned either to the least represented group in the country or to a given group on the basis of other information. Notwithstanding, nine regions are found not to present any of the features described above and are thus included in a residual group as 'other' regions.

Explaining increasing regional disparities in CEECs

Table 6.2 reports the total variance of EU-relative per capita GDP in CEECs in 1991, 2000 and 2011; it also shows separately the fraction explained by countries and by socio-economic groups. First of all, as mentioned above, intra-group variability more than doubles in the period under analysis. Coming to the impact of countries and of socio-economic groups, it is easily seen that while in 1991 countries explained 73 per cent of total variance, their explanatory power falls over time, passing to 61 per cent in 2000 and to 45 per cent in 2011. On the contrary, socio-economic groups, which in 1991 explained a minor 33 per cent of total variance, rise to 45 per cent in 2000 and reach 57 per cent in 2011, when they become a more powerful explanatory factor with respect to countries. Overall, the data clearly show the rising importance of socio-economic groups in explaining differences in per capita GDP across regions in CEECs.

In order to disentangle the role played by socio-economic factors in explaining regional disparities in per capita GDP within countries, we use both non-parametric and regression analyses. The non-parametric analysis consists in comparing, both for 1991 and for 2011, the original (country-relative) regional distribution of per capita GDP with that conditional on socio-economic factors and then formally testing whether the two are significantly different by means of the K-S test. Conditional distributions are obtained by first regressing per capita GDP (expressed as the log of the difference from the country average) on socio-economic factors, and then computing the distribution of residuals. Figures 6.17 and 6.18 show the univariate distributions of country-relative per capita GDP and of country-relative per capita GDP conditional on socio-economic groups. They also illustrate the respective contour plot for each distribution in 1991 and in 2011. In a contour plot, curves lying along the main diagonal indicate that the conditioning factor has a weak explicative power (the relative position of each region remains roughly unchanged over time). Curves that instead depart from the diagonal point to a relatively important conditioning factor. If curves were perfectly horizontal, this would mean that regions belonging to a given socio-economic group obtain very similar levels of per capita GDP – that is, regional disparities are largely explained by the conditioning factor.

Table 6.2 Fraction of variance in EU-relative per capita GDP explained by countries and socio-economic groups

Countries	Total	Between	Within	R-squared
1991	0.8756	0.6363	0.2393	0.7267
2000	1.1837	0.7274	0.4563	0.6145
2011	2.1507	0.9708	1.1800	0.4514
Socio-economic groups	Total	Between	Within	R-squared
1991	0.8756	0.2861	0.5895	0.3268
2000	1.1837	0.5389	0.6449	0.4552
2011	2.1507	1.2372	0.9136	0.5752

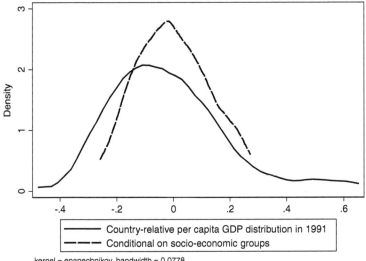

kernel = epanechnikov, bandwidth = 0.0778

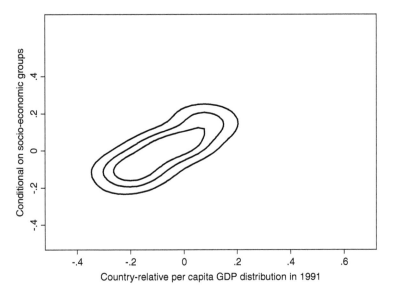

Figure 6.17 Country-relative per capita GDP distribution original and conditional on socio-economic groups in 1991 and contour plot.

Table 6.3 reports the variance, skewness and kurtosis of the distributions and the respective K-S tests.

Comparing the univariate distributions in Figures 6.17 and 6.18, the conditional ones appear to be far more concentrated around the mean with respect to the country-relative distributions. This is particularly evident in 2011. The same

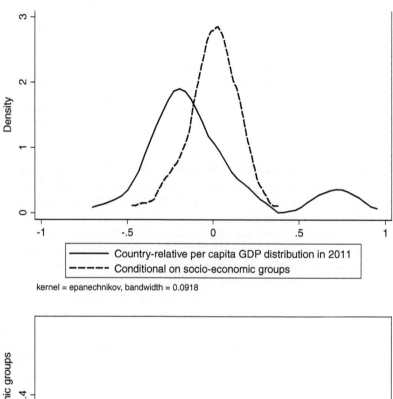

kernel = epanechnikov, bandwidth = 0.0918

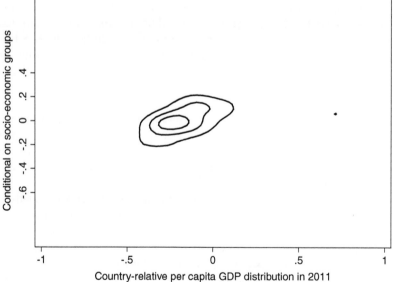

Figure 6.18 Country-relative per capita GDP distribution original and conditional on socio-economic groups in 2011 and contour plot.

Table 6.3 Variance, skewness, kurtosis and Kolmogornov-Smirnov tests for country-relative original and conditional distributions

Distribution	Variance	Skewness	Kurtosis	K-S test
Country-relative 1991	0.039	0.988	4.225	
Country-relative 2011	0.113	1.339	4.264	0.314***
Conditional on socio-economic groups 1991	0.017	0.199	2.306	0.196
Conditional on socio-economic groups 2011	0.023	-0.509	4.000	0.451***

Note: Kolmogornov-Smirnov tests compare the country-relative distribution in 2011 with that in 1991 and the distributions conditional on socio-economic groups to the country-relative distributions in 1991 and in 2011

information can be drawn also from the contour plots: while conditioning for socio-economic factors in 1991 shows only a marginal impact of these elements, the 2011 plot results in lines that, especially for the higher densities, appear to be almost parallel to the horizontal axis.

Moreover, Table 6.3 shows that while the variance of the country-relative distribution grows over time (from 0.039 to 0.113), it falls when conditioning for socio-economic factors (from 0.113 to 0.023). The skewness of the country-relative distribution in 2011 also falls when conditioning for socio-economic factors (from 1.339 to -0.509) and the distribution from right-skewed becomes left-skewed. Finally, the kurtosis decreases from 4.26 to 4.00. Conditioning for socio-economic factors in 1991 also reduces the variance, the skewness and the kurtosis of the distribution, even if the conditional distribution does not change much from the original one. In fact, the K-S test rejects equality between the original and the conditional distribution only for 2011. This result is consistent with the hypothesis of an increasing explanatory power of socio-economic groups that emerges from the analysis of variance.

Finally, Table 6.4 reports the results of regression analysis. In the first specification the dependent variable – the (country-relative) rate of growth of per capita GDP – depends only on the initial (country-relative) per capita GDP. In the second specification we add dummies for socio-economic groups (the base category is old industrial regions).

The results of the first specification signal that richer regions (country-relative) have grown more than poorer ones, indicating divergence in country-relative per capita GDP. The second specification shows that it is, indeed, the differences in the growth performance across the various socio-economic groups that account for such divergence. Results specify that the best performance is reached by capital regions that were already the richest ones in 1991. These grow at a yearly rate that is almost three percentage points higher than that achieved by old industrial regions, followed by restructuring regions that grow almost 1 per cent more than old industrial areas. The residual group grows almost 0.5 per cent more than old industrial areas while the rate of growth of peripheral areas does not differ significantly from that of old industrial regions.

Table 6.4 Unconditional and conditional convergence regressions for country-relative per capita GDP

	(1)	*(2)*
Per-capita GDP 1991	0.023 ***	−0.010
	(3.63)	(−1.56)
Urban		0.029 ***
		(7.78)
Restructuring		0.009 ***
		(3.69)
Peripheral		0.002
		(0.60)
Other		0.005 *
		(1.71)
Intercept	−0.002	−0.010 ***
	(−1.39)	(−5.18)
R-squared	0.211	0.672

Notes: Dependent variable: rate of growth of country-relative per capita GDP.
In specification (2), the reference group is old industrial regions.
t-values in brackets; *, **, *** denote respectively significance at 10%, 5% and 1%

Conclusions

This chapter focuses on within-country GDP per capita disparities in newcomer regions. Such disparities rise strongly between 1991 and 2011 in all CEECs. This is consistent with previous empirical evidence and highlights the consequences of a sudden shift from formerly centrally planned to market economy. Coming to the main factors that explain such strong divergences, the chapter argues that the socio-economic groups identified by Rodríguez-Pose to explain disparities in EU old members in the 1980s may apply also to newcomers. In particular, the role of urban areas has been extensively documented also in other studies, while the forced industrialization of many areas under socialism, mainly based on heavy industry, determined strong restructuring problems. Finally, the geographic configuration of newcomers raises the question of whether eastern regions (peripheral to the core of Europe) may encounter more difficulties with respect to areas at the border of EU old member regions. This leads to testing the explanatory power that the categories of capital regions, old industrial and peripheral regions have in CEECs. Moreover, we also test the relevance of a new category that includes regions that have restructured their economies especially thanks to considerable FDI flows.

Overall, it appears that the explanatory power of the above categories rises over time. Moreover, while in 1991 the country-relative per capita GDP distribution and that conditional on our groups did not differ significantly, in 2011 socio-economic groups become significant and explain a great part of regional GDP disparities.

These results cast some doubt on the ability of market mechanisms to generate even patterns of development. They also call for policies especially devoted to finding mechanisms to help the restructuring of old industrialized areas and promote the integration of peripheral regions with the rest of the European Union.

Appendix 6.1 The classification of CEECs regions

Nuts_id	Name	Growth employm. special. 91-00	Country-rel. special. indus. 91	Country-rel. special. indus. 11	Country-rel. special. agric. 91	Country-rel. special. agric. 11	Country-rel. special. serv. 91	Country-rel. special. serv. 11	Country-rel. special. serv. 91*	Country-rel. special. serv. 11*	Country-rel. Foreign Direct Invest.	Category
bg31	Severozapaden	-0.28	1.20	1.17	1.10	2.92	0.89	0.84	1.00	0.97	2.5	OLDIND
bg32	Severen tsentralen	-0.04	1.13	1.29	1.10	2.06	0.94	0.85	1.05	0.98	3.7	OLDIND
bg33	Severoiztochen	-0.03	0.88	0.85	1.10	1.50	1.03	1.02	1.15	1.17	9.3	PERIPHERAL
bg34	Yugoiztochen	-0.11	1.33	1.26	1.45	1.08	0.73	0.81	0.82	0.93	13.6	PERIPHERAL
bg41	Yugozapaden	0.17	0.76	0.82	0.44	0.32	1.26	1.13			62.0	CAPITAL
bg42	Yuzhen tsentralen	0.13	0.96	1.30	1.32	1.48	0.91	0.83	1.01	0.96	8.8	NEWFDI
cz01	Praha	-0.13	0.68	0.44	0.06	0.21	1.32	1.35			52.3	CAPITAL
cz02	Strední Cechy	0.09	1.21	1.24	1.18	1.39	0.86	0.88	0.93	1.00	10.6	NEWFDI
cz03	Jihozápad	0.17	0.93	1.14	1.70	2.08	0.95	0.88	1.03	1.00	6.8	NEWFDI
cz04	Severozápad	-0.11	1.22	1.26	0.61	0.81	0.88	0.85	0.96	0.97	4.4	OLDIND
cz05	Severovýchod	0.02	1.02	1.21	1.22	1.46	0.95	0.87	1.03	0.99	6.6	OTHER
cz06	Jihovýchod	0.05	1.00	1.06	1.52	1.39	0.96	0.93	1.04	1.06	8.7	NEWFDI
cz07	Strední Morava	0.01	0.93	1.28	1.68	1.15	0.99	0.82	1.07	0.94	3.4	OTHER
cz08	Moravskoslezsko	-0.14	1.33	1.27	0.73	0.51	0.82	0.88	0.89	1.01	7.2	OLDIND
hu1	Közép-Magyarország	-0.14	0.85	0.73	0.27	0.16	1.19	1.18			71.5	CAPITAL
hu21	Közép-Dunántúl	0.22	1.24	1.73	1.18	1.56	0.82	0.67	0.93	0.82	5.4	NEWFDI
hu22	Nyugat-Dunántúl	0.11	1.25	1.60	1.20	1.26	0.83	0.74	0.94	0.91	9.0	NEWFDI
hu23	Dél-Dunántúl	0.11	0.87	0.89	1.60	2.02	0.99	0.93	1.13	1.14	4.0	OTHER
hu31	Észak-Magyarország	-0.14	1.30	1.30	0.93	1.49	0.85	0.83	0.97	1.01	2.5	OLDIND
hu32	Észak-Alföld	0.09	0.93	1.05	1.78	2.38	0.91	0.87	1.04	1.07	3.0	PERIPHERAL
hu33	Dél-Alföld	-0.04	0.98	0.94	2.04	2.41	0.88	0.91	1.01	1.11	4.6	OTHER
pl11	Lódzkie	-0.02	1.02	1.32	0.84	1.74	1.07	0.83	1.09	0.89	4.2	NEWFDI
pl12	Mazowieckie	0.00	0.84	0.55	0.91	0.79	1.11	1.22			38.6	CAPITAL
pl21	Malopolskie	-0.14	0.98	0.95	0.60	0.72	1.05	0.98	1.07	1.05	6.3	OTHER
pl122	Slaskie	0.00	1.41	1.36	0.37	0.21	0.84	0.92	0.86	0.98	9.1	OLDIND
pl31	Lubelskie	-0.20	0.85	0.86	1.86	2.27	0.96	0.96	0.98	1.03	1.5	PERIPHERAL

pl32	Podkarpackie	0.03	1.06	1.08	1.12	0.62	0.92	1.00	0.94	1.07	1.8	PERIPHERAL
pl33	Swietokrzyskie	0.12	0.88	1.02	1.60	1.19	1.00	0.96	1.02	1.03	0.7	OTHER
pl34	Podlaskie	-0.02	0.67	0.63	2.08	2.31	1.06	1.09	1.08	1.16	0.7	PERIPHERAL
pl41	Wielkopolskie	-0.04	1.02	1.27	1.49	1.74	0.87	0.82	0.89	0.88	8.8	NEWFDI
pl42	Zachodniopomorskie	-0.03	0.80	0.63	1.13	0.82	1.13	1.14	1.16	1.22	5.6	NEWFDI
pl43	Lubuskie	0.20	0.69	1.16	0.90	0.86	1.27	0.96	1.30	1.03	2.8	OTHER
pl51	Dolnoslaskie	0.17	1.05	1.47	0.85	0.55	0.96	0.84	0.98	0.90	9.1	NEWFDI
pl52	Opolskie	0.04	0.90	1.01	1.73	0.91	0.97	1.01	0.99	1.08	1.9	OTHER
pl61	Kujawsko-Pomorskie	-0.10	1.04	1.13	0.97	1.92	0.99	0.87	1.01	0.93	2.3	OLDIND
pl62	Warminsko-Mazurskie	0.06	0.79	0.96	1.84	1.80	1.02	0.96	1.04	1.03	1.2	PERIPHERAL
pl63	Pomorskie	0.19	0.90	0.83	0.76	0.51	1.12	1.09	1.15	1.17	5.5	NEWFDI
ro11	Nord-Vest	0.06	0.93	1.22	1.00	1.19	1.09	0.86	1.16	0.96	4.8	PERIPHERAL
ro12	Centru	0.12	1.13	1.16	1.24	0.95	0.85	0.91	0.90	1.02	7.8	NEWFDI
ro21	Nord-Est	-0.06	0.95	0.88	0.92	1.77	1.09	0.98	1.16	1.10	3	PERIPHERAL
ro22	Sud-Est	0.03	0.82	0.90	1.30	1.58	0.97	0.94	1.04	1.05	5.5	PERIPHERAL
ro31	Sud - Muntenia	-0.22	1.18	1.33	1.12	1.47	0.83	0.76	0.88	0.85	7.2	OLDIND
ro32	Bucuresti - Ilfov	0.11	0.99	0.71	0.10	0.03	1.38	1.30			60.6	CAPITAL
ro41	Sud-Vest Oltenia	-0.11	1.08	1.06	0.90	1.62	0.90	0.86	0.95	0.96	3.5	OLDIND
ro42	Vest	0.15	0.87	1.11	1.54	0.89	0.85	0.98	0.91	1.09	7.6	NEWFDI
si01	Vzhodna Slovenija	0.03	1.13	1.39	1.72	1.65	0.83	0.84	1.00	1.00		OTHER
si02	Zahodna Slovenija	-0.04	0.89	0.70	0.37	0.50	1.15	1.13				CAPITAL
sk01	Bratislavský kraj	-0.19	0.60	0.60	0.46	0.32	1.26	1.28			61.9	CAPITAL
sk02	Západné Slovensko	0.07	1.22	1.49	1.19	1.33	0.87	0.78	0.94	0.88	19.3	NEWFDI
sk03	Stredné Slovensko	0.00	1.05	0.91	1.22	1.32	0.95	0.96	1.03	1.09	9.3	OTHER
sk04	Východné Slovensko	0.00	1.04	0.85	1.06	1.12	0.98	0.99	1.06	1.12	9.5	PERIPHERAL

*excluding the capital

Notes

1 Wiiw Report (2010), p. 5. The role of EU integration and economic disparities is discussed by Cuadrado-Roura (2001).
2 See Yoder (2003) and Chapman (2008).
3 On average, over 2000–10 the yearly growth rate of newcomers was more than double that of older members (5.1 per cent compared to 2.2 per cent). Calculated from Eurostat.
4 By 2010 the variability of per capita GDP among newcomer regions was almost double that recorded in 2000.
5 See Kallioras and Petrakos (2010).
6 See, among others, EU Commission Report (2014).
7 In a few cases peripheral regions are defined as coasting the relatively far off Black Sea.
8 In some cases we refer also to EU-relative specialization, but we report figures only for country-relative data. Results for EU-relative data are available on request.
9 Previous chapters were based on Eurostat data providing information on employment following a classification of sectors based on their knowledge intensity. This chapter is based on Cambridge Econometrics data using a different sectoral classification and providing data on a longer time span.
10 Specialization measured relative to the EU average shows that the capital region is specialized in services while all other regions specialize in agriculture.
11 See Hungarian Central Statistical Office, https://www.ksh.hu/docs/hun/xstadat/ xstadat_eves/i_qpk006.html
12 From an EU-relative perspective, instead, the whole country except Slaskie is specialized in agriculture.
13 See National Strategic Reference Framework 2007–2013, June 2007.
14 Data are from National Statistical Institute, Republic of Bulgaria, and refer to FDIs in non-financial enterprises, various years.
15 For the identification of old industrial regions, see Plostajner (2005).

References

Artelaris, P., D. Kallioras and G. Petrakos (2010), 'Regional inequalities and convergence clubs in the European Union new member-states', Eastern Journal of European Studies, vol. 1, pp. 113–33.
Aslund, A. and W.M. Orlowski (2014), 'The Polish transition in a comparative perspective', mBank–CASE Seminar Proceedings No.133/2014.
Bachtler, J., R. Downes, E. Helioska-Hughes and J. Macquarkie (1999), 'Regional development and policy in the transition countries', Regional and Industrial Policy Research Paper 36. European Policies Research Centre, Glasgow.
Boeri, T., H. Brücker, et al. (2001), The Impact of Eastern Enlargement on Employment and Labour Markets in the EU Member States, Report for European Commission's Employment and Social Affairs Directorate, European Integration Consortium (DIW, CEPR, FIEF, IAS, IGIER), Berlin and Milan (Brussels: European Commission).
Central Statistical Office (2014), 'Economic activity of entities with foreign capital in 2013'. Warsaw.
Chapman, S. (2008), 'Regional growth patterns in the enlarged EU: are new members conforming to old development schemes?', Economia, impresa e mercati finanziari, no. 2, pp. 7–34.
Condon, C. (2004), 'Business park changes tack in search of smaller victories', Financial Times, 14 January, p. 2.

Cuadrado-Roura, J.R. (2001), 'Regional convergence in the European Union: from hypothesis to the actual trends', *The Annals of Regional Science*, vol. 35, pp. 333–56.

Cucu, S.V. (1996), 'Economic geography of Romania', *Editura Glasul Bucovinei*, Iasi.

European Commission (2014), *Reindustrialising Europe: Member States' Competitiveness*, Brussels.

Ezcurra, R., P. Pascual and M. Rapun (2007), 'The dynamics of regional disparities in Central and Eastern Europe during transition', *European Planning Studies*, vol. 15, pp. 1397–421.

Finka, M., R. Janacek and D. Petrikova (2005), 'Slovakia: transforming industrial regions and preparing for EU regional policy'. In B. Müller, M. Finka and G. Lintz (eds), *Rise and Decline of Industry in Central and Eastern Europe*. Heidelberg and New York: Springer.

Gorzelak, G. (1996), 'The regional dimension of transformation in Central Europe', *Regional Policy and Development*, vol. 10. London: Jessica Kingsley.

Horváth, G. (2002), 'The perspectives of Hungarian regional development'. In G. Horváth (ed.), *Regional Challenges of the Transition in Bulgaria and Hungary*. Pécs: Centre for Regional Studies of the Hungarian Academy of Sciences, pp. 129–35.

Isfanescu, R. (2010), 'Potential clusters in Banat and their role in regional economic development', *Journal of Urban and Regional Analysis*, vol. 2, pp. 15–24.

Kallioras, D. and G. Petrakos (2010), 'Industrial growth, economic integration and structural change: evidence from the EU new member-states regions', *Annals of Regional Science*, vol. 45, pp. 667–80.

Lackenbauer, J. (2004), 'Catching-up, regional disparities and EU cohesion policy: the case of Hungary', *Managing Global Transitions: International Research Journal*, vol. 2(2), pp. 123–62.

Miron, D., A.M. Dima and S. Vasilache (2009), 'Indexes of regional economic growth in post-accession Romania', *Romanian Journal of Economic Forecasting*, vol. 10(3), pp. 138–52.

Nadejde, S., D. Pantea, A. Dumitrache and I. Braulete (2005), 'Romania: consequences of small steps policy'. In B. Müller, M. Finka and G. Lintz (eds), *Rise and Decline of Industry in Central and Eastern Europe*. Heidelberg and New York: Springer.

National Bank of Romania (2013), *Foreign Direct Investment in Romania in 2012*.

Nemes-Nagy, J. (2001), 'New regional patterns in Hungary'. In P. Meusburger and H. Jöns (eds), *Transformations in Hungary*. Heidelberg: Physica, pp. 39–64.

Okraska, E. (2005), 'Poland: redevelopment strategies at different levels'. In B. Müller, M. Finka and G. Lintz (eds), *Rise and Decline of Industry in Central and Eastern Europe*. Heidelberg and New York: Springer.

Petrakos, G. (2001), 'Patterns of regional inequality in transition economics', *European Planning Studies*, vol. 9(3), pp. 359–83.

Plostajner, Z. (2005), 'Slovenia: different types of old industrial regions'. In B. Muller, M. Finka and G. Lintz (eds), *Rise and Decline of Industry in Central and Eastern Europe*. Heidelberg and New York: Springer.

Rechnitzer, J. (2000), 'The features of the transition of Hungary's regional system', Discussion Paper, no. 32. Centre for Regional Studies of the Hungarian Academy of Sciences, Pécs.

Rodríguez-Pose, A. (1998a), *The Dynamics of Regional Growth in Europe: Social and Political Factors*. Oxford: Clarendon Press.

Skokan, K. (2009), 'Regional clusters and transformation of old industrial regions', Third central European Conference in Regional Science, CERS.

Sochulakova, J. and M. Igazova (2013), 'Foreign direct investment in Slovak regions and their impact on regional economic growth', *Economics and Management*, vol. 18(3), pp. 501–8.

Spiridonova, J. and M. Novakova (2005), 'Bulgaria: identifying regions of industrial decline'. In B. Müller, M. Finka and G. Lintz (eds), *Rise and Decline of Industry in Central and Eastern Europe*. Heidelberg and New York: Springer.

Stejskal, J. (2005), 'Czech Republic: towards the reclamation of derelict land'. In B. Müller, M. Finka and G. Lintz (eds), *Rise and Decline of Industry in Central and Eastern Europe*. Heidelberg and New York: Springer.

Visy, E., G. Zala and K. Schneller (2005), 'Hungary: an umbrella plan for the regions'. In B. Müller, M. Finka and G. Lintz (eds), *Rise and Decline of Industry in Central and Eastern Europe*. Heidelberg and New York: Springer.

Weise, C., J. Bachtler, R. Downes, I. McMaster and K. Toepel (2001), 'The impact of the EU enlargement on cohesion', DIW German Institute for Economic Research and European Policies Research Centre, European Commission Tender No. PO/00-1/RegioA4, Berlin and Glasgow. Brussels: European Commission.

Wiiw Report (2010), 'Whither growth in central and eastern Europe? Policy lessons for an integrated Europe', Bruegel Blueprint Series, vol. 11.

Yoder J.A. (2003), 'Decentralisation and regionalisation after communism: administrative and territorial reform in Poland and the Czech Republic', *Europe-Asia Studies*, vol. 552(2), pp. 263–86.

7 Conclusions

Main results

This book argues that reading the process of convergence/divergence along the lines of the neoclassical (old and 'new') growth theory and/or of the new economic geography paradigms misses important features of growth and transformation processes that are relevant for studying the evolution of regional disparities. These include the sectoral composition of the economy and processes of structural change, the way in which local territories are able to introduce and assimilate new technologies and socio-economic factors. The study of 'regional disparities', a term that we prefer to the more widely used concept of 'regional convergence', shows a great deal of variety in the behaviour of different groups of regions in different periods of time.

The huge diversity in regional behaviour can be explained only by means of a rich array of methodologies. In fact, as simple regression analysis focuses on 'average' behaviour and says little on intra-distribution dynamics, the book has always integrated this approach with the study of entire distributions via kernel density estimates. Alongside, it relies also on the analysis of variance and uses conditional distributions to disentangle the role of various groupings in explaining total variability (in per capita GDP, labour productivity and employment rates).

The book wants to explain the following main facts that strongly emerge from the analysis of regional data:

1. In the second half of the 1990s, regional disparities across EU regions fell overall. However the general trend of falling variability in per capita income across EU-27 regions actually conceals different and diverse phenomena:

    a. income disparities increase among regions of old EU member countries, in particular after the 2008 crisis, while
    b. regions belonging to newcomers reduce their distance from the EU average at the expense of increasing inequalities within countries.

2. When looking at labour productivity and employment rates, an overall process of convergence is found only for labour productivity, while regional disparities in the employment rate grow.

3. When old members are distinguished from newcomers, they are found to experience divergence in both labour productivity and employment rates. At the same time, the overall convergence in newcomers hides growing disparities in both labour productivity and employment rates at the regional level.

The principal aim of the book is to explain what factors are responsible for divergence across regions of old EU members and what explains increasing polarization between regions in newcomers. The explanatory factors considered are specialization, knowledge and socio-economic characteristics. In order to test the importance of these factors for regional disparities in per capita GDP, labour productivity and employment rates, the book classifies regions on the basis of each of these elements. The descriptive analysis shows that, although there is some overlap among groupings, each group provides additional information. For instance, while capitals mostly specialize in services (both knowledge intensive and less knowledge intensive ones), a few capitals in newcomers specialize in low-tech manufacturing. Moreover, while it is generally true that peripheral regions specialize in agriculture and have low levels of innovation and human capital, a few far-off regions in Sweden and the UK specialize in knowledge intensive services and present high levels of education coupled with high, or medium, innovation. Finally, it appears that there is a relationship between the groups and the levels of per capita GDP, of labour productivity and of employment rates. Disentangling the role of these groups for the evolution of regional disparities in Europe is the main object of the book. The main results, the questions they raise and their interpretation are summarized below:

1. For the EU as a whole country factors lose importance in explaining regional disparities in per capita GDP. However, this does not hold for older members alone, for whom country factors regain importance – especially after the crisis. This result runs counter to current wisdom concerning the most likely outcome of 50 years or so of economic integration and raises the question of what determines different reactions to exogenous shocks across countries, most of which share full monetary integration but only partial real integration.
2. Country factors explain a big (and growing) share of regional disparities in employment rates, especially in old members. The result suggests that competition from new members and the economic downturn following the financial crisis have hit particularly the weaker economies of the old Europe, while wage flexibility and migration have proved ineffective response mechanisms.
3. For all regions (belonging to either old or new EU members) innovation and socio-economic groups gain importance over time. In particular, innovation groups explain differences in EU-relative per capita income better, while socio-economic groups do so with respect to income differences within countries. The growing importance of innovation in explaining income disparities is hardly surprising in the case of the older EU members, in view of the growing difficulties faced by advanced economies in competing in global markets on the basis of cost/price factors. Interestingly, the same conclusion

applies also to newcomers where innovation and especially human capital appear to set a dividing line between catching up and lagging behind.

4. When distinguishing between labour productivity and employment rates, knowledge groups appear to be more relevant for labour productivity in the whole sample, while socio-economic groups are more relevant when old members and newcomers are taken separately (innovation explains better differences in labour productivity between old members and newcomers).

5. Over time the importance of knowledge groups and socio-economic groups in explaining disparities in the employment rate (but not in labour productivity) increases for the whole sample.

6. The importance of knowledge for disparities in the employment rate increases, especially in old members, while that of socio-economic groups grows, especially in newcomers.

7. Among the different groupings examined in the book, that based on specialization shows the lowest explanatory power. This contrasts with previous findings according to which specialization had a significant role, at least up to 2005 (Ezcurra *et al.*, 2007; Ezcurra and Rapun, 2007; Chapman and Meliciani, 2012). The falling importance of specialization could be an effect of considerable relocation processes in act whereby old members have delocalized important portions of the production chain in manufacturing, especially low-tech products, to newcomers, leading to significant growth in many CEEC regions (Marrocu *et al.*, 2014). This interpretation is supported by the fact that in the Eurozone specialization continues to play a significant role in affecting growth, with services and high-tech manufacturing offering better opportunities as compared to agriculture and low-tech manufacturing.

8. In all newcomers transition went hand-in-hand with growing disparities in per capita GDP within countries. Such disparities are increasingly explained by:

   a) economic activity concentrating in urban areas;
   b) new industrial areas forming as a result of economic restructuring processes often linked to foreign direct investment;
   c) the decline of most former industrial areas and of peripheral regions bordering non-EU countries.

Overall, the book shows the growing importance of innovation and human capital and of socio-economic groups in explaining regional disparities. The fact that such disparities increase in old EU members, especially across countries, and in newcomers (within countries) raises some doubts regarding the capacity of market mechanisms to generate even patterns of development, pointing to the importance of targeted policies.

Implications for policy

Neoliberalist approaches to economic growth and convergence argue that further European integration based on a stronger reliance on market mechanisms and a lower weight of the state in the economy ensure increasing and sustainable growth in Europe. The failure of socialist regimes and the high level of public debt in many European countries contribute to the prevalence of neoliberalism in Europe over alternative approaches that emphasize the risks of relying too much on market mechanisms and of disregarding the importance of policy instruments. This had consequences for the way in which the European Monetary Union was conceived and put into practice and on the management of the transition from centrally planned to market economies in former socialist countries. A unique monetary policy matched by a decentralized fiscal policy – but subject to strong rules involving, first, a limit to the deficit/GDP ratio and, later, also the balanced budget amendment to the Constitution – left national governments, particularly those of countries with high public debt, with almost no instrument to manage aggregate demand. At the same time, this task was not given to any European institution: the European Central Bank (ECB) has the prevalent objective of controlling inflation while the EU budget covers only about 1 per cent of the wealth generated by EU economies every year. Moreover, while the budget is mainly devoted to reducing regional income disparities, to favouring rural development and to financing environmental protection, it is already insufficient to cover these goals and cannot be used for counter-cyclical fiscal policies. In this setting, it is hardly surprising that the financial crisis originated in USA had a major and more long lasting impact in Europe than in the USA.

The growth in regional income and employment disparities in old EU members (mainly belonging to the Eurozone) in the second half of the 1990s, clearly shown in Chapters 3 and 4 of this book, cannot be fully understood without considering the macro-economic context. The fact that income and, even more, employment disparities grow, particularly across countries, raises some doubts on the effectiveness of European integration and of its mechanisms of response to the crises. Important reforms are needed to avoid future recessions leading to growth in income inequalities across EU regions and countries to the extent of creating dangers for the entire integration process. First, fiscal policy should be subject to a higher degree of centralization. Second, the governance structure of the European Monetary Union must envisage a fiscal transfer system acting as an automatic stabilizer for regions affected by region specific shocks. Such a regime could be based on a common European unemployment insurance system; or else on other social transfers on the expenditure side of the EU's budget or on business cycle-sensitive taxes such as financial transaction taxes, acting on the revenue side (Aiginger *et al.*, 2012).[1] Third, a higher degree of harmonization across countries in important domains of the real economy, including labour markets, taxation and regulation, should be achieved in order to avoid countries responding to crisis by 'beggar thy neighbour' competitive strategies. Fourth, a certain degree of coordination of unit labour costs across countries (or better across regions) is required. Countries/regions with higher productivity should allow wages to increase, thus boosting domestic demand and creating positive spillovers for other countries/regions.

Among the factors identified in this book, innovation and human capital are the ones that explain better the growth in income and employment disparities in old

EU members, especially in the Eurozone, after the financial crisis. This shows the importance of these factors in responding to the downturn in the absence of other compensating mechanisms. However, relying on these mechanisms alone appears to be dangerous for European cohesion since, without appropriate industrial policies, they appear to strengthen pre-existing technology and economic gaps. So far, the policies suggested by the European Commission to Southern European countries, mainly based on labour market flexibility, cuts in public spending and privatization have seemingly not allowed them to regain international competitiveness, while they have depressed domestic demand with negative consequences on economic growth and, even more, on employment.

The European Commission rightly recognizes the importance of innovation and human capital for sustainable growth. The specific targets identified in Europe 2020 follow in the footsteps of the Lisbon Agenda. The target of devoting 3 per cent of EU GDP to R&D expenditure is maintained, together with specific targets on human capital: the share of early school leavers should be under 10 per cent in 2020 and at least 40 per cent of the younger generation should have a tertiary degree. However, in 2008, R&D in EU-27 amounted to only 2.1 per cent, with a highly uneven distribution across countries and no sign of convergence. Since then, the recession has led to falling expenditures and greater disparities. Again, progress towards the set goals has been highly uneven and the recession has cut advances in 'periphery' countries (Pianta, 2014). Our results are consistent with the hypotheses that increasing gaps between the core of Europe (particularly northern countries and Germany) and Southern Europe in innovation and human capital are responsible for divergence in per capita GDP and employment rates after the crisis. The European Commission and EU governments should, therefore, acknowledge the difficulty of achieving the goals of Europe 2020 – that is, of devoting more resources to 'growth-enhancing activities' such as education, R&D and innovation – in the presence of stringent rules for fiscal consolidation and debt reduction. In fact, expenditure cuts in the context of fiscal consolidation strategies in Southern European countries occurred mainly at the cost of public investment, including in education and R&D. Not counting this type of expenditure in the fiscal budget would allow more consistency between the Strategy Europe 2020 and the Fiscal Compact and could help laggard countries/regions to reduce their gaps in innovation and human capital.[2]

While the book shows the increasing importance of innovation and human capital for regional growth, the evidence concerning the impact of specialization is more mixed. While specialization clusters do not appear to grow in importance for the whole sample of EU regions, they do in the Eurozone. The fact that different types of specialization can lead to different growth patterns in different regions gives support to the recent literature on 'smart' specialization (McCann and Ortega-Agilés, 2013) which highlights how each territory has its own specific comparative advantage on the basis of which it builds related diversification processes maximizing local knowledge diffusion and learning networks. However, when one looks at the sample of more advanced regions (that remain unable to allow currency devaluation and to compete on costs) the advantages of being specialized in more knowledge intensive activities (knowledge intensive services and high-tech manufacturing) become evident. This suggests that horizontal industrial policies are insufficient for long-run growth, while priorities should be identified favouring activities and industries characterized by high learning opportunities, rapid technological change, scale and scope economies, and a strong growth of demand and productivity (Meliciani, 2001; Pianta, 2014).

Another important result emerging from this book which bears relevant policy implications concerns the behaviour of newcomers. These countries converge to the EU average but face generalized and strong divergence within themselves. This raises doubts on the self-equilibrating mechanisms of market economies and calls for policies especially devoted to find mechanisms to help the restructuring of old industrialized areas and the integration of peripheral regions with the rest of the CEECs and with the EU.

Another interesting point is the fact that the socio-economic groups suggested by Rodríguez-Pose (1998a) for old members appear very relevant in explaining the behaviour also of newcomers. In these countries, urban areas (that coincide with regions hosting the capital city) are the main beneficiaries of European integration, while many old industrial areas and peripheral regions (bordering non-EU member countries) are those that suffer most. The advantages of capital cities appear to be strongly linked to the availability of high levels of human capital, confirming the complementarity between skills and cities and the importance of agglomeration for knowledge spillovers (Henderson *et al.*, 1995; Glaeser and Mare, 2001; Glaeser, 2008; Bacolod *et al.*, 2009). Overall, also in the presence of falling transportation and communication costs, many factors appear to favour the concentration of economic activity in urban areas, where economic and social actors can benefit from proximity to other economic and social actors with whom they can relate from a cognitive, organizational, social and institutional dimension (Boschma, 2005). Concentration of economic activity in urban areas creates the adequate environment for the exchange of ideas, Jacobs's type externalities, innovation and, ultimately, economic activity and growth (Rodríguez-Pose and Crescenzi, 2008). Therefore, although advances in technology and deregulation may allow economic activity to take place virtually everywhere, favouring the emergence of new actors in the global world (the 'flat world' hypothesis of Friedman, 2005), at the regional level globalization appears to have favoured large metropolitan areas which are the nodes within the global network of financial and business firms.

This poses some policy questions for both urban and peripheral areas. First, we might ask whether there is an 'optimal' size of the city, either because there are decreasing returns to agglomeration or because there are costs linked to agglomeration such as pollution, congestion, increase in prices in the housing market, crime, etc. While answering this question is outside the scope of the present book, the size of the cities observed in European countries does not suggest the need to adopt policies limiting their growth. Conversely, the main problems might rather involve the optimal organization of space and transport systems, the integration of immigrants and, more generally, creating the conditions for maximizing knowledge spillovers arising from agglomeration. In this respect, many cities in eastern countries (such as Prague and Bratislava) are performing much better than some cities in Southern European countries (such as Rome or Athens). Further studies could shed light on the reasons that lie behind the different performance of urban areas and on the most effective policies for maximizing the benefits of agglomeration while reducing its costs.

As far as peripheral areas are concerned, attention should be devoted to, first, identifying the new peripheries of the European Union. In this respect it appears that these might include, together with areas at the far eastern border in newcomers, also some Southern European regions which have started to diverge from the core of Europe, especially after the 2008 crisis. These two groups are in a different position. Southern regions suffer from competition from low-cost eastern regions that are endowed with relatively high levels of human capital. Moreover, they are constrained by fiscal consolidation and by the impossibility of regaining some competitiveness through currency devaluation. In turn, the far eastern regions have been damaged by the shift of the geopolitical centre of former socialist countries from the Soviet Union to the EU. It is apparent that all these areas will not automatically benefit from relocation processes based on low wages, since their levels of human capital, infrastructures, government efficiency, etc. do not allow endogenous development and do not attract foreign investment. Although one might argue that the consequence of European integration is the agglomeration of economic activity leading to large differences in population density across areas (similarly to what occurs in the USA), the lower mobility of labour in Europe and the much higher degree of cultural differences make such a scenario unlikely in the near future. Therefore, unemployment will continue to be, in the absence of appropriate policies, a serious problem in peripheral areas of Europe. In particular, we expect that countries undertaking fiscal consolidation will be more and more unable to invest resources in the reduction of territorial inequalities. Moreover, the cut in national investment expenditures may hurt the periphery more than the core. In these cases, as already argued, a rethinking of the long-run effects of the actual institutional set-up of the European Monetary Union is urgently needed. Only a rethinking of fiscal rules, a higher centralization of fiscal policies and some degree of debt mutualization would free new resources to be devoted to innovation and industrial policies without which peripheral areas are deemed to lag behind.

In peripheral areas, the major sector of activity is still agriculture. Therefore, the development of these areas rests on improved coordination between agricultural policy and regional policy funds as foreseen in the revision of the cohesion policy currently under way. The major goal should be to promote structural change and sustainable rural and regional development. Funds should be shifted away from subsidizing large-scale farming and directed towards enhancing the production of high-value products and to establish strong value chains in food processing and local services (Aiginger *et al.*, 2012).

Innovation and industrial policies, possibly taken mainly at the EU level, are also needed in old industrial areas. These policies should not aim at investment that does not fit existing production structures but rather at upgrading existing structures by favouring specialization in related fields, deepening the cooperation between firms, increasing investment in vocational training and favouring private–public partnerships and partnerships between local and foreign firms to maximize knowledge spillovers. The book shows that some industrial areas, especially in newcomers, have been able to restructure also thanks to foreign direct investment. FDI is the fastest way to bridge productivity gaps and to import technology. Low property prices, well-developed logistics, industrial parks or software centres near universities and near to the ports can be supportive. Fast-track administrative procedures, a strategy for reindustrialization and adequate legal institutions are also necessary (Aiginger *et al.*, 2012). Cases of particular success in newcomers are based on an initial presence of foreign actors later giving rise to the development of domestic industry thanks to industrial clusters, to the presence of skilled labour and of local universities. This model of local development should be encouraged also through the use of structural funds and by favouring the participation of local universities and firms in EU-funded research projects.[3]

Overall, the importance of the groups identified in this book for explaining regional disparities points to the relevance of taking into account regional spatial location, degree of agglomeration (also distinguishing between urban and non-urban areas), type of specialization and ability to innovate and/or to assimilate new knowledge when devising regional policies.

The way in which regional policy has been conducted so far has not halted the growth in regional disparities between the core of Europe and peripheral areas in old members and has not prevented an increase in regional disparities within CEECs. This has led to a series of new policy suggestions mainly centred on European industrial policy, and implying a much higher amount of resources to be devoted to such policy, new funding arrangements and governance mechanisms (for a thorough discussion of this topic, see Pianta, 2014).[4] We fully agree that such a shift of perspective is urgently needed since the policies adopted so far, relying mainly on reducing production costs, regulations and the weight of the public sector in the economy, have proved unsuccessful in reducing regional inequalities, thus undermining citizens' confidence in European institutions and challenging the entire process of European integration.

Notes

1 Such automatic stabilizers accommodate about one third of an asymmetric shock in the USA.
2 On this point, the European Parliament has asked the Commission to provide a report 'on the possibilities offered by the Union's existing fiscal framework to balance productive public investment needs with fiscal discipline objectives in the preventive arm of the SGP while complying with it fully' (regulation no. 473/2013, 21 May 2013, European Parliament and Council, Art. 16.2). Moreover, it argued that public expenditure related to the implementation of programmes co-financed by the European Structural and Investment Funds should be completely eliminated from the definition of structural

deficits according to the Stability and Growth Pact, inasmuch as they are devoted to achieving the goals of Europe 2020 and supporting competitiveness, growth and job creation. Furthermore, current spending and investment should be kept separate in the budget deficit calculations. See 'On the effects of budgetary constraints for regional and local authorities regarding the EU structural funds expenditures in the Member States', Motion for a European Parliament Resolution, Committee on Regional Development, 25 September 2013.

3 Previous studies show the importance of participation in European Framework Programmes for regional knowledge spillovers (Maggioni *et al.*, 2007; Hoekman *et al.*, 2013; Di Cagno *et al.*, 2013).

4 The German trade union confederation DGB suggested 'A Marshall Plan for Europe' (DGB, 2012), envisaging public investment of the magnitude of 2 per cent of Europe's GDP per year over ten years. Similarly, the European Trade Union Confederation presented the document 'A new path for Europe' (ETUC, 2013). See also Pianta (2010), Lucchese and Pianta (2012), Dellheim and Wolf (2013), EuroMemo Group (2013).

References

Aiginger, K., P. Huber and M. Firgo (2012), 'Policy options for the development of peripheral regions and countries of Europe', WWW for Europe, Policy Brief no. 2, December.

Bacolod, M., B.S. Blum and W.C. Strange (2009), 'Skills in the city', *Journal of Urban Economics*, vol. 65, pp. 136–53.

Boschma, R.A. (2005) 'Proximity and innovation: a critical assessment', *Regional Studies*, vol. 39, pp. 61–74.

Chapman, S. and V. Meliciani (2012), 'Income disparties in the enlarged EU: socio-economic, specialization and geographical clusters', *Tijdschrift Voor Economische En Sociale Geografie*, vol. 103(3), pp. 293–311.

Dellheim, J. and F.O. Wolf (2013), 'Alternative European economic policy, industrial policy, and socio-ecological reconversion', Paper presented at the EuroMemorandum conference, London, 20–22 September.

Di Cagno, D., A. Fabrizi and V. Meliciani (2013), 'The impact of participation in European joint research projects on knowledge creation and economic growth', *The Journal of Technology Transfer*, August, pp. 1–23.

DGB (2012), 'A Marshall Plan for Europe: proposal by the DGB for an economic stimulus, investment and development programme for Europe'. Available at: http://www.dgb.de/themen/++co++d92f2d46-5590-11e2-8327-00188b4dc422/#

ETUC (European Trade Union Confederation) (2013), 'A new path for Europe: ETUC plan for investment, sustainable growth and quality jobs'. Available at: http://www.etuc.org/sites/www.etuc.org/files/EN-A-new-path-for-europe.pdf

EuroMemo Group (2013), 'The deepening divisions in Europe and the need for a radical alternative to EU policies: Euro Memorandum 2014'.

Ezcurra, R. and M. Rapun (2007), 'Regional dynamics and convergence profiles in the enlarged European Union: a non-parametric approach', *Tijdschrift voor Economische en Sociale Geografie*, vol. 5, pp. 564–84.

Ezcurra, R., P. Pascual and M. Rapun (2007), 'The dynamics of regional disparities in Central and Eastern Europe during transition', *European Planning Studies*, vol. 15, pp. 1397–421.

Friedman, T. (2005), *The World is Flat: A Brief History of the Twenty-First Century*. New York: Farrar, Straus and Giroux.

Glaeser, E.L. (2008), *Cities, Agglomeration and Spatial Equilibrium*. Oxford: Oxford University Press.

Glaeser, E.L. and D. C. Mare (2001), 'Cities and skills', *Journal of Labor Economics*, vol. 19(2), pp. 316–42.

Henderson, J.V., A. Kuncoro and M. Turner (1995), 'Industrial development in cities', *Journal of Political Economy*, vol. 103, pp. 1067–90.

Hoekman, J., T. Scherngell, K. Frenken and R. Tijssen (2013), 'Acquisition of European research funds and its effect on international scientific collaboration', *Journal of Economic Geography*, vol. 13, pp. 23–52.

Lucchese, M. and M. Pianta (2012), 'Industrial and innovation polizie in the European Union'. In F. Garibaldo, M. Baglioni, V. Telljohann and C. Casey (eds), *Workers, Citizens, Governance: Socio-Cultural Innovation at Work*. Berlin: Peter Lang.

Maggioni, M.A., M. Nosvelli and T.E. Uberti (2007), 'Space versus networks in the geography of innovation: a European analysis', *Papers in Regional Science*, vol. 86(3), pp. 271–93.

Marrocu, E., R. Paci and S. Usai (2013), 'Productivity growth in the old and new Europe: the role of agglomeration externalities', *Journal of Regional Science*, vol. 53(3), pp. 418–42.

McCann, P. and R. Ortega-Argilés (2013), 'Smart specialization, regional growth, and applications to European Union Cohesion Policy', *Regional Studies*, doi: 10.1080/00343404.2013.799769.

Meliciani, V. (2001), *Technology, Trade and Growth in OECD Countries: Does Specialisation Matter?* London: Routledge.

Pianta, M. (2010), 'Industrial and innovation policies in Europe'. In A. Watt and A. Botsch (eds), *After the Crisis: Towards a Sustainable Growth Model*. Brussels: ETUI, pp. 92–5.

Pianta, M. (2014), 'An industrial policy for Europe', *Seoul Journal of Economics*, vol. 27, pp. 277–305.

Rodríguez-Pose, A. (1998a), *The Dynamics of Regional Growth in Europe: Social and Political Factors*. Oxford: Clarendon Press.

Rodríguez-Pose, A. and R. Crescenzi (2008), 'Mountains in a flat world: why proximity still matters for the location of economic activity', *Cambridge Journal of Regions, Economy and Society*, Cambridge Political Economy Society, vol. 1(3), pp. 371–88.

Index

For Product Safety Concerns and Information please contact our EU
representative GPSR@taylorandfrancis.com
Taylor & Francis Verlag GmbH, Kaufingerstraße 24, 80331 München, Germany

www.ingramcontent.com/pod-product-compliance
Ingram Content Group UK Ltd.
Pitfield, Milton Keynes, MK11 3LW, UK
UKHW020953180425
457613UK00019B/658